Church Government
According to the Bible

Church Government According to the Bible

SIMON V. GONCHARENKO

Foreword by
Gene A. Getz *and* Wayne Barber

WIPF & STOCK · Eugene, Oregon

CHURCH GOVERNMENT ACCORDING TO THE BIBLE

Copyright © 2014 Simon V. Goncharenko. All rights reserved. Except for brief quotations in critical publications or reviews, no part of this book may be reproduced in any manner without prior written permission from the publisher. Write: Permissions, Wipf and Stock Publishers, 199 W. 8th Ave., Suite 3, Eugene, OR 97401.

Wipf and Stock
An Imprint of Wipf and Stock Publishers
199 W. 8th Ave., Suite 3
Eugene, OR 97401

www.wipfandstock.com

ISBN 13: 978-1-62564-368-1

Manufactured in the U.S.A.   09/02/2014

Scripture quotations taken from the New American Standard Bible®, Copyright © 1960, 1962, 1963, 1968, 1971, 1972, 1973,1975, 1977, 1995 by the Lockman Foundation. Used by permission. (www.Lockman.org)

To my wife—for believing in me and encouraging me through some of the hardest years of our lives together.

Contents

Foreword by Gene A. Getz and Wayne Barber | *ix*
Preface | *xiii*

1. What Is Church Government? | 1
2. Key Terms and Polity Models | 7
3. Theological Considerations for Polity Models | 29
4. Theological Considerations for Polity Models (Continued) | 55
5. Multiple-Elder Congregationalism: The Most Biblically Defensible Model | 81
6. Addressing Objections and Providing Practical Recommendations | 110

Appendix: Further Thoughts from Getz and Bar | 137

Bibliography | 145
Index | 159

Foreword[1]

We believe this is a book all church leaders need to read and digest. In writing on the subject of church governance, author, pastor, and professor Simon Goncharenko has blended his superb academic experience and achievements with his current church-planting ministry.

The author also writes from a diverse cultural background. Growing up outside the American milieu has added to his hermeneutical skill in interpreting Scripture and applying biblical truth cross-culturally. His emphasis on supracultural principles that flow from the biblical story is an important presupposition in approaching the subject of church governance.

Beyond Goncharenko's abilities in interpreting Scripture, he also brings his understanding of governance to bear through the lens of church history—one of his academic specializations. Goncharenko's command of New Testament history and the eras that follow make his observations regarding past and present governance models both astute and insightful. We believe he accurately demonstrates that the New Testament story of the church does not teach that episcopalian, presbyterian, or congregational models are absolute forms for church governance per se. Furthermore, whenever these models or any others are presented as a *fixed biblical pattern*, it leads to practices that are, at least in some respects, out of harmony with biblical functions and absolute principles. This is particularly true in planting churches transculturally.

From a pragmatic perspective, we have no disagreement with Goncharenko's overall approach to church governance. Our point of divergence would be his proposal that Scripture teaches a *pattern* or *form* involving eldership and congregational governance. Even here, we acknowledge there is a "fine line," depending on how we define terms.

---

1. For further thoughts from Getz and Barber, please see the Appendix.

In essence, we believe the Holy Spirit has not given us absolutes in terms of *any* ecclesiological forms and structures. Rather, that which is absolute are normative activities and functions that yield supracultural principles, which in turn enable believers in every culture of the world and at any moment in history with the freedom to develop forms and structures that are not only culturally relevant, but are also in harmony with the timeless truths revealed in the word of God.

In this sense, we would disagree with Cartwright, whom Goncharenko cites, who states that the Scriptures provide a *single pattern* for the church that amounts to a perpetual and immutable law for all succeeding generations living under the Gospel. If Cartwright were correct, it would mean that God would have imposed on us patterns that are uniquely related to various first-century cultures, which would have restricted the progress of the Gospel. Furthermore, it would have violated Paul's clear statement regarding church planting—to "become all things to all people so that 'we' may *by all means* save some" (1 Cor 9:23). Here "the means" Paul refers to are clearly not the absolutes of Scripture, but the patterns, forms, structures, and methodologies that are culturally relevant without violating the absolutes in Scripture.

From our perspective, there are no structural patterns that are comprehensive or even clearly discernible in the New Testament story of the church. It's definitely true that we cannot function without form, but the Holy Spirit guided the authors of Scripture to describe numerous functions without describing their forms. And when references to forms for church governance are mentioned, they are always partial and incomplete. We believe this ambiguity is intentional and by divine design, since social history demonstrates a universal tendency, even among Christians, to be more "form conscious" than "function-oriented." In fact, if we're not careful, we tend to superimpose forms and patterns on Scripture that are missing in the biblical text. When this occurs, it naturally leads to the variations in organizational church polity that proponents claim to be supracultural. In fact, their different conclusions regarding governance affirm the ambiguity in the New Testament story, supporting "freedom in form."

All this leads us differ from Goncharenko with regard to his conclusions that the biblical model for church governance is one of multiple elders in each local church blended with congregationalism. We readily agree, however, that the model he supports is an extremely viable form with many positive values that are in harmony with supracultural principles for church governance. In fact, there are also some biblical and pragmatic values in all the governance models he cites. In other words, we believe all of these approaches reflect the "freedom in form" that Scripture illustrates rather than being, as Goncharenko cites, an "organizational blueprint."[2]

Frankly, we prefer the term "functional blueprint." Furthermore, we would also cautiously use the term "biblical model" to describe church governance—unless we're using this term "functionally" rather than "structurally."

Having said this, we believe the best illustration of a biblical and "functional model" for church governance is the biological family or the "household model." The Scriptures reveal that, with few exceptions, most of the New Testament churches grew out of extended households that came to Christ. For example, we see this illustrated in Colossae, where the church evidently grew out of Philemon's household. The same thing happened in Corinth, where Crispus and his entire household believed in the Lord (Acts 18:8), and in Philippi, where Lydia and her whole household believed. And we find that this church expanded quickly after the jailor's entire household became a part of the believing community (Acts 16:15, 34). We can also conclude that these godly fathers may have become some of the first elders/overseers in these city churches.

This observation correlates with one of the most important qualifications for serving as elders/overseers (terms Goncharenko correctly notes are interchangeable). Paul wrote to Timothy that a man who is selected for this position should be "one who manages his own household competently, having his children under control with all dignity. (If anyone does not know how to manage his own household, how will he take care of God's church?)" (1 Tim 3:4–5). Paul repeats this same basic qualification in his letter to Titus, who was appointing elders/overseers in the various towns on the island of Crete (Titus 1:6).

Both of us come from different traditions in terms of church polity. However, we have arrived at the same conclusion in terms of absolutes in functions and non-absolutes in forms. This gives us great freedom to develop a system of governance that is in harmony with supracultural principles, but also culturally relevant. In conclusion, both of us want to affirm this work as researched and written by Simon Goncharenko. He welcomes dialogue and discussion—hence this foreword. May it be said of all of us, as

---

2. Waldron, "Plural-Elder Congregationalism," 66.

Foreword

it was said of the Bereans: "They . . . examined the Scriptures daily to see if these things were so" (Acts 17:11).

Gene A. Getz
Wayne Barber

Preface

Another book on elders? The answer is "Yes," and, at the same time, "Not exactly." There are several factors that make this work unique and different from all the other material on elders as part of the biblical idea for church government. Before I start listing these factors, however, perhaps an interesting tidbit on the origin and the long journey of this manuscript from its creation to its publication is in order here. This work originated as an attempt at a doctoral dissertation in one of the seminaries of the Southern Baptist Convention. As the conclusions of this research regarding a particular style of church government ended up diverging from the majority view of the seminary, the project was set aside, for there was no way to move forward to a successful degree completion. So I wrote a brand new dissertation on a completely different subject and received an excellent mark on its defense. Following the graduation, I revisited this subject and, since the conclusions of this work represent my deep seated biblical and theological convictions, I decided to make my research available to you, the reader, so that you too can judge for yourself the validity of the evidence presented here. There are some other unique characteristics about this work.

First, the author's multicultural background adds an inimitable perspective that is not limited to North America alone. As someone born behind the Iron Curtain, yet who spent a large part of his formative years in the United States, this author recognizes God's providential hand in his upbringing and understands all life as preparatory for the next divinely assigned task. In the case of this work, here is what led him to the point of making it available to the reader.

The journey that led to this work started with God's providential removal of one of the many thousand young men in the former Soviet Union to be placed in the middle of the USA at the age of sixteen. The credit for this young man's preparation for life and maturation at this relatively young age can only be given to God, whose sovereignty kept him on the straight and narrow even while far from the home he knew and everything that was familiar to him. God's enabling hand oversaw this young man's rapid progression through American university, though he had never studied in a foreign language before.

The kind hand of the Almighty availed an unusually smooth transition for this young man from college to Dallas Theological Seminary, the school of his dreams. The merciful hand of his creator led this young man to meet the most wonderful woman in the world on that campus. The odds of such an encounter at an institution with such a skewed ratio of male to female students was quite unbelievable.

By God's grace, having graduated from Dallas Theological Seminary, my wife and I—the aforementioned young man—moved to Houston, Texas, where the Lord opened an opportunity to work with junior high school students at a large Bible church. His blessings were poured out abundantly on our family in the form of two beautiful children. In continuing to follow the Lord's plan, we subsequently found ourselves in East Texas, where God blessed us with two more children and where I was almost supernaturally directed to the PhD program at Southwestern Baptist Theological Seminary. It was there, in the midst of the period of intellectual rigor and spiritual stretching, that I was challenged to examine biblical data with reference to church polity.

My interest was initially limited to the issue of Scripture's sufficiency with regard to church polity. Having answered the question in the affirmative, my mind wanted to push the question one step further and find the form of church government that is most consistent with biblical precedent. Thus, the birth of *Church Government According to the Bible*.

The second factor that makes this work unique is the method of the argument employed here. While seemingly circular in nature, the argument presented here progresses from identifying common theological foundations for any ecclesiological polity type, to analyzing these foundations in light of the biblical data, to synthesizing the resultant information with multiple-elder congregationalism emerging as the primary form of church government. So the support for the thesis presented here is derived from two avenues: biblical/exegetical and theological, which end up intersecting as they really ought to.

As I mentioned earlier, my multi-faceted, multi-cultural, and multilingual background affords me a unique perspective from which to

Preface

consider the question at hand. My story also crosses between a number of denominations from Russian Baptist Union to American Bible Church movement to Southern Baptist Convention. This constitutes the third factor contributing to the distinctiveness of this manuscript compared to other relevant material on the market today. Having spent equal time within the nondenominational Dallas Theological Seminary-established Bible church movement and the Southern Baptist Convention, the author's perspective is not restricted by the denominational lenses or narrow vision of the traditional way of doing things. Yet, at the same time, as more and more churches within the Southern Baptist Convention are transitioning from single-elder governance to multiple-elder congregationalism, the reader may find it helpful to see this work address some common objections to this form of church government within Baptist circles. Additionally, those pastors who are convinced by the biblical, theological, historical, and practical argumentation within this work will find some practical advice from those within the Southern Baptist Convention who have successfully led their churches through transitions in government structure.

Finally, the fourth element of this work that makes it stand out from the rest is the dual benefit it offers the worlds of academia and the church alike. The research presented here is carefully documented and can be easily verified for academic pursuits. The multiplicity of the footnotes, while not as common in the books for the church, will provide additional resources for the pastor and the layman alike, should they desire to pursue an issue further than the boundaries of this work allow.

As for the quick synopsis of the chapters of this book, they proceed as follows. Chapter 1 introduces the reader to the argument. It sets the context for the issue at hand and provides a historic preamble. Chapter 2 defines the terms frequently used in this work and provides a broad overview of the main models of ecclesiastical organization. Chapters 3 and 4 identify, examine, and analyze the six theological principles that form hermeneutical parameters for one's choice of polity. Chapter 5 synthesizes the information at hand, resulting in the emergence of multiple-elder congregationalism as the most defensible model of church polity. Finally, Chapter 6 more deeply explores the key elements of the model that chapter 5 introduces, addresses objections to it, and offers recommendations for its successful practical implementation on a local church level.

Preface

May God bless your reading and open your eyes to discern his best plan for the governance of the body that to him is the most important organization on earth!

Midway, TX

1

What Is Church Government?

HISTORICAL INTRODUCTION

The year was 1572. Arguably the most important theological development of the time in Elizabethan England was a duel—a literary one—between Archbishop of Canterbury John Whitgift and Presbyterian theologian Thomas Cartwright.[1] This debate would last until 1577 and center around the six propositions Cartwright set forth in his exposition of the model of the primitive church based on the first two chapters of Acts. Cartwright's propositions dealt with orders of clergy and with their offices, duties, and calling.[2] At the center of the controversy was the governmental form of the

---

1. Credit and appreciation for this introduction should go to Dr. Malcolm B. Yarnell III, who suggested the parallel between the events of Elizabethan England and the focus of this project. As a result, the Whitgift-Cartwright-Harrison debate makes, in my opinion, an interesting introduction to the present work.

2. The six propositions may be summarized as follows: "(1) The names and functions of archbishops and archdeacons should be abolished. (2) The ministry of the church should be brought in line with the apostolic church. There should be only two orders of clergy, bishops to preach and pray, and deacons to care for the poor. (3) Each church should be governed by its own minister and presbyters, not by bishops, chancellors, etc. (4) Ministers should be confined to the care of particular flocks. They should not be at large. (5) No man should be a candidate for the ministry, or solicit an appointment. The ministry is a divine calling. (6) Bishops should not be appointed by secular authority; they should be selected by the church" (Gane, "Sixteenth-Century Puritan Preachers," 26). See Jones, *Thomas Cartwright 1535–1603*; Collinson, *Elizabethan Puritan Movement*, 112; Carlson, "Archbishop John Whitgift," 295.

church. Was it to be Episcopal or reformed, in the direction of the Presbyterian model?[3]

John Whitgift, adopting a relativistic stance on church polity, considered experience and convenience to be appropriate yardsticks for a viable form of church government.[4] With his stringent view of human depravity, Cartwright argued that episcopacy had no foundation in Scripture and that a system not commanded by God should not be tolerated.[5] In response, Whitgift claimed that the Scriptures were authoritative for all things pertaining to redemption, but permissive in matters indifferent to it.[6] Or, in the words of Stephen Brachlow, "Since he could find no evidence in the New Testament that Christ had delineated an organizational structure for the church with the precision and clarity Christ had employed in other doctrinal matters, Whitgift reasoned that ecclesiology must therefore be an *adiaphora*[7] issue, an indifferent matter, secondary to the more substantive doctrinal teachings of the gospel."[8] Cartwright believed that the Scriptures

---

3. New, "Whitgift-Cartwright Controversy," 203.

4. Ibid., 205. Since the question of church government lay outside matters of salvation, Whitgift felt justified in exercising more freedom upon arriving at his position. Additionally, the Archbishop's somewhat soft view of human depravity, which he likened to a spiritual infirmity that impaired man's natural capacity for reason, contributed to the development of his understanding.

5. The Presbyterian-Reformed tradition, as affirmed by Cartwright, insisted on a stricter standard: A biblical *command* was needed for anything that was to be included in worship. See Frame, "Questions about the Regulative Principle," 357. Cartwright distrusted human intellect because his notion of man's corruption was far more thorough—he considered every faculty deficient. Man could and should not frame a church organization because "the infirmity of man can neither attain to the perfection of anything whereby he might speak all things that are to be spoken of it, neither yet be free from error in those things which he speaketh" (Whitgift, "Works of John Whitgift," 148, 176–77).

6. New, "Whitgift-Cartwright Controversy," 206. In general, his approach was common to Roman Catholic, Anglican, and Lutheran theologies in their agreement that the church's worship practices ought to be scriptural in the sense of not *contradicting* the Bible.

7. From *adiaphora*, or morally indifferent.

8. Brachlow, *Communion of Saints*, 22. "Even where Scripture seemed to offer an apparently clear directive, Whitgift insisted that this did not mean Christ intended to shackle his church with 'that precise form that is there set down.' On the contrary, Whitgift argued that the form of ceremonies, orders, and discipline in the church depended largely upon historical conditions. Therefore, Christ intended that ecclesial matters should be left to the authority of the bishops, aided by the civil magistrate, who together could determine an appropriate polity for the church not according to biblical

revealed a model for church organization—a single pattern for the church that amounted to a perpetual and immutable law for all succeeding generations living under the gospel.[9] Thus, people were to put into practice what was in the Bible and abstain from doing what was not in it.

Who was right and who was wrong in this theological duel? Was Whitgift right in his more adiaphorist, or normative, approach to biblical treatment of church polity? Or was Cartwright correct in using Scripture as a regulative principle in this debate?[10] And if Cartwright was right, then what does this imply about the more adiaphorist stance that he himself took in his later controversy with such separatists as Robert Browne and Richard Harrison?[11]

There seems to be a degree of arbitrariness about Cartwright's approach. Having professed that the practice of biblical church discipline was a matter of salvation in his debate with Whitgift, Cartwright conveniently failed to mention the soteriological significance of ecclesiology in his correspondence with Harrison. This same type of inconsistency is apparent in most major Protestant denominations' exposition of church polity today, for although they all look to the same source of support for some or all of their views, each seems to emerge with a different argument.

The aim of this work is to provide assistance in eliminating the fog of random exegesis by fleshing out hermeneutical assumptions shared by the adherents of all polity models and grounding these in the word of God, and in so doing, present the most biblically defensible model of church government.

SUFFICIENCY OF SCRIPTURE AND CHURCH POLITY

Prior to diving into the deep waters of theology, a more foundational matter must be addressed—that of Scripture's sufficiency in the area of polity. To put it in the form of a question: Is the Bible sufficient to address

---

prescription, but by their good judgment" (ibid., 22–23).

9. Whitgift, "Works of John Whitgift," 190–91. See also Brachlow, *Communion of Saints*, 23.

10. The idea of regulative principle comes from the Puritan "regulative principle of worship" by which whatever is commanded in Scripture with regard to worship is required, and whatever is not commanded is forbidden. See Smith, "What Is Worship?" 16–17.

11. Brachlow, *Communion of Saints*, 47–49.

Church Government According to the Bible

the issues of church polity? Or is Schweizer right in asserting that "there is no such thing as *the* New Testament Church order?"[12] The same notion is echoed by Frost: "In the New Testament and the early church up to the second century, in spite of incipient legal thinking, there was no fixed form of church government."[13]

The arguments put forth by Schweizer and Frost must be rejected for at least two reasons. The first reason is biblical and the second is theological. Biblically, careful examination of the New Testament provides ample evidence of specific set patterns or frameworks within which early church members structured their time together. They gathered together at set times for worship and prayer (Acts 2:42, 47), practiced the ordinances of baptism and the Lord's Supper (Acts 2:41–42, 46), received offerings in an organized fashion (1 Cor 16:2), sent letters of recommendation from one church to another, maintained official lists of those who needed care or assistance from the church (1 Tim 5:9), and practiced church discipline (1 Cor 5; 2 Cor 2:5–11), among other things.[14]

Theologically, if the church is indeed the body of Christ, then Waldron is correct in stating that it is unthinkable that God would leave it here on earth without any distinguishable organizational blueprint.[15] That church polity is significant to God is evidenced by the fact that "for every time that Paul used the word 'church' of the organism" in Scripture, "he used it six times of the organization."[16] Furthermore, "if Paul can say of the Old Testament Scriptures that 'everything that was written in the past was written to teach us' (Rom 15:4), how much more so is it true that the principal instruction that the apostle gives concerning church government in the New Testament applies to us?"[17]

Historically, there have been three basic responses to the question, "What is the relationship between the New Testament and church polity?" First, there is the view that the New Testament provides no "system" or "pattern" of church government, and thus churches in later centuries should be guided by "expediency" in matters of polity, often conforming to

---

12. Schweizer, *Church Order*, 13, emphasis Schweizer's.
13. Frost, "Church Government: Church History," 2.1.
14. Brand and Norman, *Perspectives on Church Government*, 3–4. See also Saucy, *Church in God's Program*, 98.
15. Waldron, "Plural-Elder Congregationalism," 66.
16. Ryrie, "Pauline Doctrine of the Church," 65.
17. Knight, "Church Government," 90.

What Is Church Government?

the political order or the societal norms under which particular churches exist.[18] Second, others have held that the New Testament provides a single, divinely-given "precise model" of church polity, which is applicable to "all ages and circumstances" and is to be rigidly enforced, leaving nothing to be determined in later centuries and in diverse cultures.[19] Third, there has been a mediating position which finds in the New Testament "a pattern of ecclesiastical organization and discipline in *outline*, not in *detail*," according to which certain "principles" or essentials are clearly taught, although their application is left "to the judgment of Christians" in diverse contexts according to a "wise expediency."[20]

Here I will argue for a position that lies somewhere between the second and third views; namely, that Christ has gifted the church with all that she needs to pursue her ministry, and this gift is presented within the context of how the Lord established his church from the beginning.[21] Careful

---

18. Garrett, "Congregation-Led Church," 171. Those who subscribe to this view include Knox, *Early Church*, 15; Schweizer, *Church Order*, 13; Frost, "Church Government: Church History," 2.1. In addition, this is the de facto way that Russian Baptist churches were historically organized during the years of the Soviet Union—the structure of the Baptist Union of the USSR closely mirrored the civil organizational pattern of the country such that superintendents were appointed over regions of churches, thus bringing about an amalgam of congregationalism and episcopacy within the denomination.

As to the scholars who hold to a flexible form of church government, several recurring suggestions have been made as to why God has left us no definite order. Among these is the lack of evidence—the New Testament does not give enough clear evidence for us to decide how they organized their churches. See Davies, *Normative Pattern of Church Life*, 17; Morris, *Ministers of God*, 111; Fung, "Function or Office?" 36; Cox, "Emerging Organization," 35. For the view that God never intended to use the New Testament to establish a blueprint for church government, see Harper, "Duplicating the New Testament Church," 24; Von Schlatter, *Church in the New Testament Period*, 77. For the argument that our situation today is so different from the one in the first century that there is little relevance in seeking to emulate early church polity, see Schaeffer, *Church at the End*, 67; Lambert, "Church," 1:650; Martin, "Authority in the Light of the Apostolate," 81. For a more detailed discussion, see Daughters, *New Testament Church Government*, 10–14.

19. This view is represented by Reymond's forceful presentation of Presbyterian polity discussed later in this chapter. See Reymond, "Presbytery-Led Church."

20. Garrett, "Congregation-Led Church," 172, emphasis Garrett's. This is the view that Garrett himself endorses.

21. My view is more in line with those expressed in White, "Plural-Elder-Led Church," 258; Saucy, *Church in God's Program*, 118.

examination of the New Testament provides ample evidence of the early church's understanding of polity.[22]

The importance of reevaluating biblical data in the area of church polity is clearly evidenced by the wide variety of different Protestant approaches to structuring church. As was the case some 450 years ago in Whitgift and Cartwright's day, so it is today: Any given Sunday morning reveals a plethora of ways in which God's people understand and practice church polity. They all look to the Bible to derive support for all or some of their beliefs and practice. But can the Bible truly support all of their different views?

A close evaluation of the various models of church polity yields a number of hermeneutical issues that each model has to address, even if just on the level of assumption. The particular positions taken by the proponents of each specific government style with regard to these hermeneutical issues influences their exegesis and affects their conclusions.

Therefore, in order to assure an accurate understanding of the biblical passages on polity, we must line up this position on the guiding theological parameters and issues against Scripture. This will assure that the New Testament passages on polity are understood, interpreted, and applied carefully and faithfully in accordance with the intent of the original authors.[23]

First, however, a quick definition of some frequently used terminology is in order.

---

22. To be discussed in detail in chapters 5 and 6.

23. Liefeld is correct in his observation that when it comes to scriptural warrant for different ideas of church polity, "the issue is not simply between different forms of government, but between different appraisals of the biblical sources" (Liefeld, "Leadership and Authority," 30). If this is so, then there is a great need to establish the rule for a more streamlined appraisal process, which is precisely the focus of this work.

2

Key Terms and Polity Models

Among the concepts that need to be defined at this point are such articles as sufficiency of Scripture, church polity, and hermeneutics. The success of any foregoing discussion can be greatly impeded when writer and reader find themselves operating with different meanings of the terms. Outlined below, then, are the definitions of some of the most common concepts discussed in this work.

DEFINITION OF TERMINOLOGY

Sufficiency of Scripture

The doctrine of sufficiency generally answers the question of whether the Bible is enough in knowing what God wants us to think or do.[1] According to Wayne Grudem, "the sufficiency of Scripture means that Scripture contained all the words of God he intended his people to have at each stage of redemptive history, and that it now contains all the words of God we need

---

1. Enjoying a measure of recent popularity, the topic of sufficiency of Scripture has received much attention in print. The following few titles are recommended for those interested in further research in the area of sufficiency: Yarnell, *The Formation of Christian Doctrine*, 25–28; Weeks, *Sufficiency of Scripture*; Murray, *Claims of Truth*, ch. 3; Pipa and Wortman, *Written for Our Instruction*.

for salvation, for trusting him perfectly, and for obeying him perfectly."[2] Sufficiency of Scripture, according to Yves Congar, means that "God has given us everything necessary or useful for the conduct of our lives."[3]

Church Polity

Polity, according to the *Oxford Dictionary of English*, is "A form or process of civil [or in our case, religious] government or constitution."[4] The *Concise Dictionary of Christian Theology* contains the following definition of polity: "the organization or governmental structure of a local church or fellowship of churches."[5] Dargan, a nineteenth-century Baptist theologian, defines polity as "the method of organization and rule under which a church, or churches, live and act."[6] Brand and Norman espouse the following particularly helpful definition of polity in the introduction to their *Perspectives on Church Government*: "As the church corporately submits herself to the lordship of Christ, the process, expression, and structure of her submission can be designated church polity."[7]

Hermeneutics

Since the two foundational chapters of this work, chapters 3 and 4, center on the issue of biblical hermeneutics, a quick working definition of this concept is called for here. The English word "hermeneutics" comes from the Greek verb *hermeneuō*[8] and the noun *hermeneia*.[9] These words point back to the wing-footed messenger god, Hermes, in Grecian mythology. As Zuck points out:

---

2. Grudem, *Systematic Theology*, 127.

3. Congar, *Tradition and Traditions*, 381. While his definition may sound similar to Grudem's, Congar's true meaning is something entirely different, for only a few pages later Congar espouses, "There is no one who holds that the letter of the Text alone is sufficient," (ibid., 409).

4. *Oxford English Dictionary*, 3rd ed., s.v. "Polity."

5. Erickson, "Polity," 155.

6. Dargan, *Ecclesiology*, 11.

7. Brand and Norman, *Perspectives on Church Government*, 5.

8. Unless otherwise noted, quotations have been transliterated from the original Greek.

9. Zuck, "Why of Bible Interpretation," 22.

He was responsible for transmuting what is beyond human understanding into a form that human intelligence can grasp. He is said to have discovered language and writing and was the god of literature and eloquence, among other things. He was the messenger or interpreter of the gods, and particularly of his father Zeus.[10]

Thus the verb *hermeneuō* came to refer to bringing someone to an understanding of something in his language or in another language.[11] Of the nineteen times *hermeneuō* and *h.ermeneia* occur in the New Testament, they are more frequently used in the sense of translation (John 1:42; Luke 24:27), which can be understood as an explanation in one language of what is conveyed in another language.[12]

Hermeneutics, therefore, is the science (principles) and art (task) by which the meaning of biblical text is determined.[13] It should be distinguished from *exegesis*, which is the determination of the meaning of the biblical text in its historical and literary contexts, and *exposition*, which is the communication of the meaning of the text along with its relevance to present-day hearers.[14] Zuck likens hermeneutics to a cookbook, comparing exegesis to the preparation and baking of the cake and exposition to serving the cake.[15]

Hence, hermeneutics provides the rules or guidelines, the principles and theory governing a proper approach to understanding the Bible.[16]

OUR MAIN FOCUS

In his book, *Gospel and Spirit*, which deals primarily with hermeneutical issues in the Pauline epistles, Gordon D. Fee ends his chapter entitled "Observations on Church Order" by raising some questions regarding the proper application of the New Testament "church order." For "if we do think in terms of 'modeling' after the New Testament church," asks Fee, "which of the various models do we opt for, and why?"[17] In answering Fee's

---

10. Ibid.
11. Ibid.
12. Ibid.
13. Ibid., 23.
14. Ibid.
15. Ibid., 24.
16. Ibid., 25.
17. Fee, *Gospel and Spirit*, 142.

question, I will argue based on the research conducted that multiple-elder congregationalism, unlike any other form of church government, enjoys the unequivocally overwhelming support of the Bible. Because any biblical argument for a model of church government relies upon the particular position that one takes on the basic hermeneutical/theological principles—a position that functions as a presupposition—I will delineate my own position in the next chapter. In order to validate the contention of this manuscript, it will be necessary to demonstrate that both the theological principles that form our pre-understanding *and* the exegesis of the biblical data in polity that rests on this pre-understanding are in line with Scripture.[18]

Because our understanding of church polity is directly related to our position on the following hermeneutical principles, it is my contention that the way to the multiple-elder congregationalism as the most biblically defensible form of church government lies through a position for the above-mentioned principles that is in line with the teachings and general intent of the word of God, as follows: (1) Scripture reigns over tradition; (2) literal interpretation is the best way of understanding the Bible consistently; (3) the New Testament church originated at Pentecost; (4) the offices of apostle and prophet were the foundation blocks of the spiritual building—the church; (5) the offices of elder, overseer, and pastor are interchangeable in nature and function; (6) application of any biblical passage and principle must follow interpretation. Conversely, a disregard for the above-mentioned six principles will yield a church government structure that does not comply with the biblical ideal, does not achieve its full potential, and opens itself to abuse, as is evidenced by history.

The next two chapters are devoted to further explication of these principles, while the following two chapters examine how they affect our understanding and practice of church polity. At this point, however, it may be of benefit to examine the most popular models of church polity.

---

18. Pre-understanding is to be differentiated from a definitive understanding. The latter is the final understanding of the text which is produced through eisegesis rather than exegesis, while the former is the theological "baggage" that the interpreter brings to the text and which will influence how he sees the text (Bultmann, "Is Exegesis without Presuppositions Possible?" 294).

PRIMARY POLITY MODELS

A brief survey of the main polity models is in order. Perhaps a disclosure regarding a limitation for this section needs to be made first. The scope of this segment is limited to a survey. It is a survey because, with the number of writing theologians boasted by each tradition, it is not possible to cover every single nuance in their respective literature, nor is this the focus of the present work.

What follows, therefore, is a representative sampling that is designed to examine closely some of the larger elements that make each tradition's exposition of church polity distinctive. With that in mind, perhaps the following will suffice as the simplest list of views available: (1) episcopal polity; (2) presbyterian polity; and (3) congregational polity. What is perhaps most striking about the wide variety of Protestant views on polity is that, whether in part or as a whole, they point to the Scripture as their source. In the words of Henry Craik, a nineteenth-century theologian in the Brethren tradition,

> there are passages in the inspired writings that seem, to some extent, to favour a species of Episcopacy; others that may appear to support Presbyterianism; very many, again, that uphold Congregationalism, and others, as clearly teaching what may be described as less systematic than any of the above organizations.[19]

Below is the more in-depth examination of the three ecclesiastical structures.

Episcopal Polity

The episcopal group is made up of those denominations that emphasize a distinct role for the *episkopos*.[20] Among their number are Roman Catholics,

---

19. Craik, *New Testament Church Order*, 3–4.
20. This is the Greek term that is used in the New Testament to designate an "overseer." Presently, those denominations that practice the episcopal model of church government translate *episkopos* as "bishop."

Eastern Orthodox, Anglican/Episcopal, Methodist,[21] many Lutheran[22] fellowships, and some Holiness and Pentecostal denominations.[23] For the purposes of this study, we will consider the Anglican/Episcopal ecclesiology to be a fair representative of the episcopal group and examine it next.[24]

Modern Anglicans believe that there is no blueprint in the New Testament for the polity and government of the church.[25] Thus the Anglican form of church government, in the words of Peter Toon, "is an attempt to conform in general terms to the pattern in place in the early church in the third, fourth, and fifth centuries."[26] Prior to Toon's "mature" version of Anglican ecclesiology, earlier Anglican divines derived the basic idea of church polity from the presupposition that the church was not a new organization on this earth, but "only the Jewish church perfected and enlarged."[27] This link between the two "churches" allowed the Church of England to model many of its governmental structures after the Israeli religious hierarchy: a high priest, with lower priests under him, and Levites a level below.[28] As to the explicit support for the office of a bishop enjoying a "seniority" over that

---

21. One of the major distinctions of Methodism is that, in adopting an episcopal polity, it lessened the power of the bishop. For an introduction of the Methodist concept of this office, see Moede, *Office of Bishop in Methodism* and Erickson, *Christian Theology*, 1081. For a more in-depth overview of the Methodist polity, consult Kern, *Christianity as Organized*, 493–520.

22. For a helpful overview of the Lutheran polity, see Kern, *Christianity as Organized*, 463–69.

23. Such as the Church of God (Anderson, IN) and the Church of God (Cleveland, TN).

24. Peter Toon prefers to call this form of church government synodical rather than episcopal. Anglican polity is considered to be somewhat of a "mid-range" on an episcopal scale, with Methodist churches being the simplest, authorizing only one level of bishops, and Catholic churches the most complex, with multiple layers of bishops. For an additional source on Anglican polity, see Toon, "Episcopalianism."

25. Toon, "Episcopalianism," 28.

26. Ibid., 24.

27. Potter, *Church Government*, 3, 24. By "Jewish church," Potter, a nineteenth-century Archbishop of Canterbury, means Israel's Old Testament covenant relationship with YHWH. Incidentally, having claimed that the Bible contains no blueprint for church organization, Toon resorts to following in the footsteps of earlier theologians from whom he had previously distanced himself by using the Old Testament in support of the episcopal ecclesiastical hierarchy. See Toon, "Episcopalian's Response," 102.

28. Potter, *Church Government*, 95, 101. Thus, inherent in the episcopal structure is the idea of different levels of ministry or different degrees of ordination (Erickson, *Christian Theology*, 1070).

of presbyter/elder in the New Testament, it is generally recognized that a third office distinct from presbyters is not found there.

Advocates of the episcopal polity sometimes use the following arguments in support of their view. First, there is the historical development that resulted in three orders of ministers—deacons, presbyters, and bishops—as early as the middle of the second century. Second, there are passages where, according to the adherents of this model, implicit support for hierarchical government may be found: The Bible documents Paul and Barnabas "appointing" elders in each church (Acts 14:23), James exercising a special leadership role in Jerusalem (Acts 15:13), and Paul instructing Titus "to appoint Testament Elders in every town" in Crete (Titus 1:5).

The bishop is the key to the functioning of church government within Episcopal polity.[29] He inherits this centrality of position from the apostles themselves, according to the Anglican understanding of the apostolic succession.[30] Richard Hooker, in drafting his great treatise, *Of the Lawes of*

---

29. Erickson, *Christian Theology*, 1070. Bishops are a quasi-independent body of teachers/overseers. There are differences among the denominations that practice some type of episcopal polity. In the Eastern Orthodox churches, the patriarch of Constantinople is *primus inter pares* (first among equals) and together with four other patriarchs, forms a pentarchy. Scandinavian Lutheranism has retained the title and office of "bishop," but with less than clear claims to apostolic succession. In Methodism, the bishop is consecrated but not ordained, without apostolic succession, and functions with and through the annual conference. Garrett, *Systematic Theology*, 585.

30. A notion that can be traced back as far as the late second to early third centuries a.d. when Irenaeus of Lyons and Tertullian argued in their respective writings that apostolic succession was verifiable since there existed lists of bishops. See Irenaeus, "Irenaeus: Against Heresies," 5.20.2; Tertullian, "Prescription against Heretics," 32. However, not every denomination that follows an episcopal structure affirms apostolic succession. Some would prefer the term "historic episcopate," believing this to be the primitive model, yet recognizing that they cannot actually historically trace such a succession to the first and second generations of church leadership. See Brand and Norman, *Perspectives on Church Government*, 298; Saucy, *Church in God's Program*, 106. The Anglican Church's understanding of early ecclesiastical structures is largely shaped by its own form of government, which was inherited from the Roman Catholic Church. As a result of its determination to find biblical support for its own structure, the Anglican Church can miss the unique nature of the early years of the church. So when the apostles are involved in ordaining ministers, matters of church discipline, or restoration of repentant church members, the Anglican position sees only the authority possessed by the apostles to command such actions, completely missing the vital role that the local church played in each situation and the care with which the apostles exhorted the church, rather than ruling over them. Unfortunately, this thinking runs counter to passages like Eph 2:19–22, which plainly state that Christ's job, along with those of the apostles and prophets, was to erect a solid foundation for the new building—the church. Chapter 4 will discuss

Ecclesiasticall Politie, in the late sixteenth century, forcefully argues for the office of the bishop:

> A thousand five hundred years and upward the Church of Christ hath now continued under the sacred Regiment of Bishops. Neither for so long hath Christianity been ever planted in any Kingdom throughout the world but with this kind of government alone, which to have been ordained of God, I am for mine own part even as resolutely perswaded [sic], as that any other kind of Government in the world whatsoever is of God.[31]

Thus, episcopal polity has historically built itself upon the diocesan bishop, who is regarded as successor to the Twelve in an unbroken succession.[32] Hooker confirms this:

> From hence it may happily seem to have grown, that they whom now we call Bishops were usually termed at the first Apostles, and so did carry their very names in whose rooms of spiritual authority they succeeded.[33]

The succession of bishops held by the Anglicans constitutes the channel of grace whereby the life of the church is sustained.[34] Cyprian first enunciated this principle in the significant statement, "*Ecclesia est in episcopo.*"[35]

Within Anglicanism, the duties of a bishop include the ordination of priests, the placement of priests in pastoral assignments, the confirmation of the baptized, the preservation and teaching of true doctrine, and the exercise of discipline.[36] The main basis for the Anglican Church's teachings regarding its leadership is a logical derivation from a comparison to the way things work in civil government, as well as the duties assigned to the Old Testament office of a priest. In response to a more congregational government, Anglicans claim that the powers exercised by the officers of the church are of such a nature as can only be derived from God, or those

---

apostolic succession further.

31. Hooker, "Seventh Book," 7.1.4.

32. Garrett, *Systematic Theology*, 585. By the laying on of hands in the ceremony of ordination, the authority of the apostles has been transmitted down through history to today's bishops. See Erickson, *Christian Theology*, 1071.

33. Hooker, "Seventh Book," 7.4.4.

34. Dana and Sipes, *Manual of Ecclesiology*, 145.

35. "The Church is in the bishop" (Cyprian, "Epistles of Cyprian," 68.8).

36. Garrett, *Systematic Theology*, 585.

who act by his special commission, namely, the apostles.[37] For further support, they cite such ministers as Timothy and Titus, who seemed to enjoy a higher level of authority than that of deacons or elders/overseers.[38] In the case of Titus, Potter points out that he was ordained and appointed to his office not by the people's choice, but by Paul, who had converted the Cretans to the Christian faith,

> and by virtue of his appointment he was empowered to teach all degrees of men, and to exhort and rebuke them with authority; to take cognizance of heretics, and to reject from his own and the church's communion, such of them as did not repent upon the second admonition; to set in order whatever St. Paul had left wanting. Lastly, to ordain those whom he himself should approve to be bishops and elders.[39]

Moreover, in considering who may be ordained for different church offices, Anglicans recognize Scripture's silence, yet conclude "from the different kinds of officers whom Christ hath entrusted with the care and government of his church, not only that private Christians are excluded from the ordinary execution of an ecclesiastical power; but that some powers are appropriated in such a manner to the chief officers, that they cannot lawfully be exercised by those of lower orders."[40]

Additionally, Anglicans view the structure of the church, made up of apostles and prophets with Christ himself as the chief cornerstone (Eph 2:19–20), as something that was established on this earth during Jesus' own

---

37. Potter, *Church Government*, 102. Thus the bishops are not chosen from below, but from above.

38. "Whether or not the positions of James and Timothy and Titus were actually taken by the early church as the link between apostolic superintendence and that of the later bishop," Saucy points out, "this office does gradually appear around the turn of the first century, first in Asia Minor, and a generation later in the West. Appearing first as more or less a headship among equals, it develops into a position of independent supremacy during the second and third centuries. Instrumental in bringing this about were the needs of the church. The bishop provided a unifying factor amid churches of diversified character, many of which were suffering persecution. As an authoritative doctrinal voice, he was also a safeguard against heretical intrusions. And finally, there was the practical need for someone to represent the churches of one locality in communicating with others. According to Episcopalians, these needs were met through the guidance of the Spirit by the establishment of this form of government" (Saucy, *Church in God's Program*, 108).

39. Potter, *Church Government*, 117. They also view the seven angels of the seven churches in Rev 2–3 to be seven bishops who presided in the seven principal cities of the proconsular Asia.

40. Potter, *Church Government*, 181–82.

lifetime. In other words, they trace the origins of the Christian church to a time before the descent of the Holy Spirit upon the disciples in Jerusalem on Pentecost. With regard to baptism, the Church of England views circumcision as the forerunner to the sacrament, attaching to it remission of sins, the grace of the Holy Spirit, and eternal life.[41] Potter sees baptism at the center of different gospel presentations in the Scripture.[42] He cites Acts 22:16, in which Ananias instructs Paul to be baptized and wash away his sin immediately following his conversion: "Now why do you delay? Get up and be baptized, and wash away your sins, calling on His name." Then there is Peter exhorting his converts in Acts 2:38: "Repent, and each of you be baptized in the name of Jesus Christ for the forgiveness of your sins; and you will receive the gift of the Holy Spirit."[43]

Even Christ, in Potter's opinion, joins faith and baptism together as necessary conditions for salvation in John 3:5: "unless one is born of water and the Spirit he cannot enter into the kingdom of God." And in Mark 16:16: "He who has believed and has been baptized shall be saved." Potter concludes that these and the like passages of Scripture led the primitive church to infer that where the gospel had been sufficiently propounded, "no man could be saved without baptism actually obtained, or earnestly desired."[44] The rejection of baptism in the New Testament, according to this tradition, was tantamount to declining the covenant of God, as was the case with circumcision in Israel.

It may come as a surprise, in view of such high importance being ascribed to baptism within the Church of England, that Anglicans consider it one of the lowest ministries, with the power to perform it belonging chiefly and primarily to bishops, though it could be delegated to presbyters and deacons operating under the authority and within the "jurisdiction" of the bishop. Whether a layman can perform baptism in the Anglican Church is a delicate issue. In consulting the works of early church fathers, there is somewhat of a consensus that it can be done only in extreme situations where no ordained clergy can be procured.[45]

---

41. Potter, *Church Government*, 8.
42. Ibid., 8–9.
43. Ibid., 184–85.
44. Ibid., 10.
45. According to O. C. Quick, "it is recognized that if an ordained minister is not available, a layman or woman should preform [sic] the rite [of baptism] in case of need" (Quick, "Doctrine of the Church of England," 126).

Another responsibility belonging strictly to priestly office within this denomination is the right to consecrate the Lord's Supper. As Christ consecrated the bread and the wine and commanded his disciples to continue this practice in remembrance of him, the act of consecration, according to the Anglican theology, falls within the command to continue. Unlike baptism, the right to perform the consecration of the Lord's Supper is open only to the bishop or the presbyter, but not to the deacons, because:

> Baptism was always reckoned one of the lowest ministries, and, therefore, was usually committed by the apostles to ministers of the lower orders . . . or that baptism, being the right of admission into the church, was thought more necessary than the Lord's supper; which reason is commonly assigned by the ancient fathers for permitting laymen to baptize when any person was in danger of leaving the world unbaptized. But there is yet a farther reason why none but bishops and presbyters have ever consecrated the Lord's supper; viz. because the Lord's supper was always believed to succeed in the place of sacrifices; consequently, as none beside the high-priest and inferior priests were permitted to offer sacrifices under the Jewish law, so the Lord's supper was consecrated by none but bishops and presbyters, who alone are priests in the Christian sense of that name.[46]

In the exercise of church discipline, Anglicans believe that the power to determine and pronounce the disciplinary measures resides with the "rulers" of the church, and not the whole assembly. As the ones invested with the authority to make laws, it is natural for the governors of the church to "pass sentence on those who break them."[47] These disciplinary judgments were pronounced in the public assemblies (Matt 18:19) but received their force from the leadership of the church.

Presbyterian Polity

The presbyterian system of church government places primary authority in a particular office as well, but puts less emphasis on the individual office and office holder than upon a *series of representative bodies* that exercise that authority.[48]

---

46. Potter, *Church Government*, 225–26.
47. Ibid., 297.
48. Erickson, *Christian Theology*, 1074, emphasis mine.

Presbyterianism originated in the Protestant Reformation, particularly in Calvin's Geneva.[49] In this reformer's *Institutes of the Christian Religion*, as in the later Presbyterian and Reformed tradition, the key to both the doctrine and the order of the church is found in God's sovereignty, rather than in the explicit testimony of Scripture.[50]

The key officer in the presbyterian structure is the elder.[51] Accordingly, this model traces its name from the two Greek words: *presbuteros*, which occurs sixty-six times in the Greek New Testament[52] and means "older man" or "elder," and *presbuterion*, which occurs three times in the Greek New Testament (Luke 22:66; Acts 22:5; 1 Tim 4:14) and means "body of elders." Presbyterians believe that *presbuteros* (elder) and *episkopos* (overseer) are descriptive synonyms designating a function for the same office holder:

> Beyond dispute, for Paul the elder was an overseer and the overseer was an elder. The two terms simply describe two roles of the same officeholder: as an elder this officer exercises authority; as an overseer this same officer performs the functional role of spiritual supervision and oversight.[53]

According to this model, the elders or overseers governing the church, distinct from those charged with teaching, are chosen by the congregation, which must recognize that "their officer's election is Christ's will and that in the final analysis, as Paul states in Acts 20:28, it is the Holy Spirit who is placing these men in the office of elder/overseer."[54] Thus, "in choosing officers, the church does not grant them authority, but recognizes Christ's authority and calling."[55] The Presbyterian congregation recognizes that the church is not a pure democracy, so the job of the elders/overseers does

---

49. Clowney, "Presbyterianism," 530. For another exhaustive source on Presbyterianism, see Hodge, *Discussions in Church Polity*.

50. Clowney, "Presbyterianism," 530.

51. For a detailed explanation of this office and its correlation with the offices of pastor and overseer, see chapter 3.

52. Luke 15:25; John 8:9; 1 Tim 5:1; Matt 16:21; 21:23; 26:3, 47; 27:1, 3, 12, 20, 41; 26:57; Acts 11:30; 14:23; 15:2, 4, 6, 22; 16:4; 1 Tim 5:17, 19; Titus 1:5; Jas 5:14, to list a few.

53. Reymond, "Presbytery-Led Church," 92. They support this assertion with Paul's intertwining usages of the words in Acts 20:17 and 20:28; 1 Tim 3:1–7; Titus 1:5–9; Phil 1:1; 1 Pet 5:1–2, pointing out that although *episkopountes* is a variant reading, the very fact that many manuscripts include it gives evidence that many adult Christians in the early church believed that "elders" were also "overseers."

54. Ibid., 94.

55. Clowney, "Presbyterianism," 530.

Key Terms and Polity Models

not consist of simply carrying out the congregation's will.[56] Instead, their responsibility is "to rule and oversee the congregation, not primarily in agreement with the will of the congregation but primarily in agreement with the revealed word of God, in accordance with the authority delegated to them by Christ, the head of the church."[57]

Presbyterians recognize that the scriptural pattern of government is necessary for the wellbeing of the church, but is not essential for its existence.[58] At the same time, they insist that the governmental structure of the New Testament church, especially the one described in Acts, provides a warrant for their "governmental connectionalism." In other words, by logical deduction from the passages describing the practices and organization of the early church, the theologians of this tradition hold that the Scripture supports their connectional government of graded courts: local "session," regional "presbytery," and "general assembly."

> The local council of elders/overseers referred to as the session or consistory exercises authority over the local congregation. Some of these same elders/overseers, together with elders/overseers from other local churches, serve periodically as members also of a presbytery or classis that usually meets quarterly to exercise authority over the several local churches in its geographically circumscribed area, and more specifically to examine and to ordain ministers of the gospel and to exercise discipline over the same when the need arises. Of these elders/overseers, along with elders/overseers from other presbyteries, in turn, some serve as members of a national General Assembly or synod that usually meets annually to exercise authority over the several presbyteries in a region or country, to worship God together, to hear reports on the spiritual health and future plans of the church's mission agencies and educational institutions, and to adjudicate disciplinary cases that come before it from the lower courts.[59]

This system of graded assemblies, or courts, reflects the unity of the church catholic, regional, and local.[60] In passages like Acts 13:1–3; 15:3,

---

56. Berkhof, *Systematic Theology*, 584.

57. Reymond, "Presbytery-Led Church," 95. See also Berkhof, *Systematic Theology*, 582.

58. Clowney, "Presbyterianism," 530.

59. Reymond, "Presbytery-Led Church," 123–24. See also Berkhof, *Systematic Theology*, 588–89.

60. Clowney, "Presbyterianism," 531.

35, Presbyterians see the elders/overseers of the Antioch and Jerusalem congregations forming themselves into local presbyteries.[61] Much of their system is based on the account of the conference in Jerusalem described in Acts 15, which was convened with the purpose of identifying the terms of Gentile conversion—that is, faith alone versus faith plus circumcision and observation of dietary laws. Presbyterianism considers the Jerusalem council to have set a precedent for their general assembly.

Their interpretation of Acts 15 is as follows: When the local church in Antioch did not believe that they had sufficient authority to settle for themselves the terms of membership in their churches, a request was made for the assembly of elders to convene in Jerusalem.[62] Furthermore, the Presbyterians consider the dissemination of Acts 15 decisions, as evidenced in Acts 16:4, to be further proof that the apostles and elders did not regard the congregations to which they wrote as independent and autonomous, but rather as "mutually submissive to, mutually dependent upon, and mutually accountable to one another."[63] Additionally, Christ's high priestly prayer for the "visible unity" of his followers in John 17:20–21, as well as the interdependent nature of the gifts of the Spirit, are put forth as further arguments for Presbyterian connectionalism:

> In light of the biblical emphasis, then, on *visible* Christian unity and "oneness" (see John 10:10–13; Rom 15:5–6; Gal 3:28; 1 Cor 1:10–13; 12:12–13; Eph 2:14–16; 4:3–6; Phil 2:2; Col 3:12–14), why, Presbyterians wonder, do Congregationalists put so much

---

61. Needless to say, the texts nowhere explicitly state anything about local presbyteries, but that does not stop Presbyterian scholars like R. L. Reymond, in whose opinion theologians must wean themselves away "from reading Scripture texts in an unnatural, wooden, *literalistic* way," (quoted in Brand and Norman, *Perspectives on Church Government*, 81, emphasis mine). From a more objective perspective, Berkhof admits that "Scripture does not contain an explicit command to the effect that the local churches of a district must form an organic union. Neither does it furnish us with an example of such a union. In fact, it represents the local churches as individual entities without any external bond of union" (Berkhof, *Systematic Theology*, 590). Berkhof then proceeds to argue for Presbyterian connectionalism from the "essential nature of the church . . . a spiritual organism in which all the constituent parts are vitally related to one another" (ibid.).

62. Reymond, "Presbytery-Led Church," 108. Reymond notes the presence of the apostles in the council (Acts 15:4), but dismisses the uniqueness of that element by deducing that the apostles were acting as elders in the church. He also speculates that the Jerusalem Council included some Antioch elders/overseers meeting as delegated commissioners with the Jerusalem presbytery in a general assembly (ibid.). See also Taylor, "Presbyterianism," 80.

63. Ibid., 109.

emphasis upon—indeed, even glory in as one of their distinctives—local church autonomy, self-consciously making their *independency* from each other and from other denominational churches a major reason for claiming "bragging rights" over Presbyterian connectionalism so far as their form of church government reflecting the teaching of the New Testament is concerned?[64]

Under the presbyterian system, there is a deliberate coordinating of clergy and laity.[65] Both groups are included in all of the various governing assemblies and neither has special powers or rights that the other does not have.[66] However, their exegesis of 1 Tim 5:17 draws a distinction between ruling elders and teaching elders.[67] Ruling elders are non-ministerial elders of the church who are elected by the local congregation. Teaching elders are those who have been set apart for the ministry of the Word and are called by the local congregation to labor among them, but ordained and installed in their work by presbyteries.[68] The Presbyterian recognition of the ruling elder is based on the distinction of teaching and ruling gifts (1 Tim 5:17; Rom 12:8; 1 Cor 12:28), and the divinely authorized role of the elders of the people in the Old Covenant (Num 11:16, 17), continued in the New (Acts 11:30; cf. Matt 13:52; 23:34).[69]

---

64. Ibid., 110. The "visible Christian unity" and the spiritual gifts that teach the interdependent nature of the body seem to make much better sense when applied on a local church level rather than a denominational level. Furthermore, Reymond may find himself far out on a limb in making such a statement, considering Berkhof's affirmation of the autonomy of the local church: "Every local church is a complete church of Christ, fully equipped with everything that is required for its government. It has absolutely no need of it that any government should be imposed upon it from without. And not only that, but such an imposition would be absolutely contrary to its nature . . . The idea that a classis (presbytery) or synod can simply impose whatever it pleases on a particular church is essentially Roman Catholic" (Berkhof, *Systematic Theology*, 589–90).

65. Erickson, *Christian Theology*, 1077.

66. Ibid.

67. 1 Tim 5:17 reads: "The elders who rule well are to be considered worthy of double honor, especially those who work hard at preaching and teaching." The Presbyterian understanding of this passage is that "the elders who direct the affairs of the church well are worthy of double honor [namely, both 'honor' and 'honoraruim']" (Reymond, "Presbytery-Led Church," 121). As Knight observes, Paul is speaking here of "a subgroup of the 'overseers' that consists of those who are *especially* gifted by God to teach, as opposed to other overseers, who must all 'be *able* to teach'" (Knight, *Pastoral Epistles*, 233, emphasis Knight's).

68. Reymond, "Presbytery-Led Church," 121–23.

69. Clowney, "Presbyterianism," 531.

The presbyterian model views the office of the deacon as one of ministry rather than spiritual government. It is charged with the service of mercy to the poor and needy among the saints, and, as God grants opportunity, to the world.[70]

When it comes to church discipline within this branch of Christianity, although the ordinary members of the church are frequently called upon to take part in the application of discipline, it is generally applied by the officers of the church and can be applied *only by them* when discipline becomes censure.[71] Distinguishing between private and public sins, Presbyterians have a different way to deal with each. In case of private sins (trespasses dealing with interpersonal relationships), the pattern of Matt 18:15–17 is usually followed, with a personal confrontation preceding a confrontation by a group of people and possibly resulting in a confrontation by the church. Public sins, however, render the sinner subject to disciplinary action by the consistory at once, without the formality of any preceding private admonitions, even if there is no formal accusation.[72]

Elaborating on the disciplinary process exercised by the consistory, Berkhof unveils its three stages:

> (a) The *excommunicatio minor*, restraining the sinner from partaking of the Lord's Supper. This is not public, and is followed by repeated admonitions by the consistory, in order to bring the sinner to repentance. (b) If the preceding measure does not avail, it is followed by three public announcements and admonitions. In the first of these the sin is mentioned, but the sinner is not named. In the second the name is made known in accordance with the advice of classis, which must first be obtained. And in the third the imminent final excommunication is announced, in order that this may have the consent of the congregation. During all this time the consistory, of course, continues its admonitions. (c) Finally, this is followed by the *excommunicatio major*, by which one is cut off from the fellowship of the Church, Matt 18:17; 1 Cor 5:13; Titus 3:10,11.[73]

---

70. Ibid.

71. Berkhof, *Systematic Theology*, 600, emphasis Berkhof's.

72. Ibid. Public sins encompass not merely sins that are committed in public, but also sins that give public and general offense.

73. Ibid., emphasis Berkhof's. One would naturally wonder how many Presbyterian churches today still practice a disciplinary process that is similar to the one outlined by Berkhof in the first part of the twentieth century.

Berkhof adds that according to 2 Cor 2:5–10, it is always possible to reinstate the sinner, provided he or she shows due repentance and confesses his or her sins.[74] All church power, according to Presbyterianism, is wholly moral and spiritual.[75] Church officers possess no civil jurisdiction; they may not inflict civil penalties nor seek the aid of the civil authority in the exercise of their jurisdiction.[76]

Congregational Polity

Congregational polity, as defined by James Leo Garrett, is "that form of church government in which final human authority rests with the local or particular congregation when it gathers for decision-making."[77] Thus, congregationalism locates the authority of the church in each local body of believers.[78] Saucy summarizes well how this works out on a local level:

> Emphasis is upon the democratic structure of the church whereby the ultimate authority is vested in the members themselves. This does not preclude ministers elected in recognition of their divine gifts to serve as leaders, but their authority rests in their relation to the congregation and is generally less extensive in practice than either the episcopal or presbyterian ministers. In the ultimate sense, officers have no more ecclesiastical authority than any other member. Each has but one vote on any issue.[79]

Whereas the historical roots of episcopal (which date to the rise in prominence of the office of the bishop in the second and third centuries a.d.) and presbyterian (which most trace back to the writings of John Calvin) forms of church government are generally better known, it may be of value to take a moment here to review the origins of congregationalism. According to Kern's work, *A Study of Christianity as Organized*, the original motive for the establishment of congregationalism was neither doctrinal nor legislative, but disciplinary: "It was distinctly a moral motive—not a desire for a scriptural in place of an unscriptural creed, nor a scriptural

---

74. Ibid.
75. Clowney, "Presbyterianism," 531.
76. Ibid. It is noteworthy that this concept of later Presbyterianism is quite divergent from the actual practice in Calvin's Geneva.
77. Garrett, "Congregation-Led Church," 157.
78. Akin, "Single-Elder-Led Church," 27.
79. Saucy, *Church in God's Program*, 114.

Church Government According to the Bible

in place of an unscriptural form of government, but the desire for a scriptural in place of an unscriptural state of discipline."[80] In the course of their study and further investigation of Scripture, the early Separatists did reach the conclusion that their newly adopted polity was in accordance with the teachings of Jesus and his apostles, rather than their own invention.[81] Most date this new phenomenon to around the year 1580, when, in the city of Norwich, England, Robert Browne, "the father of modern Congregationalism," became pastor of what may be called the first Congregational Church of modern times.[82]

Aside from Browne, other well-known early English congregationalists include Henry Barrowe, John Owen, Isaac Watts, Phillip Doddridge, William Jay, Thomas Binney, Robert William Dale, Joseph Parker, and Andrew Martin Fairbairn.[83]

The congregational model of church government today has two different variations: democratic congregationalism,[84] which itself can take a number of different practical venues: single-elder-led, deacon-board-led, trustee-led, etc., and multiple-elder-led congregationalism, which is exercised by a good number of Baptist churches, all Plymouth Brethren churches, and Bible churches, among others.[85] "It is the intention under congregational polity," writes Garrett, "that the congregation govern itself under the lordship of Jesus Christ (Christocracy) and with the leadership of the Holy Spirit (pneumatophoria), with no superior or governing ecclesial bodies (autonomy) and with every member having a voice in its affairs and

---

80. Kern, *Christianity as Organized*, 376.

81. Ibid.

82. Ibid., 377. It was Browne, who, due to the violent reaction to his severe opposition to the Establishment, was forced to flee, along with his whole congregation, to the town of Middleburg, Holland, where he wrote a well-known tract in defense of the congregational views named "Reformation without Tarrying for Any." To be fair, a man called Richard Fitz formed the first Separatist church in Britain in 1567 London, but it had a very checkered and short history. D. Martin Lloyd-Jones considers the first real Congregational church to be the one established by Henry Jacob in Southwark, London, in 1616. For more on Lloyd-Jones' logic, see Lloyd-Jones, "First Congregational Church."

83. Kern, 380.

84. This style of government can be seen most often in Baptist churches.

85. These varieties are most common within the congregational model. Grudem adds a few others, such as leadership by a corporate board, pure democracy, and "no government but the Holy Spirit" (Grudem, *Systematic Theology*, 935–36). Additionally, a staff-led model seems to have gained popularity in the last decade among larger churches with multiple staff.

Key Terms and Polity Models

its decisions (democracy)."[86] The principle of autonomy, as explained by Erickson, means that each local church is self-governing: Each congregation may call its own pastor, determine its own budget, purchase its own property, make decisions that do not require outside ratification or approval, and enter into cooperative affiliations that are strictly voluntary in nature.[87] Accordingly, the concept of democracy means that, on the basis of the doctrine of the priesthood of all believers, authority within the local congregation rests with the individual members.[88]

When it comes to the biblical warrant for congregational structure, there are at least six Scripture passages that, according to Garret, offer explicit support for democratic congregationalism: Matt 18:15–20; Acts 6:3; 13:2–3; 15:22; 1 Cor 5:2; and 2 Cor 2:6.[89] Second, such support can also be derived from examining the predominant meaning of *ekklesia*, a Greek term that refers to a local assembly in some ninety-three of the 114 times it is used in the New Testament. The third argument for congregationalism is derived from the New Testament's complete silence regarding any territorial organization of the church or churches.

There is no reference in Acts or the Epistles to any structure above or beyond the local church. There is no command to form inter-church unions of any type. We find no evidence of control over a local church by outside organizations or individuals. The apostles made recommendations and gave advice, but exercised no real rulership. Even Paul had to argue for his apostolic authority and beseech his readers to follow his teachings (2 Cor; Gal 1:11–24).[90] Fourth, the interchangeability of the Greek terms *episkopos*, *presbuteros*, and *poimēn*, defended in Chapter 4, can provide further—though indirect—support for congregational polity, which is more

---

86. Garrett, *Systematic Theology*, 586–87.

87. Erickson, *Christian Theology*, 1079. Dana and Sipes cite the following examples in support of this assertion: "(a) When Paul secured an offering from the Gentile churches of the West for the destitute saints in Palestine he had the local churches to appoint messengers to accompany him in carrying the offering to its destination (2 Cor 8:19, 23). (b) New Testament churches determined their own customs (1 Cor 11:16). (c) Each church settled its own difficulties without any interference from without, except in the capacity of advice (1 Cor 5:4, 5; 6:4). (d) A local church had the right to determine its own policies (Acts 15)" (Dana and Sipes, *Manual of Ecclesiology*, 36–37).

88. Erickson, *Christian Theology*, 1080.

89. There are additional texts that provide indirect evidence of Congregationalism present in Scripture, including: Acts 1:21–26; 9:26–28; 1 Cor 16:3; 2 Cor 8:22–24; Phil 2:25; Rev 2:14–16, 20–25.

90. Erickson, *Christian Theology*, 1079.

than can be said of the basis for views advocating a monarchical or diocesan bishop.[91]

Fifth, the doctrine of the priesthood of all Christians,[92] "affirmed in the early patristic age, overcome and supplanted for centuries by the clerical priesthood, and rediscovered by Martin Luther,"[93] provides a powerful support for congregational theologians' position.

In the congregational form of government, as in the presbyterian, there is only one level of clergy.[94] The New Testament offices of elder, overseer, and pastor are believed to be one and the same and are usually referred to as "pastor" within the single-elder-led branch of this tradition.[95] In this kind of government, the pastor is seen as the only elder in the church, and an elected board of deacons serves under his authority and gives him support.[96]

The following evidence is often used in support of single-elder-led government. First, there is the fact that the early church would meet in the homes of the believers.[97] It is reasonable to suppose, therefore, that each household was led by one elder.[98] Second, Eph 4:11 makes reference to the pastor-teacher: "And He gave some as apostles, and some as prophets, and some as evangelists, and some as pastors and teachers." According to Akin, as the only office of the four mentioned in the passage that is directly related to the local church, it is extremely likely that the pastor-teacher is an elder.[99] The third argument for single-elder-led churches is a pattern found in both the Old and New Testaments. That pattern is a plurality of leaders

---

91. Garrett, "Congregation-Led Church," 171.

92. Taught in 1 Pet 2:4–10; Rev 1:5b–6; 5:9–10; 20:6

93. Garrett, "Congregation-Led Church," 184.

94. Consistent of two grades: elders and deacons (Erickson, *Christian Theology*, 1080).

95. Merkle, "Elder and Overseer."

96. Grudem, *Systematic Theology*, 928.

97. See Acts 2:46; 12:12, 17; 21:18; Rom 16:3–5, 10–11; 14–15, 23; Phlm 2; Col 4:15; 1 Cor 16:15, 19.

98. Akin, "Single-Elder-Led Church," 65. See also Strong, *Systematic Theology*, 914–17; Carson, "Church, Authority in," 249. Campbell suggests that the leadership of each group was naturally assumed by the head of the household—the one who would have a house large enough to fit the group and who would open it for such meetings (Campbell, *Elders*, 151–53).

99. Akin, "Single-Elder-Led Church," 65.

with a senior leader over them.[100] This can be observed in Exod 18, in which Moses, the senior leader, is assisted by a group of "under-leaders" who help him with judging the nation of Israel. The same can be said of James, the half brother of Christ, who according to Paul (Gal 1:19; 2:9, 12), served as the main, though not sole, leader of the Jerusalem church. Acts 15 provides a beautiful illustration of how James functioned in that capacity. Fourth, some believe that the "angels of the church" addressed in Rev 2:1, 8, 12, 18; 3:1, 7, 14 are best interpreted to mean pastors. If this understanding is correct, it is clear that each church had not many pastors, but one.[101]

Those advocating plurality of elders within a local church differ in that they recognize a pastor as one among the elders—an elder in office.[102] He does not have authority over the other elders, nor does he work for them as an employee. His distinction from the rest, however, is that he is engaged in the full-time work of preaching and teaching and derives his income from that work.[103] In this system of government, there is always more than one elder, a point that distinguishes this form of government from the "single-elder system" discussed above.[104]

The scriptural support for a plurality of elders in a local church can be found first in the fact that whenever elders are mentioned in the New Testament, they are always spoken of in the plural.[105] Second, the fact that the leadership of the church at Ephesus is identified by "elders" in Acts 20:17 provides yet further proof for plurality of eldership in the New Testament. It was not a single pastor that Paul wanted to see; it was a body of elders that was entrusted with leading the Ephesian church.

Within congregationalism, church officers are generally viewed as representatives and servants of the church, answerable to those who have chosen them.[106] They are not to exercise their authority independently of,

---

100. Ibid., 66.

101. Strong, *Systematic Theology*, 916. However, we know for a fact that at least one of the churches listed in Rev 2–3 had multiple-eldership and not a single elder/pastor. See Ephesians; Acts 20:17.

102. Campbell, *Elders*, 160.

103. Grudem, *Systematic Theology*, 933. See 1 Tim 5:17–18.

104. Ibid.

105. See Acts 14:23; 16:4; 20:17; 21:18; 1 Tim 5:17; Titus 1:5; Jas 5:14; 1 Pet 5:1. Pointing to Acts 14:23, White adds that understanding "elders" merely in the sense of one elder per church runs counter to the plain meaning of "elders for them in every church" (White, "Plural-Elder-Led Church," 271).

106. Erickson, *Christian Theology*, 1080.

or contrary to, the wishes of the people.[107] Proponents of congregationalism believe that biblical church discipline is a function of a congregation, citing passages like Matt 18:17, 1 Cor 5:4–5, 2 Cor 2:6, and 2 Thess 3:6, 14–15 in support of this view. In Matthew, the last resort in the discipline process is for the whole congregation to be involved. In 1 Corinthians, Paul directs the church to deal with the incest among them on a congregational level. In 2 Corinthians, he speaks of the benefits of disciplinary action exercised by the majority. Finally, in 2 Thessalonians, the whole church is commanded to withdraw from the one with "disorderly" conduct. As Gerald P. Cowen explains, "the final court of appeal in matters of discipline is the church as a whole, not the officers or any representative body."[108] MacArthur's understanding may be used as a universal example of the common sentiment within this tradition: "Our Lord clearly teaches here that ultimately the entire assembly of believers has a responsibility to follow through in seeking restoration of a sinning member."[109] Having introduced the concept of Church Polity and various polity models, it is now time to examine the hermeneutical principles which form the foundation of the argument within this work.

---

107. Ibid.

108. Cowen, *Who Rules the Church?* 85. See also Samuel E. Waldron, "Plural-Elder Congregationalist's Response," 118–21.

109. MacArthur, *Master's Plan*, 236.

3

Theological Considerations for Polity Models

THE NEED FOR UNDERSTANDING FOUNDATIONAL THEOLOGICAL PRINCIPLES

To use the words of Rex A. Coivisto, "we all interpret the Bible if we read it. It would do us all well then to think about whether we are doing so appropriately or not."[1] Since it is a known fact that the Scriptures do not speak with equal clarity on all matters they touch upon, the concern of this chapter, therefore, is to discover and lay out a position on some hermeneutical principles common to the discussion of polity that can function as a theological paradigm for accurate exegesis of ecclesiological passages in the New Testament.[2] Or, stated differently, what position should we take on the theological principles in question when approaching Scripture for the purpose of determining what it teaches about church polity?

THE GENESIS OF THE FOLLOWING SIX GUIDING THEOLOGICAL PRINCIPLES

I realize that the idea of a theological paradigm that guides Scriptural reading may cause some to cry, "FOUL!" How dare I suggest that we should

---

1. Koivisto, *One Lord, One Faith*, 152.

2. Ibid., 132. The theological paradigm would be the rule that helps to produce more clarity for the modern understanding of church polity.

approach Scripture with preconceived notions regarding what it says? Have we not all been taught to come to the Bible with open minds and hearts and let its message determine what we believe?

The answer to the last question is a resounding "Yes!" and at the same time, "Not exactly." We all come to the Bible with some preconceived notions about it, which themselves may or may not be based on Scripture.[3] For example, when reading the Bible, everyone is guided by one of two theological presuppositions regarding its inerrancy and infallibility. One either assumes that it is, in fact, inerrant—containing no alleged error in doctrine, history, chronology, or physics, and infallible—or it is not. Much of one's interpretation of and general attitude towards Scripture is going to depend on this theological presupposition regarding its trustworthiness. Klein, Blomberg, and Hubbard put it this way: "Though we must always submit to the teachings of the Bible as our sole and final authority, our actual pre-understanding of the Bible as God's revelation guides our interpretation of its pages" and "our commitment to the authority of the Bible derives from our prior conviction of its truthfulness."[4]

Furthermore, we all are steeped in some type of tradition that also affects the way we read and interpret the Bible. Brown is right in stating that none of us can practice the "leapfrog" model of interpretation, which claims the ability to go directly to the Bible, uninfluenced by tradition. He believes that no one approaches the Bible free of denominational or theological presuppositions or unaffected by our contemporary situation, arguing,

> When it comes to the theological or denominational presuppositions, Lutherans tend to read the Bible in the light of the interpretive principle of justification by faith, Presbyterians in terms of the sovereignty of God. The sect groups read it from the perspective of their own practices, which may range from snake handling to speaking in tongues. Liberal Protestants find the Bible a handbook for social justice, while conservatives find it depicting an everlasting hell fire designed for liberals . . . From the contemporary

---

3. As the only infallible and the inerrant word of God, Scripture should norm all such notions. Bultmann argues that insofar as the exegete is not a *tabula rasa*, but on the contrary, approaches the text with specific questions or with a specific way of raising questions—and thus has a certain idea of the subject matter with which the text is concerned—"*there cannot be any such thing as presuppositionless exegesis*" (Bultmann, "Is Exegesis without Presuppositions Possible?" 289–90, emphasis Bultmann's).

4. Klein et al., "Preunderstandings and Intepreter," 76. See also Osborne, *Hermeneutical Spiral*, 407.

situation standpoint, Americans in East Lansing hear Rom 13 in a different way from Germans in East Berlin. When Mississippi Senators and Afrikaner nationalists read Paul's speech on Mars Hill, they draw different conclusions about racial discrimination than do natives of Indonesia or Ghana who read the same passage ... No one is trying to be dishonest. Everyone claims to be hearing the word of God. But the indisputable fact of the matter is that Lutherans, Presbyterians, sectarians, liberals, conservatives, Lansingites, East Berliners, southern Americans, southern Afrikaners, Indonesians, and Ghanaians all read the same Scripture and hear different things.[5]

Fee similarly argues that it is simply impossible for us to *not* bring our own experience of faith and church to biblical texts.[6] "Presuppositionless understanding," according to Schneiders' blunt assessment, "is a figment of the imagination of nineteenth-century historicism."[7] Likewise, Fred H. Klooster concludes that "presuppositionless exegesis is impossible."[8]

The issue of the "hermeneutical circle" or "spiral," as it is sometimes called, needs to be mentioned in passing here insofar as it pertains to our present discussion. "Hermeneutical circle" assumes that understanding a whole stretch of language or literature depends on a grasp of its component parts, while comprehension of these smaller units likewise depends on an understanding of the total import of the whole.[9] Admittedly, there is an inevitable circularity in interpretation.[10]

When we posit the requirement of faith to understand the Bible fully and then look to the Bible to understand God's self-revelation in Christ in whom we have faith, the process has a definite circularity to it.[11] Recognizing the role of our pre-understanding, however, does not doom us to a closed circle—that we find in the text what we want to find in the text. The honest, active interpreter remains open to change, even to a significant transformation of pre-understandings.[12]

---

5. Brown, *Spirit of Protestantism*, 215–16. Also see Bultmann, "Is Exegesis without Presuppositions Possible?" 289–96.

6. Fee, *Gospel and Spirit*, 70. See also Vanhoozer, *Meaning in This Text?* 381ff.

7. Schneiders, "Faith, Hermeneutics," 722.

8. Klooster, "Role of the Holy Spirit," 464.

9. Thiselton, *Two Horizons*, 104.

10. Klein et al., "Preunderstandings and Intepreter," 80.

11. Ibid.

12. Ibid., 81.

Hence, the important thing is not whether we come to the Bible with total neutrality (none of us really do), but whether our guiding theological presuppositions conform to Scripture. Klooster correctly concludes that "a sound biblical hermeneutic demands that one approach Scripture with a pre-understanding that is wholly consonant with it."[13] When our presuppositions are not formed by Scripture, then we are left with some sort of tradition setting itself up to be *normative* and *irreformable* over the Scriptures, to use Lane's words.[14]

One final explanation regarding the origin of the following principles may be appropriate before delving into the principles themselves. In other words, from where did they originate? Were they randomly picked with the purpose of ultimately "conforming" polity passages to our own theological system, or was there more objectivity to it?

The process of compiling the principles outlined below was neither random nor prejudiced. In reading through the various models of church polity, I found that they depend largely on their understanding of the six guiding theological principles that formed the nucleus of this work. The position that each of us takes with regard to these guiding principles, therefore, affects our understanding of church polity. These six guiding theological principles deal with (1) the relationship between Scripture and tradition; (2) literal versus allegorical readings of the Bible; (3) the timing of the origin of the church; (4) the nature of the New Testament offices of apostle and prophet; (5) the relationship between the New Testament offices of elder, overseer, and pastor; and (6) the connection between interpretation and application of biblical passages. Each of the principles is either directly drawn from or indirectly sanctioned by the word of God and enjoys the support of not just one stray verse, but a number of related passages.

---

13. Klooster, "Role of the Holy Spirit," 464.

14. "Our teaching today is not, cannot be, a simple summary of the Scripture," (Lane, "Scripture, Tradition and Church," 48). Writing in the last century, Lane was absolutely correct in his conviction that twentieth-century theology, even when most firmly based on Scripture, is clearly the outcome of nineteen centuries of Christian thought. But this awareness does not mean that the Protestants have to abandon the *sola Scriptura* in the sense that Scripture is the sole norm, the *norma normans non normata* (the rule that rules, but is not ruled).

SIX GUIDING FOUNDATIONAL THEOLOGICAL PRINCIPLES

Listed below is a position on the six principles that is closely linked with the word of God and will serve as a springboard for subsequent inquiry into the most biblically defensible model of church polity.

First Principle: The Supremacy of Scripture

The first principle delineates the supremacy of Scripture over human traditions, including the church, reason, and experience. In saying this, I do not deny the value of tradition, the community within which we live and develop our interpretation of Scripture, our ability to reason, or our personal experiences. Each is valuable and helpful in its own right, though with various degrees of import. None of them, however, can enjoy the same level of authority as the word of God.

Since we have already discussed the role of tradition in our understanding of Scripture, it may be helpful to pick up the discussion where we left it and add to it here. William Kiffin, a seventeenth-century British theologian, ably outlined the importance of careful and complete obedience to the Lord exactly as prescribed in Scripture, especially in those areas where it may be "enhanced" by human traditions:

> If the Conquest of an Enemy against the Command of his General, cost a *Roman* Gentleman his life, though his own Father were the Judge: If the killing of a Lion contrary to the Laws of the Kings Hunting (though to rescue the King himself) cost a poor *Persian* his Head: If the Architect that brought not the same (but as he judged a fitter) piece of Timber than he was commanded, to a *Roman* Consul, was rewarded with a bundle of Rods: If *Nadab* and *Abihu* came to a Tragical [*sic.*] end for their prohibited service, in offering not the *same* that was *commanded,* but *strange* fire before the Lord, what shall we say to such as mix their Inventions with the Sacred Institutions and Prescripts of the Great Sovereign? . . .

> And may it not be truly said that whoever Practices any Institution otherwise than as was appointed by the Supreme Law-giver *does not Honour the Ordinance, but an Idol of his own making? Mixtures* are useful for two purposes; *viz.* either to slaken and abate something that is *excessive*, or to supply something that is *deficient*: and so all *Heterogeneous* mixtures do plainly intimate, either a Viciousness to be Corrected, or a Defect to be Supplyed [*sic*.]. Now it is no less than *Blasphemy* to charge either of these upon the Pure and Perfect Word of God, and any Glosses that take away or diminish the force of it, or human Traditions that argue any defect, are equally dangerous and impious. To stamp anything of a humane Original with a Divine Character, and father it upon God, is one of the highest and most daring Presumptions the Pride of man can aspire unto, and is provided against by special prohibitions and threatening.[15]

Later, Kiffin emphasizes again the high import that the Scripture places on meticulous compliance with its propositions:

> . . . if Military Commanders expect a punctual and regular Obedience from their Soldiers; and severely punish such as break their Array, or quit their Stations; The *Lord* (who is a Jealous God with respect to his Worship, and positive Institutions) will call any, that presume to break the Order he has prescribed, to a severe account.[16]

But what is tradition?[17] Fee identifies at least five levels of tradition, which we may acknowledge, embrace, reject, or utilize, consciously or otherwise:

> "Tradition" tends to have five distinct nuances, which can be illustrated in the following nearly impossible sentence: The New Testament documents record the tradition (1) of Christ and the apostles, which early church tradition (2) understood to be inspired and authoritative Scripture; the later church codified tradition (3) so that it became equally authoritative with Scripture, an understanding which those within the evangelical tradition (4)

---

15. Preface to Kiffin, *Sober Discourse of Right to Church*.
16. Ibid., 20.
17. The English word "tradition" derives from the Latin equivalent of the Greek word *paradidomi*, which means to "hand down."

reject, but who nonetheless frequently interpret Scripture through the lenses of their own personal and theological traditions (5).[18]

It is tradition in the third sense with which I am mainly concerned in this section. This is the tradition found especially in the Roman Catholic communion, where church tradition holds an official and authoritative role in the church's life, equal to Scripture itself.[19] The official Roman Catholic position is that the Spirit's activity did not cease when the last New Testament book was completed, but that he also makes his will known through the traditions of the living organism that is the church.[20]

Before engaging in any further discussion of this topic, a short historical overview of the relationship between Scripture and tradition may be helpful. Following the establishment of the New Testament church,

> . . . well into the second century, the Old Testament remained the early Christians' only authorized text, but the needs of churches and the assaults of heretics led to a relatively rapid formation of the canon of the New Testament by the late second century and its fixation by the mid-fourth. The essential criterion was that these writings contain authentic *apostolic tradition*.[21]

Thus, the earliest view of the relationship between Scripture, tradition, and church may be called the *coincidence view*: that the church teaches what the apostles taught, which it receives from the apostolic Scriptures and from the apostolic tradition.[22] During this period, Scripture, tradition, and church were assumed to teach one apostolic message.[23]

---

18. Fee, *Gospel and Spirit*, 67.
19. Ibid., 68.
20. Brown, *Spirit of Protestantism*, 214.
21. Van Engen, "Tradition," 1211.
22. Lane, "Scripture and Tradition," 631, emphasis Lane's. The early church fathers often appealed to an orthodox "rule of faith," a kind of summary of the gospel possibly related to early baptismal creeds and later issuing in full-fledged creedal documents; this rule was not originally fixed in writing or anything contrary to—or wholly outside of—Scripture (Van Engen, "Tradition," 1211–12).
23. Lane, "Scripture and Tradition," 631.

There is no conflict between them, and the whole Christian message is found in each.[24] This approach proved extremely useful to Irenaeus[25] and Tertullian[26] in their struggle against the Gnostics who appealed to their own Scriptures and to their own secret traditions. In his response, which provided the most effective answer to Gnostic heresy, Irenaeus claimed that the apostles' teaching, found in their genuine writings, was handed down in an open public tradition of teaching in those churches which they had founded, where it was still taught.[27]

In time, the coincidence view gave way to the *supplementary view*: that tradition is needed to supplement Scripture by providing teaching not found in Scripture.[28] In the fourth century, Saint Basil of Caesarea became one of the first to apply such a method in his defense of the deity of the Holy Spirit when he stated that some Christian beliefs are not found in Scripture.[29] To count as authentic apostolic tradition, such fathers as Saint Augustine[30] and Saint Vincent of Lerins[31] in the fifth century West required

---

24. Ibid. The early church fathers also appealed to "apostolic succession," the public teaching (as distinguished from the Gnostics' secret wisdom) in those churches where bishops stood in a direct line with their apostolic founders, especially the See of Rome, which was believed to have been founded by Peter and Paul. Between the first and fourth centuries, they prepared a whole series of anonymous manuals (Didache) that claimed to contain the apostles' teachings, especially on cultic and ethical matters. These were not set against Scripture, but rather constituted the means by which the living church carried forward its witness (Van Engen, "Tradition," 1212).

25. Irenaeus, "Irenaeus against Heresies," 1.10.2–3.

26. Tertullian, "Chaplet," III.

27. Irenaeus, "Irenaeus against Heresies," 3.4.1; 3 Elucidation 2.

28. Lane, "Scripture and Tradition," 631, emphasis Lane's. Once the New Testament canon was fixed and the whole Bible complete, the great church fathers of the fourth and fifth centuries distinguished tradition and Scripture more clearly, but not antithetically. Tradition was understood as the church's enriching and interpretive reflection on the original deposit of faith contained in Scripture. This pertained preeminently to christological interpretation of the Old Testament. But it included as well the writings of earlier "fathers" considered to be products of the Spirit's guidance to help buttress the true faith, the decisions of bishops who met in council under the Spirit's aegis, and various rites that had become central to the practice of the faith (Van Engen, "Tradition," 1212).

29. Saint Basil, "Book of Saint Basil," 10.25–26. Among other church practices that were ascribed to apostolic tradition were praying while facing east, baptizing infants, immersing three times, and fasting on certain days.

30. Augustin, "Letters of St. Augustine," 54.1.1.

31. Vincent also gave us the maxim that the Roman Church used as its standard to distinguish true from false tradition. We must hold "what has been *everywhere, always*, and *by all* believed" (Saint Vincent, "Commonitory," 2.6, emphasis mine).

Theological Considerations for Polity Models

that these be recognized and practiced throughout the whole church. Dale Johnson provides a helpful synopsis of the development of tradition during this particular period:

> Tradition is a weed in the Christian garden. It germinated in the rocky soil of the church fathers, some of whom watered it. The Bishop of Rome sometimes fertilized this tender houseplant called tradition, and it eventually grew into the theological equivalent of kudzu. The growth of tradition as a coordinate source of authority, however, did not emerge from a church council or papal pronouncement. It grew out of a process, not an event. The history of the early church and the development of tradition are so closely intertwined that it is nearly impossible to separate them. This happened in part because the canon of Scripture was not fully recognized for the first few centuries of the Church.[32]

In the Middle Ages, this approach resulted in the emergence of unscriptural doctrines, such as indulgences and Mariology.[33] It is these extrabiblical doctrines, which were held and promoted on the same level as those found in Scripture, that played a major role in the monstrous abuses by the Catholic Church of its power over the lives of men and prompted Martin Luther to revolt against Rome's view of tradition. In Lane's opinion, it was not justification by faith alone that lay at the center of Reformation, but rather the relationship between Scripture and the church, with the key question being: "Does the gospel define the church or vice versa?"[34] One can certainly see how the other issues raised by the Reformers may ultimately trace back to this crucial point.

Luther's battle cry, therefore, soon became one the distinguishing feature of the Protestant Reformation from which its other distinctions ultimately originated, was his emphasis on *sola Scriptura*. In fact, it was from this principle that the rest of Luther's "solas" ultimately originated. As one of the most important priorities of his life's work, Luther's focus

---

32. Johnson, "Time, Scripture and Tradition," 35.

33. Mariology is the Roman Catholic Church's study of Mary, the mother of Jesus. By this period, the Eastern church effectively parted ways with the Western church, resulting in different understandings of what constituted authoritative tradition. For the Eastern Orthodox, ecumenical councils represented the highest authority in defining tradition, while the Catholic Church found itself placing an ever-increasing emphasis on the papacy as the normative spokesman for apostolic tradition (Van Engen, "Tradition," 1212).

34. Lane, "Scripture and Tradition," 632.

on Scripture alone is ever-present in his writings, for as *The Babylonian Captivity of the Church* affirms, "what is asserted without the Scriptures or proven revelation may be held as an opinion, but need not be believed."[35] Calvin similarly asserted:

> For the truth is vindicated in opposition to every doubt, when, unsupported by foreign aid, it has its sole sufficiency in itself. How peculiarly this property belongs to Scripture appears from this, that no human writings, however skillfully composed, are at all capable of affecting us in a similar way. Read Demosthenes or Cicero, read Plato, Aristotle, or any other of that class: you will, I admit, feel wonderfully allured, pleased, moved, enchanted; but turn from them to the reading of the Sacred Volume, and whether you will or not, it will so affect you, so pierce your heart, so work its way into your very marrow, that, in comparison of the impression so produced, that of orators and philosophers will almost disappear; making it manifest that in the Sacred Volume there is a truth divine, a something which makes it immeasurably superior to all the gifts and graces attainable by man.[36]

What this meant was that all church teaching, including the teachings of the early fathers, needed to be tested by Scripture.

In reaction to the Reformation tide, the Roman Catholic Council of Trent in 1546 issued its *Decree Concerning the Edition and the Use of Sacred Books*. It stated that "the truth and discipline [of the gospel] are contained in the written books and in unwritten traditions—those unwritten traditions, that is, which were either received by the apostles from the mouth of Christ himself, or were received from the apostles (having been dictated by the Holy Spirit) and have come down even to us, having been transmitted as it were hand by hand."[37] Furthermore, Scripture and tradition were to be venerated "with equal affection of piety and reverence."[38] The First Vatican

---

35. Luther, *Babylonian Captivity*, 29.

36. Calvin, *Institutes of the Christian Religion*, 1.8.1.

37. Waterworth, "Fourth Session," 17–21. With the phrase, "the written books," Rome included both the canonical books and all the books rejected by Protestants as apocryphal. Further, it endorsed the Latin Vulgate as the only reliable and authoritative translation, and gave Rome the exclusive patent on interpretation. At the conclusion of this gathering, the official Roman Catholic position posited tradition as a separate, unwritten *source* handed down by apostolic succession, especially through an infallible papacy (Van Engen, "Tradition," 1212).

38. Lane, "Scripture and Tradition," 632. In Johnson's opinion, the fundamental issue of the sufficiency of Scripture was championed by Protestants leading up to the Council

Ecumenical Council completed this line of thought when it declared the church's teaching office to be centered in an infallible papacy.[39] The notion of tradition's equality with Scripture was further upheld at the Second Vatican Council in 1962–1965.[40]

While outlining the danger of elevating tradition to the same level as Scripture, the first theological principle is not meant to reject the importance or validity of tradition. Lane is absolutely right when he states that "we must honour our theological forbears and listen with respect to the voice of the past, but we are not bound to it."[41] For "Tradition is worthy of respect," he goes on, "but is subject to the word of God in the Scriptures."[42]

Hence, what the first principle advocates is Scripture's superiority over tradition.[43] John Calvin so fervently affirmed this principle that he included it as part of the title of the seventh chapter of the first book of the *Institutes of the Christian Tradition*: "It is a Wicked Falsehood that Its [Scripture's] Credibility Depends on the Judgment of the Church." He then ends the second section of the same chapter with these words: "Indeed, Scripture exhibits fully as clear evidence of its own truth as white and black things do of their color, or sweet and bitter things do of their taste."[44] Several hundred years later, John Webster reiterated the same idea, writing that "Scripture is not the word of the church, the church is the church of the Word."[45] The

---

of Trent and, as a result, was emphatically rejected by Rome (Johnson, "Time, Scripture and Tradition," 47).

39. Tanner, "On the Infallible Teaching Authority."

40. "Sacred tradition and sacred Scripture form one sacred deposit of the word of God," and both flow "from the same divine wellspring, in a certain way merge into unity and tend toward the same end" (Abbott, *Documents of Vatican II*, 117).

41. Lane, "Scripture and Tradition," 633.

42. Ibid.

43. By tradition I also mean the church, such that Scripture reigns not only over human traditions, but also over the church. Schwöbel states this clearly: "The Church is *creatura verbi divini*: the creature of the divine Word. The Church is constituted by God's action and not by any human action . . . As the creature of the divine Word the Church is constituted by divine action" (Schwöbel, "Creature of the Word," 122). In proclaiming scriptural superiority here, I do not deny a place for tradition, experience, or reason for informing Scripture. Fully agreeing with Yarnell, I do, however, affirm the active and overwhelming supremacy of Scripture as the authority in orthodox theology (Yarnell, *Formation of Christian Doctrine*, 28). For an instructive source on the proper usage of tradition, see ibid., 127–38.

44. Calvin, *Institutes of the Christian Religion*, 1.7.2.

45. Webster, *Holy Scripture*, 44.

Bible must remain "the decisive and *final* authority, the norm by which all the teaching of tradition and the church is to be tested."[46] Webster masterfully sets straight the proper biblical relationship between church and Scripture when he states:

> The church exists in the space which is made by the Word. Accordingly, it is not a self-generated assembly and cannot be adequately described only as a human historical trajectory or form of human culture. The church exists and continues because God is communicatively present; it is brought into being and carried by the Word; it *is* (as the Reformers often put it) *solo verbo*. The "Word" from which the church has its being is thus the lordly creativity of the one who, as Father, Son and Holy Spirit *calls* into being the things that are not.[47]

Webster continues his argument by establishing a connection between the Word and faith, which entrusts itself to the gospel as a divine declaration in the life of the church.[48] Having done so, he depicts the consequences of this inseparability of the Word and faith for the place of Holy Scripture in the life of the church:

> The basic ecclesiological effect of the primacy of Word and faith is to give priority to the action of God in the being of the church: "As the creature of the divine Word the Church is constituted by divine action."[49]

Why should the Bible reign over tradition? First, because the Holy Spirit illuminates believers, thus enabling them to interpret Scripture without the necessity of any church's magisterial office and its accompanying reliance on human traditions. The doctrine of illumination is frequently reiterated in Scripture with passages like 2 Cor 4:6, "For God, who said, 'Light shall shine out of darkness,' is the One who has shone in our hearts to give the Light of the knowledge of the glory of God in the face of Christ," and 1 Cor 2:12–13, "Now we have received, not the spirit of the world, but the Spirit who is from God, so that we may know the things freely given to us by God, which things we also speak, not in words taught by human wisdom, but in those taught by the Spirit, combining spiritual thoughts

---

46. Lane, "Scripture and Tradition," 633, emphasis Lane's.
47. Webster, *Holy Scripture*, 44, emphasis Webster's.
48. Ibid., 45.
49. Ibid.

with spiritual words," and Eph 1:17–18, "that the God of our Lord Jesus Christ, the Father of glory, may give to you a spirit of wisdom and of revelation in the knowledge of Him. I pray that the eyes of your heart may be enlightened," and 1 John 5:20, "And we know that the Son of God has come, and has given us understanding so that we may know Him who is true."[50] Calvin believed and propagated the doctrine of illumination, pointing out that "the Word will not find acceptance in men's hearts before it is sealed by the inward testimony of the Holy Spirit."[51] William G. T. Shedd echoes Calvin's words, adding to the discussion:

> Illumination or instruction by the Holy Spirit implies then the production of an experimental consciousness of religious truth. In this respect, it differs from human teaching. This is alluded to in John 6:63: "The words I speak unto you, they are spirit, and they are life," that is, they are spiritual life. Vital and conscious knowledge of religious truth is the effect of the operation of the Holy Spirit in the human understanding. One man can teach religious truth by grammatical propositions to another, but he cannot illumine his mind in respect to it.[52]

Through the process of illumination, the Holy Spirit enables the believer to understand the message contained within God's Word—the Bible. Since the canon is closed, the experience of revelation is not by direct revelation. As a rule, the Spirit uses those whom God has blessed with the gift of teaching, as well as one's personal study and meditation in the Word, together with the awareness of what others believe about it, in his ministry of illuminating humankind.[53] One would do well to understand, then, that although illumination is a supernatural event, it usually comes as a result of careful and prayerful pursuit of "accurately handling the word of truth" (2 Tim 2:15), or interpreting the Bible in accordance with fundamental principles of hermeneutics and an awareness of the rich history of biblical ex-

---

50. In addition to the passages quoted above, there are others that may be cited here for the biblical basis of this doctrine: 1 Cor 2:9–3:3; Eph 3:16–19; Phil 1:9; Col 3:10; 1 John 2:20, 27; 4:7; John 16:12–15; 17:3; Pss 19:7–8; 43:3–4. Illumination is generally considered among the works of the Holy Spirit that testify to his divinity.

51. Calvin, *Institutes of the Christian Religion*, 1.7.4.

52. Shedd, *Dogmatic Theology*, 764.

53. Keathley, "Bible: Understanding Its Message." See Rom 12:7; 1 Cor 12:28; Eph 4:11; Acts 2:42; 5:21, 25, 42; 11:26; 18:11; 20:20; 21:28; 28:31. 1 John 2:27 does not mean that we do not need teachers. Otherwise, why would the Spirit give this gift? In context, John was speaking of discerning truth from error (ibid.).

egesis.[54] As Klooster puts it, "The Holy Spirit works in individual persons, but His work is not individualistic."[55] The Spirit's illumination takes place within the believing community, "yet the responsibility of every believer before the word of God remains."[56]

The Holy Spirit's illumination is indispensable in discerning the true meaning of the Spirit-breathed Scripture.[57] In the words of I. Howard Marshall, "the relationship between . . . ourselves and the Spirit is one that cannot be explained in human terms."[58]

For he is active in our understanding, so that without him our sinful minds cannot understand Scripture, and yet it is we who carry out the task of understanding.[59] As Marshall puts it, "We are . . . dealing with two incommensurable quantities, neither of which can be reduced to the terms of the other."[60]

The second reason why Scripture is to reign supreme over human tradition is because the word of God is "perspicuous," i.e., requires no apostolic tradition to interpret it correctly.[61] Rome, by contrast, advocated Scripture's obscurity and the need for church hierarchy to act as interpreter.[62] The clarity, or perspicuity, of Scripture was enunciated by Saint John Chrysostom, repeated by Luther, and echoed by Protestant confessions: "All things are clear and open that are in the divine Scriptures; the necessary things are all plain."[63] According to the Reformers, the Bible's basic message of salvation by grace through faith and the basic outline of Christian obedience was

---

54. For a more detailed and helpful discussion on the role and the method of the Holy Spirit in illuminating Scripture, see Zuck, "What and Why of Bible Interpretation," 26–28.

55. Klooster, "Role of the Holy Spirit," 465.

56. Ibid.

57. Ibid., 452.

58. Marshall, "Holy Spirit and the Interpretation," 67.

59. Ibid.

60. Ibid.

61. It was the belief in Scripture's perspicuity, in part, that drove the efforts in making the Bible available in the vernacular translation of its potential readers, thus effectively ending the dictatorial domination of Rome's magisterial office.

62. Yves Congar states plainly, "Scripture is not self-explanatory" (Congar, *Tradition and Traditions*, 382).

63. Saint Chrysostom, "Homilies on the First Epistle," 13.388. See also Callahan, "*Claritas Scripturae*," 359.

what lay at the foundation of those "necessary things."[64] In explaining the actions of the Reformers, Johnson states,

> to offset the idea that Scripture could be interpreted only by the elite church clergy, who at times imposed on the biblical texts their own views and extraneous philosophical systems with excessive allegorizations, the Reformers insisted that the Bible in its message of salvation can be understood by all Christians (priesthood of all believers), and is self-interpreting. However, they also insisted that the message of the Scriptures as the word of God was tied up with the meaning of the biblical author's language in its ancient cultural and historical sense.[65]

Perspicuity is implied by Scripture's authority.[66] Charles Hodge argued that the perspicuity of Scripture meant that the "The Bible is a plain book," that "is intelligible by the people," and that Scripture was addressed to the "people." Therefore, "to them are directed these profound discussions of Christian doctrine, and these comprehensive expositions of Christian duty. They are everywhere assumed to be competent to understand what is written."[67] The perspicuity of Scripture is precisely the reason why an organization like Gideons International can justify its existence, generating countless testimonies of how simply giving someone a copy of the word of God can change their eternal destiny—a change that is often irrespective of church tradition in that person's life.

Scripture's divinely instituted authority over church is the third reason why it must reign over tradition. Webster defines the church's authority as "its Spirit-bestowed capacity to quicken the church to truthful speech and righteous action."[68] In contradistinction to the Catholic theologians who rebut Protestant claims surrounding Scripture's authority over church by pointing to the process of the formation of the canon, Webster asserts, "Very simply, the church is not competent to confer authority on Holy Scripture, any more than it is competent to give itself the mandate to be

---

64. Johnson, "Problems of Normativeness in Scripture," 267.
65. Ibid., 266.
66. Callahan, "*Claritas Scripturae*," 365.
67. Hodge, *Systematic Theology*, 1.183–84. For a more detailed treatment of perspicuity, see Brewster, "Perspicuity of Scripture," 16–34; Callahan, "*Claritas Scripturae*"; Maddox, "Scripture, Perspicuity, and Postmodernity," 555–85; Osborne, *Hermeneutical Spiral*, 27.
68. Webster, *Holy Scripture*, 52.

apostolic."[69] A careful examination of the process of canonization requires one to set it in proper context, which, according to Webster, does not begin with the church but instead with Christology and pneumatology.[70]

It begins with Christology because the church's speech is generated and controlled by Christ's self-utterance: "there exists prior to and above and after every *ego dico* [I said] and *ecclesia dicit* [the church said] a *haec dixit Dominus* [thus said the Lord]; and the aim of Church proclamation is that this *haec dixit Dominus* should prevail and triumph, not only before, above and after, but also *in* every *ego dico* and *ecclesia dicit*."[71] The act of canonization is precipitated by pneumatology because, "if the church's speech is governed by the self-communication of Christ, the church's acts of judgment (its 'decisions') are governed by the Holy Spirit who animates the church and enables its perception of the truth."[72]

Understanding canonization within the context of Christological and pneumatological backgrounds enables us to gain an accurate historical perception of the proper relationship between Scripture, church, and tradition. Calvin comments on the relationship:

> a most pernicious error widely prevails that Scripture has only so much weight as is conceded to it by the consent of the church. As if the eternal and inviolable truth of God depended upon the decision of men![73]

And elsewhere:

> That it is the proper office of the Church to distinguish genuine from spurious Scripture, I deny not, and for this reason, that the Church obediently embraces whatever is of God. The sheep hear the voice of the shepherd, and will not listen to the voice of strangers. But to submit the sound oracles of God to the Church, that they may obtain a kind of precarious authority among men, is blasphemous impiety. The Church is, as Paul declares, founded on the doctrine of Apostles and Prophets; but these men speak as if they imagined that the mother owed her birth to the daughter.[74]

---

69. Ibid., 53.
70. Ibid., 59.
71. Barth, *Doctrine of the word of God*, I/2:801.
72. Webster, *Holy Scripture*, 60.
73. Calvin, *Institutes of the Christian Religion*, 1.7.1.
74. Ibid., "True Method of Giving Peace," 267.

In summarizing his argument, Webster comments on Calvin's observations, noting that "The language of discipleship is not incidental here" because "affirming the canon is a matter of the church 'obediently embracing' what comes from God, or of the sheep hearing the shepherd's voice; that is, it is an act of humble affirmation of and orientation towards what is already indisputably the case in the sphere of salvation and its communication in human speech."[75]

Then what of the church's role in the canonization of Scripture? In light of the criteria detailed above, Webster offers the following perspective:

> First, the church's judgment is an act of confession of that which precedes and imposes itself on the church . . . and which evokes a Spirit-guided assent . . . To put it differently: this decision has noetic but not ontological force, acknowledging what Scripture is but not making it so. Second, this act of confession, the church's judgment with respect to the canon, is an act of submission before it is an act of authority . . . "The Church has exactly as much authority as it exercises obedience" . . . Third, as an act of confession and submission, the act of canonisation has a *backward* reference. Through it, the church affirms that all truthful speech in the church can proceed only from the prior apostolic testimony. Canonisation is recognition of apostolicity, not simply in the sense of the recognition that certain texts are of apostolic authorship or provenance, but, more deeply, in the sense of the confession that these texts, "grounded in the salvific act of God in Christ which has taken place once for all," are annexed to the self-utterance of Jesus Christ . . . Fourth, as an act of confession, submission and retrospection, the church's judgment with respect to the canon is its pledging of itself to be carried by this norm in all its actions. Canonisation is commitment to operate by a given norm, and thereby to have speech and action mastered by that norm.[76]

Webster concludes with the following verdict: "In a very real sense, the canon spells the end of free speech in the church."[77]

It is impossible to overstate the importance of Scripture's superiority over tradition to the study of church polity, for the proper recognition of this principle establishes the Scripture alone as the final authority on what we are and are not to do in the local church. In effect, this ground rule

---

75. Webster, *Holy Scripture*, 62.
76. Ibid.
77. Ibid., 65.

identifies much of the ecclesiology of the Roman Catholic Church as faulty and erroneous because its foundation cannot be drawn from Scripture.

While it would be interesting to investigate the questions of Scripture and tradition in more detail, in the words of Cardinal Joseph Ratzinger, "such an inquiry would take us too far afield from the present subject."[78] In this work, and for the sake of the present argument, the main point has been that whereas biblical exegesis must use any and all of those tools legitimately available to it (including tradition, the history of church's interpretation, reason, etc.), it must preserve the autonomy and supremacy of the text and assume its integrity.[79] In matters of ecclesiology, then, only that which Scripture prescribes should be implemented.[80] Where it is silent, we should not grow vocal. Where it stops, we should halt immediately, lest we be charged with adding to God's Word, and so be guilty of allowing a well-meaning tradition that is nevertheless only a *human tradition* to supplement the revealed will of God. Kiffin weighs in on this matter quite eloquently: "It is commendable to keep the Ordinances of Christ pure, as they were delivered, because it prevents the creeping in of the Inventions of Men in the Worship of God."[81] Jeremiah Burroughs' words resonate with this point:

> All things in Gods worship must have a warrant out of Gods Word. It must be commanded; it's not enough that it is not forbidden . . . It is not enough to say that a thing is not forbidden, and what hurt is there in it? But it must be commanded . . . when we come to matters of religion and the worship of God, we must either have a command, or something out of God's Word drawn from some command, wherein God manifests his will; either by a direct command, by comparing one thing with another, or drawing consequences plainly from the words. We must have a warrant for the worship of God.[82]

Burroughs adds to this:

> In the matters of worship, God stands upon little things. Such things as seem to be very small and little to us, yet God stands

---

78. Ratzinger, *Called to Communion*, 51.

79. Kaiser, *Toward an Exegetical Theology*, 66.

80. This means that there is no room for many Lutheran and Anglican ecclesiastical practices that are not contrary to Scripture.

81. Kiffin, *Sober Discourse of Right*, 48.

82. Burroughs, *Gospel-Worship*, 11.

Theological Considerations for Polity Models

much upon them in the matter of worship ... though men would think it a little matter whether this fire or that fire, and will not this burn as well as that? But God stands upon it. And so it was with the ark. When Uzzah did but touch the ark when it was ready to fall, we would think it no great matter; but one touch of the ark cost him his life ... And so when the men of Bethshemesh did but look upon the ark, it cost the lives of fifty thousand threescore and ten men.[83]

Scripture, indeed, must reign supreme over tradition!

Second Principle: Literal Interpretation of Scripture

The second principle that will contribute to clarifying our understanding of biblical teaching on church polity is that of literal interpretation of Scripture, or grammatical-historical hermeneutics.[84] It was the commitment to this principle of interpretation that, by and large, drew Luther to lead in reforming the medieval church, a decision to which we, as Protestants, owe our very theological existence. "Brother," Luther writes, "the natural meaning of the words is queen, transcending all subtle, acute sophistical fancy."[85]

What is literal interpretation, or the literal sense of Scripture? It is simply the meaning that was originally intended by the human author.[86] As Terry postulates,

> A fundamental principle in grammatico-historical exposition is that words and sentences can have but one signification in one and the same connection. The moment we neglect this principle we drift out upon a sea of *uncertainty* and *conjecture*. It is commonly assumed by the universal sense of mankind that unless one designedly put forth a riddle, he will so speak as to convey his meaning as clearly as possible to others.[87]

In other words, a grammatical-historical hermeneutic seeks to ascertain authorial intent from the meaning expressed through the written

---

83. Ibid., 14–15.
84. The grammatical sense is essentially the same as literal, the one expression having been derived from the Greek, the other from the Latin. See Terry, *Biblical Hermeneutics*, 203.
85. Luther, "Against the Heavenly Prophets," 189–91.
86. Schneiders, "Faith, Hermeneutics," 726.
87. Terry, *Hermeneutics*, 205, emphasis mine.

language of the biblical authors, assuming that their intention was not to convolute their message.[88] Sometimes this interpretation is described as "normal" or "plain," but the idea is that it does not spiritualize the passage. While most agree on the necessity of grammatical interpretation and historical interpretation, as well as on the legitimacy of literal interpretation, not everyone applies these methods with equal consistency.

Literal interpretation is the only set of "spectacles" that will *consistently* make sense of the biblical data.[89] As there seems to be an increasing desire "to know what the Scriptures really say and to face the challenge that the unmitigated word of God offers,"[90] the literal interpretation is the only method that can satisfy it. Literal interpretation applies to the sacred books the same principles, the same grammatical process and exercise of common sense and reason, that we apply to other books.[91] After all, the main reason for the Bible's inscripturation in the first place, and for its preservation through the years, was so that we can read it, learn from it, and live by it. Or as Bennetch writes, "The Bible has been inspired, preserved and circulated in the world not with a view to hiding but rather to disclosing truth."[92] The best way to do this is to understand it as literally as the text allows.[93]

Therefore, the first argument in defense of the literal basis of biblical hermeneutics is that this particular method of interpretation is the usual practice in the interpretation of literature.[94] In other words, since the literal is the most usual signification of a word, and therefore occurs much more frequently than the figurative, any term should be regarded as literal until

---

88. Tan, "Recent Developments in Redaction Criticism," 614.

89. For an excellent exposition of the many values of such hermeneutics when it comes to exegesis in general, and not only related to polity passages, see Ryrie, *Dispensationalism*, 89–119; Klooster, "Role of the Holy Spirit"; Radmacher, "Response to Author's Intention."

90. Schneiders, "Faith, Hermeneutics," 720.

91. Terry, *Biblical Hermeneutics*, 173.

92. Bennetch, "Literal Interpretation," 350.

93. "It is an old and oft-repeated hermeneutical principle that words should be understood in their literal sense unless such literal interpretation involves a manifest contradiction or absurdity" (ibid., 353). Incidentally, Luther equated the literal sense of Scripture with its perspicuity (Callahan, "*Claritas Scripturae*," 362). In a connection of this sort, disregarding the former will necessarily annihilate the latter.

94. Ramm, *Protestant Biblical Interpretation*, 123.

Theological Considerations for Polity Models

there is good reason to come to a different understanding.[95] The non-literal is always a secondary meaning that presumes an already existing literal understanding of literature.[96] Ramm provides a helpful illustration of this principle, saying, "If we attempt to read some oriental, mystical book we shall first attempt to understand it literally and when we see that procedure is not doing justice to the text we then forsake the literal program for a mystical, allegorical, or metaphorical one."[97]

The second reason why literal interpretation is to be preferred is because all secondary meanings of documents depend upon the literal stratum of language.[98] This means that all parables, types, allegories, symbols, figures of speech, myths, and fables presume that there is a level of meaning in language *prior* to the type of language typical to this kind of literature.[99] Ramm illustrates this point further:

> The parable of the sower is understood only within the context of literal "farm" language. The symbolism of a lion is based upon what is asserted about lions in literal speech. Incense as a symbol of prayer is understood again within the context of the use of incense in daily life and expressed in the literal language of daily conversation.[100]

The third reason for the superiority of grammatical-historical hermeneutics is because, to use Ramm's terminology, "only in the priority of literal exegesis can there be control on the exegetical abuse of Scripture."[101] When secondary or tertiary meanings of passages are invoked as proof of our doctrinal suppositions, we leave ourselves open to subjective conjectures and unbiblical philosophizing that is not anchored in the word of God. As Ramm states it, "To rest one's theology on the secondary strata of meaning is to invite interpretation by imagination. That which supplies the imagination with its content is, unfortunately, too often non-biblical ideas

---

95. Bennetch, "Literal Interpretation," 356.
96. Ramm, *Protestant Biblical Interpretation*, 123.
97. Ibid.
98. Ibid., 124.
99. Ibid.
100. Ibid.
101. Ibid. By the "exegetical abuse of Scripture" is meant all interpretation in the history of the church and in the histories of cults that force strange and unbiblical meanings into Scripture by allegorical interpretation.

or materials."[102] The solution—the only sure way to know the meaning of Holy Scripture—is to anchor interpretation in literal exegesis.[103]

Finally, the example of the Bible itself provides another reason for literal interpretation. A precedence for interpreting the Bible in this manner can be seen in the way Old Testament prophecies like Ps 22, Isa 7:14; 53:1–12; and Mic 5:2 have been fulfilled literally, according to their plain meaning.[104] Though there are seven Old Testament prophecies whose fulfillment is documented by the New Testament in a non-literal way, the vast majority of them (hundreds to be exact) are fulfilled literally in the New Testament.

A historical-grammatical interpretation is a consistent, contextual understanding based upon the text seen in the immediate context.[105] The immediate context is that which immediately precedes or follows a given word or sentence.[106] "Such a contextual reading and understanding," according to Elliott E. Johnson, "considers two controlling issues—the reading is limited to the grammatical senses of the text and is expressed within the historical occasion and *sitz im leben*[107] of the text."[108] It is the context—one of the most basic and yet profound rules of hermeneutics—that is the main determinant of whether the passage is to be understood literally or figuratively.

Historical context includes both the expectations of the occasion for which the book was written and the subject matter the book addresses.[109] However, if our understanding is based upon the text itself, the historical context neither dictates the meaning of a text nor determines meanings unexpressed in the text, but rather fills in the exegete's knowledge of shared historical meanings expressed in the text.[110]

---

102. Ibid., 125.

103. Ibid.

104. Keathley, "Bible: Understanding Its Message."

105. Johnson, "Historical-Grammatical Interpretation," 158–59. "The word *context*, as the etymology intimates (Latin, *con*, together, and *textus*, woven), denotes something that is woven together, and, applied to a written document, it means the connexion [sic] of thought supposed to run through every passage which constitutes by itself a whole" (Terry, *Biblical Hermeneutics*, 210).

106. Terry, *Biblical Hermeneutics*, 210.

107. *Sitz im leben* is German for "place in life," denoting context.

108. Johnson, "Historical-Grammatical Interpretation," 159.

109. Ibid.

110. Ibid. For a specific example of how this method is used in interpreting Old Testament passages, see ibid., 159–69. For a more comprehensive discussion of historical

Theological Considerations for Polity Models

In addition to taking immediate and historical contexts into consideration, Scripture is to be interpreted grammatically. That is why there is value in learning the original languages in which the Bible was written. Every word of the Bible is important, and because thoughts are expressed in words that stand in relationship to each other, grammatical relationships are vital to sound interpretation.[111] Neglecting the meaning of the words and how they are used will therefore result in a complete inability to arrive at correct interpretation.[112] Grammatical interpretation, then, is the process of studying the text of Scripture to make four important determinations: (a) the meaning of words (lexicology); (b) the form of words (morphology); (c) the function of words (parts of speech); and (d) the relationship of words (syntax).[113]

To the consideration of the immediate context, historical context, and grammatical relationships must be added the principle of Scripture interpreting Scripture. Popularized during the Reformation, this concept was a reaction against the Roman Catholic Church's claim to possess the mind of Christ and the mind of the Spirit in its teaching magisterium such that it could render obscure doctrines clear.[114] This principle means that the entire Holy Scripture is the context and guide for understanding the particular passages of Scripture.[115]

Finally, recognizing the progressive nature of God's revelation can assist all readers in accurately interpreting Scripture. God did not reveal either himself or his plan all at once. Instead, God meets people where he finds them and then, over time, develops and expands his purposes and program in the world and with his people.[116] Ryrie further elucidates this issue, stating that:

> . . . in the process of revealing His message to man, God may add or even change in one era what He had given in another. Obviously

---

and cultural backgrounds of Scripture, see Osborne, *Hermeneutical Spiral*, 158–80.

111. Keathley, "Bible: Understanding Its Message."

112. The assertion, "You can make the Bible mean anything you want it to mean," is true only if grammatical interpretation is ignored, see Zuck, *Basic Bible Interpretation*, 99.

113. Keathley, "Bible: Understanding Its Message." For a more thorough discussion of the issues pertaining to grammar, semantics, and syntax for the accurate interpretation of Scripture, see Osborne, *Hermeneutical Spiral*, 57–157.

114. Ramm, *Protestant Biblical Interpretation*, 104.

115. Ibid., 105.

116. Klein et al., "Preunderstandings and Intepreter," 78.

> the New Testament adds much that was not revealed in the Old. What God revealed as obligatory at one time may be rescinded at another (as the prohibition of eating pork, once binding on God's people, now rescinded, 1 Tim 4:3). To fail to recognize this progressiveness in revelation will raise unresolvable contradictions between passages if taken literally. Notice the following pairs of passages which will contradict if understood plainly unless one recognizes changes due to the progress of revelation: Matt 10:5–7 and 28:18–20, Luke 9:3 and 22:36, Gen 17:10 and Gal 5:2; Exod 20:8 and Acts 20:7. Notice too the crucial changes indicated in John 1:17; 16:24; 2 Cor 3:7–11. Those who will not consistently apply this principle of progressive Rev in interpretation are forced to resort to figurative interpretation or sometimes simply to ignore the evidence.[117]

Adopting a literal interpretation must necessarily mean the rejection of allegorical interpretations of Scripture.[118] Instead, attention should be paid to the meaning that is intended in the text.[119] Such a hermeneutical approach does not preclude, or exclude, a correct understanding of types, illustrations, apocalypses, and other genres within the basic framework of literal interpretation.[120] As Rowan Williams states,

> The literal sense is not dependent on a belief that all scriptural propositions uncomplicatedly depict real states of affairs detail by detail; it can and does . . . allow for a plurality of genres within it; it is the failure to see and to develop this insight that has led to those narrow and sterile definitions of the literal sense against which recent hermeneutics has so sharply reacted.[121]

Rather than "spiritualizing" the Old Testament passage, for example, or interpreting it in light of the fuller New Testament revelation, thereby

---

117. Ryrie, quoted in Keathley, "Bible: Understanding Its Message."

118. Bultmann correctly believes that one of the ways to achieve an unprejudiced approach to Scripture is by rejection of allegorical interpretation. He clarifies this idea, stating that if there is actually an allegory in the text, then of course it is to be explained as an allegory. However, such an explanation is not allegorical interpretation; it simply asks for the meaning that is intended by the text (Bultmann, "Is Exegesis without Presuppositions Possible?" 289, 314).

119. As in the previous note, in agreement with Bultmann, I believe that texts containing allegory should be interpreted allegorically. Such a method is not allegorical interpretation but constitutes faithfulness to the original meaning intended in the text.

120. Ryrie, *Dispensationalism*, 47.

121. Williams, "Literal Sense of Scripture," 124.

Theological Considerations for Polity Models

necessarily altering its original meaning, a grammatical-historical method allows later revelation to enrich our understanding of the earlier meaning, like a flower already contained in the bud.[122] The New Testament interpretation, according to this method, is the comprehension of the completed meaning intended as introduced but left undeveloped in the Old Testament.[123] Therefore, instead of reinterpreting all or most of the Old Testament prophecies and other milestones in light of the Christ event[124] or any other significant New Testament occurrence—a practice styled after the manner with which the apostles often handled the Old Testament—consistent literal interpretation would allow the New Testament to fill in what is left unexpressed in the Old Testament.[125]

In the words of Ramm:

> To interpret Scripture literally, therefore, is not to be committed to a "wooden literalism," nor to a "letterism," nor to a neglect of the nuances that defy any "mechanical" understanding of language. Rather, it is to commit oneself to a starting point and that starting point is to understand a document the best one can in the context of the normal, usual, customary, tradition range of designation which includes "facit" understanding.[126]

While there is some controversy surrounding literal interpretation of Scripture, most of the debate centers on the Old Testament prophecies and whether the mode of their fulfillment in the New Testament is literal or allegorical/spiritual.[127] Since the focus of this work is mainly ecclesiological

---

122. Johnson, "Historical-Grammatical Interpretation," 165.

123. Ibid.

124. Promoted by Ladd, "Historic Premillennialism," 21–23.

125. Johnson, "Historical-Grammatical Interpretation," 165. One must be careful, however, in invoking the apostles' example as "prescriptive hermeneutics," for they had a special enabling and inspiring assistance from the Holy Spirit, the enabling which assured that, through their writings, the very word of God was inscripturated. The illuminating power of the Holy Spirit that we enjoy as the interpreters of the text today is important but not similar to his inspiring power. Furthermore, the decision of which Old Testament prophecies are to be interpreted literally and which non-literally is highly subjective, often differing from one exegete to another, using criteria that are questionable at best.

126. Ramm, *Protestant Biblical Interpretation*, 121.

127. See, for example, Longman's address to the Dispensational Study Group in Longman, "Historical-Grammatical Exegesis," 137–55. Longman's general attitude towards Old Testament prophecy interpretation is reflected in the following sentence: "the New Testament leads us to allow for if not expect nonliteral fulfillments to Old Testament prophecies" (ibid., 152). To agree with this statement is to introduce much subjectivity

rather than eschatological, it should not be too difficult to convince the reader to adopt grammatical-historical hermeneutics, at least when it comes to the passages employed by this research.

For our purposes, there are at least two benefits of literal interpretation. Using literal interpretation, for example, will help the reader to distinguish between Israel and the church. The former is the nation that the Lord had chosen in the Old Testament, through which he dealt with the world. The latter is a transnational phenomenon established in the New Testament, through which God worked out his plan after the birth, death, resurrection, and ascension of his Son. Since the two entities are not interchangeable, we cannot look to the Old Testament for the support of ecclesiological practices of an institution that was established in the New Testament.

Furthermore, a commitment to literal interpretation could have prevented the sacramentarianism and hierarchy of the Roman Catholic Church, which derived its support for these from the Old Testament using allegorical interpretation. Other examples of similar inaccuracies today, even within Protestant circles, include infant baptism (often connected with circumcision), church elders patterned after Israel's elders of Exod 18, and the origin of the church as identical to the birth of Israel as a nation.[128] The origin of the New Testament church is precisely the issue that will be addressed in the exposition of the next theological principle.

---

into the interpretive process.

128. For the appropriate biblical corrective to such thinking, see Patterson, "Single-Elder Congregationalist's Response," 109–111.

4

Theological Considerations for Polity Models (Continued)

THIRD PRINCIPLE: PENTECOST—THE BEGINNING OF THE NEW TESTAMENT CHURCH

Over the course of history, a number of different opinions regarding the time of the origin of the church have been proposed. Below is a list of these various views and the defense of the one that seems to be most biblically credible. Before proceeding, however, a disclaimer should be made regarding the extent of this exploration. Due to the focus of the present work, the following list is neither comprehensive nor exhaustive, but it is representative of the various opinions expressed during the history of the study of the church.

In the process of theological development, there have been at least seven different views concerning the time of the origin of the New Testament church. First, according to the understanding of some early church fathers, the foundation of the church antedated the creation of the world. The Pastor of Hermas most clearly reflects this understanding when he writes that the church "was created the first of all things and for her sake was the world established."[1] Second, there was another prevailing notion shortly following the first century a.d. that regarded the question of the timing of the church's origin as a matter of indifference to early Christians:

---

1. Pastor of Hermas, "Visions," 2.4.1.

> To them the unity between Christ and the Holy Spirit was so perfect—they were so confident that the work which went on under their hands was the work of God—that it was a matter of comparative indifference to them at what stage in His career the Lord had given the first impetus to the movement. It might have been when St. Peter made his famous confession; it might have been during the forty days when the Lord spoke to His disciples of the things concerning the Kingdom of God; it might have been after His ascension, when He began in a new sense to give gifts unto men.[2]

The proponents of this view urge today's Christians to follow the position of their early counterparts and not concern themselves with determining the exact timing of the origin of the church. Third, the time of Jesus' calling of his first disciples and his kingdom sayings has been proposed as the beginning point of the New Testament church.[3] Fourth, the Last Supper has also been identified as the church's point of origin.[4] Fifth, the church has often been said to have come into existence at or after the resurrection of Jesus.[5] Sixth, some attempts have been made to develop a composite answer that gathers up all or most of the previous answers to this question.[6] The final, and perhaps the most biblically defensible, view is that the New Testament church did not begin *before* the day of Pentecost, when the Holy Spirit's descent upon the earth instituted a new era in the history of humanity.

Acts 2 chronicles the birthday of the church.[7] Paige Patterson argues with succinct clarity when he writes, "The church was launched, if not born, on the day of Pentecost and developed rapidly under apostolic and subapostolic direction."[8] The first local assembly, as reported in the pages of the New Testament, convened in Jerusalem for a prayer meeting on the

---

2. Mason, "Conceptions of the Church," 5.

3. Flew, *Jesus and His Church*, 35–39. Flew's understanding lies relatively close to that of Thomas F. Torrance, who essentially views the church as an offshoot of Israel, and thus the disciples as the true representatives of Israel. See Torrance, "Israel of God," 316; Nelson, *Realm of Redemption*, 27.

4. Von Schmidt, "Die Kirche des Urchristentums," 295.

5. Brunner, *Mediator*, 563; Johnston, *Doctrine of the Church*, 56–57; Lewis, "Constructive Statements: Evangelical," 478; Küng, *The Church*, 70–79; Dodd, *Founder of Christianity*, 97; Von Schlatter, *Church in the New Testament Period*, 4–14.

6. Dana and Sipes, *Manual of Ecclesiology*, 72. A helpful summary of some of these views may be found in Garrett, *Systematic Theology*, 466–67.

7. Brand and Norman, *Perspectives on Church Government*, 155.

8. Patterson, "Single-Elder Congregationalism," 148.

Theological Considerations for Polity Models (Continued)

day of Pentecost. This was done in obedience to Jesus' last instructions to his disciples just before his ascension (Acts 1). There was a powerful and visible descent of the Holy Spirit upon those gathered in the room that instituted the age of the church. The Spirit's mighty movement caused these Christians to experience a dramatic manifestation of the unity of the Spirit and the love of Christ, triggering a rapid growth.[9]

On the first day of its existence, in fact, the church acquired three thousand new members (Acts 2:41). Scripture provides a number of reasons for viewing the day of Pentecost as the origin of the New Testament church. First, it is significant that out of 109 New Testament verses containing the Greek term *ekklēsia*,[10] only three are in the Gospel portion of the New Testament. Moreover, these three references are found *only in two* passages of *only one* Gospel—Matt 16:18 and 18:17. Of Jesus' two references to the church here, one promises the church's future constitution (Matt 16:18), and the other provides a manual for church discipline (Matt 18:17). Neither of these passages assumes or necessitates the church's existence at the time of pronouncement. Or rather, in the words of Hammett, both passages seem to look to a future situation.[11] MacArthur concurs with this conclusion when he comments on Matthew's usage of *ekklēsia*, arguing that although it "does not specifically refer to the church born at Pentecost," this term in Matthew "certainly anticipates the New Testament church that comes about by the baptism of the Spirit of God in Acts 2."[12] The implication is that the church was not given birth until after Christ's earthly ministry.[13]

---

9. MacArthur, *Master's Plan*, 82.

10. This Greek term is one of the most common designations for "church" in the New Testament.

11. Hammett, *Biblical Foundations*, 28. See also Küng, *The Church*, 73. According to Earl D. Radmacher, that this pronouncement of Christ's refers to an event in the future can be illustrated by the grammar of Matt 16:18. Grammatically, *oikodomēsō* is in the future indicative. Because the future is primarily an indicative tense, the element of time is very pronounced. Thus, the future indicative expresses anticipation of a future event (Radmacher, *Nature of the Church*, 205).

12. MacArthur, *Master's Plan*, 236.

13. Ibid. In arguing for congregationalism, Hammett indirectly contributes further to the understanding of the church's genesis taking place at Pentecost: "In the area of choosing leaders, some see the action of the believers in Acts 1 in choosing a replacement for Judas as indicative of congregationalism, but since this is *a pre-Pentecost act, and thus prior to the actual birth of the church, it is questionable*" (Hammett, *Biblical Foundations*, 148, emphasis mine).

Second, the fact that Luke never uses *ekklēsia* in his Gospel, but does employ it twenty-four times in Acts, is also of consequence.[14] Erickson correctly assumes that the evidence must mean that in Luke's mind the church was not present until the period covered in Acts.[15] Third, the concept of the church as a mystery, which Paul expresses in Eph 3:1–10, proves its foundation at Pentecost. In his *The Nature of the Church*, Earl D. Radmacher furnishes detailed arguments supporting this assertion. He concludes his commentary on Eph 3:1–10 with these words:

> The grammatical usage allows for the possibility of such an interpretation and the argument of the passage and the study of parallel passages demand this interpretation. With this evidence in view, it may be definitely concluded that, although Gentile blessing was predicted in the Old Testament, the mystery of Jew and Gentile in one body, the church was not made known. The church, the body of Christ," Radmacher continues, "must be confined, then, to this present dispensation.[16]

As the foundation on which the church was built, the necessity of the death, resurrection, ascension, and exaltation of Christ constitutes the fourth proof that the New Testament church could not have been in existence before Pentecost.[17] Acts 20:28 contains Paul's explanation to the Ephesian elders that the church was purchased with Christ's own blood. Moreover, Eph 1:22–23 declares that God gave Christ to be head over all the church, which is his body.[18] Pointing the reader to the previous two verses (vv. 20–21), Radmacher states that they "indicate two very important events . . . which necessarily precede this headship. First, God raised Christ from the dead . . . Second, God exalted Christ to a place of honor at His own right hand. Thus, the body of Christ had the necessary Head to whom it is intimately united and from whom it receives its direction."[19] Furthermore, in Eph 4:8–11 it is revealed that Christ first had to ascend in order to give gifts to the body.[20] Ryrie explains that the body's "functioning

---

14. Erickson, *Christian Theology*, 1048.
15. Ibid.
16. Ibid.
17. Ibid., 209.
18. Ibid., 210.
19. Ibid.
20. Ibid.

Theological Considerations for Polity Models (Continued)

is dependent upon the giving of gifts to individual members, which gifts in turn are dependent upon the ascension of Christ (Eph 4:7–12)."[21]

Fifth, as Ferguson notes, when Peter speaks in Acts 11:15, he looks back to the events of Acts 2 as being "the beginning."[22] The beginning of what? A careful examination of Acts 2 yields a list of several items that occur here for the first time in the history of humanity.[23] Ferguson correctly concludes, "these together mark the occasion as the beginning of a new age, the gathering of a new community, the beginning of the church."[24] What follows is a list of at least five new events that trace their beginning to the day of Pentecost, and which together, in Ferguson's accurate understanding, mark that day as the commencement of the New Testament church.

First, Acts 2 reports the beginning of the age of the Holy Spirit. Ferguson elaborates further:

> The coming of the Holy Spirit is what Peter particularly had in mind in Acts 11:15 when he designated the events of Acts 2 as "the beginning." "The Holy Spirit fell upon them just as it had upon us at the beginning" (Acts 11:15). He referred to the coming of the Holy Spirit on the household of Cornelius, the Gentile centurion (Acts 10:44–46). He proceeded to recall "the word of the Lord, how he had said, 'John baptized with water, but you will be baptized with the Holy Spirit'" (Acts 11:16). These words from the resurrected Jesus are recorded by Luke in Acts 1:5. At the close of his first volume, Luke included in the commission of Jesus the promise, "I am sending upon you what my Father promised; so stay here in the city until you have been clothed with power from on high" (Luke 24:29). He commences his second volume with further reference to the coming of the Holy Spirit: "You will receive power when the Holy Spirit has come upon you; and you will be my witnesses in Jerusalem, in all Judea and Samaria, and to the ends of the earth" (Acts 1:8) ... Acts 1:5 and 11:16 identify the particular event of Acts 2 and the like experience in Acts 10 as a "baptism in the Holy Spirit." The description of the event in Acts 2 speaks of a "sound like the rush of a violent wind" that "filled the entire house where they were sitting" (Acts 2:2), so they were indeed in a sense immersed in the Spirit.[25]

---

21. Ryrie, *Biblical Theology*, 190.
22. Ferguson, *Church of Christ*, 63.
23. The following list was created in consultation with ibid., 63–67.
24. Ibid., 63.
25. Ibid., 63–64.

The baptism by the Holy Spirit, which occurred for the first time in Acts 2, is perhaps the chief argument for the beginning of the church on the day of Pentecost. In 1 Cor 12:13, Paul explains that entrance into the body of Christ is dependent upon the baptism by the Holy Spirit.[26] This event had not yet occurred in John 7:39, "for the Spirit was not yet *given*, because Jesus was not yet glorified." In John 14:17, Christ declares that the disciples will experience a new and distinct relationship to the Holy Spirit "because He abides with you and will be in you."[27] While they had not yet experienced it in Acts 1:5, the event had taken place by the time of Acts 11:15. "To discover when it happened, therefore," writes Radmacher, "is to discover the commencement of the body of Christ, and the only possible occasion between Acts 1 and Acts 11 is found on the day of Pentecost (Acts 2)."[28]

Second, the day of Pentecost marked the beginning of the public proclamation of Jesus as Christ. At the climax of his sermon in Acts 2, Peter publicly proclaims the deity and the Messiahship of Jesus Christ: "Therefore let all the house of Israel know for certain that God has made Him both Lord [*kurion*, or the New Testament way of identifying Israel's YHWH] and Christ [*christon*, translated as the Messiah, the Anointed One]—this Jesus whom you crucified." The twelve were witnesses already in the sense that they had seen the Lord, both before and after his resurrection.[29] Now, for the first time, the disciples were witnesses in the sense of giving testimony to tell what they had seen.[30] Ferguson adds:

> During his ministry, Jesus would not allow his followers to proclaim their faith that he was the Messiah (Mark 8:29–30; 9:9). Jesus had to perform the messianic work involved in his death and resurrection before this truth could be openly proclaimed. Now the wraps were taken off.[31]

Third, Acts 2 contains the record of the beginning of the preaching of the gospel as an accomplished fact. Again, Ferguson states:

---

26. Radmacher, *Nature of the Church*, 211.
27. Ibid.
28. Ibid.
29. Ferguson, *Church of Christ*, 65.
30. Ibid.
31. Ibid.

Theological Considerations for Polity Models (Continued)

> The gospel had been preached beforehand in promise to Abraham (Gal 3:8). Jesus had preached the gospel of the kingdom in preparation (Mark 1:14–15). Now for the first time it was preached in fullness as an accomplished fact.[32]

In 1 Cor 15:1–5, Paul defines the gospel as a message that contains the death, burial, and resurrection of Christ. This is precisely the substance of Peter's message in Acts 2.

Fourth, the day of Pentecost brought with itself the beginning of the offer of forgiveness in Jesus' name. God had forgiven sins in the Old Testament (e.g., Lev 4–5; 16; Ps 78:38),[33] and during his earthly ministry, Jesus offered forgiveness to individuals, as is chronicled in Mark 2:1–12. However, it was not until the Pentecost that the message of forgiveness was extended to the world at large "in the name of Jesus Christ" (Acts 2:38).

And fifth, Acts 2 marks the beginning of corporate worship and life. The common life that Jesus and his disciples had shared (cf. Luke 8:3; John 13:29) continued without the Messiah's personal presence. Some of the most beautiful descriptions of the early Christian community abiding in peace and unity are recorded in Acts 2 as the depiction of the state of affairs of the newly founded church. Luke describes these believers as "continually devoting themselves to the apostles' teaching and to fellowship, to the breaking of bread and to prayer" (Acts 2:42). The verses that follow may be seen as elaborating on this description.[34] They had "all things in common" (Acts 2:44), selling their possessions in order to provide for those in need (Acts 2:45), and "Day by day continuing with one mind in the temple, and breaking bread from house to house, they were taking their meals together with gladness and sincerity of heart, praising God and having favor with all the people" (Acts 2:46–47).

What are the benefits of adhering to this theological principle? The understanding that the church came to existence on the day of Pentecost will preclude Presbyterian notions of deriving the support for elder-ruled-congregations from the Old Testament.[35] It will also keep us from mining the gospels for clues about church structure or organization, a practice common to the proponents of episcopal polity. This applies especially to Christ's prediction of Peter's leadership in the foundation of the early

---

32. Ibid., 66.
33. Ibid., 67.
34. Ibid.
35. Reymond, "Presbytery-Led Church," 87–138.

church (Matt 16) and the monstrous abuse of power that resulted in the course of ecclesiastical history in the name of this misused passage.

Fourth Principle: Apostles and Prophets—The Church's Foundation

Scripture teaches that the offices of apostle and prophet were established specifically for the time of the inauguration of the New Testament church on this planet.[36] The apostles and prophets had the special task of laying the foundation for the church.[37]

The word "apostle" was a special designation that Jesus Christ gave to the twelve men he selected from the larger group of disciples (Luke 6:13; Matt 10:1–4). The Greek word *apostolos* means literally "a delegate," "a messenger," or "one sent forth with orders." So the term itself encompasses a fairly broad concept, though its New Testament usage is purposefully limited in the primary sense of its meaning to the following people: (1) the original twelve apostles who were a part of Christ's earthly ministry; (2) Matthias, who replaced Judas following his betrayal (Acts 1:26); and (3) Paul, the "great apostle to the Gentiles, who in a special way left the ranks of Judaism and penetrated the pagan world with the gospel of Jesus Christ."[38]

In the secondary sense, Luke calls Barnabas an apostle when referring to his "ministry" with Paul (Acts 14:4–14).[39] Paul refers to Silas and Timothy as fellow apostles in 1 Thess 2:6–7, and seems to apply the same title to Andronicus and Junias when calling them "outstanding among the apostles," in Rom 16:7. The latter category can certainly be thought of as apostles in a broader sense of the word, namely, as messengers who were chosen and commissioned to share the good news of salvation. But it was the narrower sense of the word that was a determining factor in the selection of the canon at the Council of Nicaea, when a connection to one of the twelve apostles was a key factor in a book's inclusion within the canon. So even in the very early years of the church there was an understanding that:

---

36. See Eph 2:19–22; 3:5; 4:11–12; 1 Cor 3:6, 10; 12:28–31.

37. Berkhof, *Systematic Theology*, 585.

38. Getz, *Sharpening the Focus*, 92. 1 Cor 9:1–2; 15:8–9; 2 Cor 12:11–12; Gal 1:1, 11–12; 2:8; 1 Tim 2:7; 2 Tim 1:11.

39. Getz accurately points out that although Barnabas is described as an apostle (that is, as one who is engaged in an apostolic work), he seemingly recognized in Acts 9:27 that there was a special group of men who were designated as apostles of which he was not a part (Getz, *Sharpening the Focus*, 93).

Theological Considerations for Polity Models (Continued)

> In a primary sense, apostles were those men who were eyewitnesses of Jesus Christ, and who were taught by Him personally and particularly selected for an initial ministry in bringing into being the body of Christ—His church. Luke verifies this particular apostolic role in the book of Acts when he records their work. The apostles "solemnly testified" and "exhorted" (2:40), they taught (2:42), worked signs and miracles (2:43; 5:12), and gave witness to the resurrection of Jesus Christ (4:33).[40]

Schweizer agrees with this view when he points out that:

> As eyewitnesses, the twelve are primarily the guarantors of the resurrection. Just as, according to Acts 1:13, they are the sole witnesses of the ascension, so, according to 4:33, they alone preach the resurrection, while the Church speaks "the word of God" (4:31).[41]

John Calvin evidenced the same understanding in the *Institutes of the Christian Tradition*, writing, "Apostles, then, were sent out to lead the world back from rebellion to true obedience to God, and to establish his Kingdom everywhere by the preaching of the gospel, or, if you prefer, as the first builders of the church, to lay its foundations in all the world [1 Cor 3:10]."[42] Similarly, Berkhof lists five criteria that made apostleship an extraordinary office limited to the time of the early church alone:

> (1) they received their commission directly from God or from Jesus Christ, Mark 3:14; Luke 6:13; Gal 1:1; (2) they were witnesses of the life of Christ and especially of His resurrection, John 15:27; Acts 1:21, 22; 1 Cor 9:1; (3) they were conscious of being inspired by the Spirit of God in all their teaching, both oral and written, Acts 15:28; 1 Cor 2:13; 1 Thess 4:8; 1 John 5:9–12; (4) they had the power to perform miracles and used this on several occasions to ratify their message, 2 Cor 12:12; Heb 2:4; and (5) they were richly blessed in their work as a sign of the divine approval of their labors, 1 Cor 9:1, 2; 2 Cor 3:2, 3; Gal 2:8.[43]

Thomas Torrance agrees in his own understanding of the apostolic foundation of the church:

---

40. Ibid., 93.
41. Schweizer, *Church Order*, 194.
42. Calvin, *Institutes of the Christian Religion*, 4.3.4.
43. Berkhof, *Systematic Theology*, 585.

> Thus, in the apostles as the receiving end of His revealing and reconciling activity, Jesus Christ laid the foundation of the Church which He incorporated into Himself as His own Body, and permitted the Word which He put into their mouth to take the form of proclamation answering to and extending His own in such a way that it became the controlled unfolding of His own revelation within the mind and language of the apostolic foundation.[44]

The office of a prophet, another one of the foundation blocks of the New Testament church, was also a temporary establishment.[45] To prophesy literally means "to speak forth" or "to speak out"; hence a prophet was a person who "spoke forth."[46]

Prophets were a familiar feature in both the Old and New Testaments, and their main function was to communicate God's truth received by means of divine inspiration. The gift of prophecy was a supernatural ability that granted prophets access to special information revealed by God for the purposes of instructing the people. Thus, their service is widely regarded in the New Testament as a direct gift of the Spirit, for the church no more chooses prophets than it chooses apostles.[47]

---

44. Torrance, *God and Rationality*, 152. See also Wasser, "Pastor-Elder-Overseer," 68.

45. See Eph 2:19–22; 4; 1 Cor 3:6, 10; 12. Berkhof, Davidson, and others add evangelists to the list of apostles and prophets. They believe that the chief employment of evangelists consisted in preaching the gospel and gathering new churches among the Gentiles. The evangelists seem to have usually been chosen by the apostles, who entrusted them with special commissions as occasion required. They had the gift of tongues, enabling them to preach the gospel to every nation in its native language, and also the gift of miracles, for confirmation of their doctrine. Their authority seems to have been more general and somewhat superior to that of regular ministers. Timothy, Titus, Philip, one of the Acts 6 deacons, and Mark have been counted among their number. While some see this office in continuation today among those with the gift of evangelism, a distinction needs to be made between the office and the gift. The office of evangelist was temporary, but the gift of evangelism is permanent. Davidson is right to point out that there are no apostles in the present day to send forth evangelists on special errands; neither do men possess the extraordinary gifts that belonged to the primitive evangelists. Further proof of this contention may be found in the fact that Paul made no mention of the office of evangelist alongside of elders/overseers and deacons in his directions to Timothy. See Davidson, *Ecclesiastical Polity*, 114–15; Berkhof, *Systematic Theology*, 585.

46. Getz, *Sharpening the Focus*, 94.

47. Schweizer, *Church Order*, 197. The church can recognize them, and it also has to test them (like the "superlative apostles" of 2 Cor 10–12), and either allow or refuse them a place for prophesying in the meeting for worship (1 Cor 14:29ff.).

Theological Considerations for Polity Models (Continued)

The New Testament apostles were also prophets,[48] as is evidenced by their works in Acts and confirmed by the writings that they left for the early church. These were letters, inspired by God, which encouraged, exhorted, informed, and instructed his people on how they were to conduct their lives until the return of Jesus Christ. Among them are Gospels according to Matthew and John, and numerous letters authored by Peter, James, John, and Paul.

Additionally, there were other prophets in the New Testament who were not apostles. Acts 11 tells of one such man in Antioch whose name was Agabus, and who prophesied an impending worldwide famine that the church was able to prepare for adequately. Later in Acts, Agabus predicts Paul's imminent arrest and persecution in Jerusalem (Acts 21:10–14). Luke names other individuals who possessed the gift of prophecy in the early church. Barnabas, Simeon, Lucius, and Manaen were such men in the Antioch church (Acts 13:1). Judas and Silas were the prophets in the Jerusalem church (Acts 15:22, 32). Philip, one of the original seven deacons[49] appointed in Acts 6, had four daughters, all of whom prophesied (Acts 21:9). Considering Paul's instructions to the Corinthian believers in 1 Cor 14:27–35, there must have been some women who prophesied in that church as well. Other New Testament writers, such as Luke, Mark, Jude, must have had the gift of prophecy also, considering the books they left for the edification of the church. Getz aptly summarizes:

---

48. Davidson takes this even further, claiming that "the apostolic office may be said to have included in itself all inferior offices. An apostle had a right to do all things which an evangelist, a presbyter, a bishop, a pastor and teacher, and a deacon, were called to perform in virtue of their respective offices. He was furnished with an extraordinary commission, universal in its range. He was empowered to preach the gospel infallibly, to work miracles in attestation of the divinity of his doctrine, and to found churches . . . In organizing Christian societies he was divinely guided, so that he could not err. He acted under the express direction and approval of the great Head of the church; and therefore his arrangements were of necessity right" (Davidson, *Ecclesiastical Polity*, 109).

49. I recognize that some disagree with the designation of Acts 6 appointees as deacons. Since their primary job description in verse 2 was "to deacon" (diakoneō, translating to serve, render assistance, wait upon, etc.), which happens to match the design for the office in 1 Tim 3:8–13, as outlined in their qualifications, I find no reason to assume some unnecessary complexity by viewing Acts 6 as a temporary unidentified office. As Dana and Sipes state, although "a literary study of the passage as such would afford no final conclusion, but an historic view of the whole fact of the diaconate in New Testament life renders it practically certain that these seven were really the first deacons" (Dana and Sipes, *Manual of Ecclesiology*, 88–89).

Once again then on the basis of biblical evidence, we are forced to conclude that the gift of prophecy, referred to in 1 Cor 12 and Eph 4, refers to a special group of individuals in New Testament days who were given special revelations from God, in order to help the new and infant church grow and develop into a mature organism. As with the gift of apostleship, it was also a "foundational" gift. You have been "built upon the foundation of the apostles and prophets," wrote Paul to the Ephesians.[50]

While some suggest that the prophets in Eph 2:20 were Old Testament prophets,[51] implying that there is a continuity between the Old and New Testament "churches," it is my opinion that a better case can be made for viewing them as New Testament prophets.[52] Lincoln states plainly, "The prophets are NT prophets."[53] First, this identification is confirmed by the order of the wording—it is difficult to suppose Old Testament prophets would be placed second—and particularly by the other references to apostles and prophets in Eph 3:5 and 4:11, where New Testament prophets are unambiguously in view.[54] Second, the parallel and proximate expression at Eph 3:5, "his holy apostles and prophets," which seems to refer to the same group as in 2:20, cannot be Old Testament prophets since the mystery has been revealed to them *now*, that is, in the new age; the salvation-historical *nun* definitely forbids us from interpreting them as Old Testament prophets.[55] Third, in Eph 4:11 the ascended Christ is said to have given apostles, prophets, evangelists, and others *after* his ascension.[56] Lincoln identifies

---

50. Getz, *Sharpening the Focus*, 96. See also Davidson, *Ecclesiastical Polity*, 115–16.

51. In the ancient church this position can be found in the writings of Chrysostom, Theodoret, Ambrosiaster, Jerome, and Aquinas. See Saint Aquinas, *Commentary on Saint Paul's Epistle*, 111–13. More recently this position has been represented by the likes of George Stöckhardt, who suggests that *profētōn* points to the Old Testament prophets and their writings, "which are accounted on an equality with the writings of the Apostles and with them constitute one genus, since both of these genitives, *apostolōn* and *profētōn*, are governed by one and the same article" (Stöckhardt, *Commentary on St. Paul's Letter*, 153).

52. Some take the phrase "apostles and prophets" to mean the apostles who prophesy; however, this suggestion cannot be upheld either grammatically or theologically. For a more detailed discussion, see Uprichard, *Commentary on Ephesians*, 146–47.

53. Lincoln, *Ephesians*, 153. See also Perkins, *Ephesians*, 76; Foulkes, *Letter of Paul to the Ephesians*, 94; Mitton, *Ephesians*, 112; Gaebelein et al., *Ephesians-Philemon*, 42; Schnackenburg, *Ephesians*, 122.

54. Uprichard, *Commentary on Ephesians*, 146–47.

55. O'Brien, *Letter to the Ephesians*, 214.

56. Ibid.

Theological Considerations for Polity Models (Continued)

these prophets by stating that they "are presumably the men and women who exercise the gift of prophecy under discussion in 1 Cor 11 and 14 and whose activities are mentioned elsewhere in Rom 12:6; 1 Thess 5:20; Acts 11:27; 13:1, 2; 15:32; 19:6; 21:9, 10; Rev 1:3; 10:11; 16:6; 18:20, 24; 19:10; 22:6–10, 18, 19."[57]

Calvin confirms the foundational nature of the ministry of the apostles and prophets, declaring that the three functions of apostles, prophets, and evangelists "were not established in the church as permanent ones, but only for that time during which churches were to be erected where none existed before, or where they were to be carried over from Moses to Christ."[58] Even Hooker, a well-known Anglican divine, admits that:

> The Apostles were sent as special chosen eye-witnesses of Jesus Christ, from whom immediately they received their whole Embassage, and their Commission to be the principal first founders of an House of God consisting as well of Gentiles as of Jews: In this there are not after them any other like unto them.[59]

Since Scripture nowhere identifies apostles and prophets as officers in the local churches, their office, job description, and special abilities were not passed down to those who came after them.[60] As Hammet explains, "Apostles and prophets are most commonly seen as extraordinary ministries, serving an important foundational purpose (Eph 2:20), but are not intended to be ongoing offices in the church."[61] Saucy correctly points out that the understanding of apostolic succession, whereby the apostles ordained others to succeed them as the only valid ministers, is not found in the New Testament.[62] Lindsay further clarifies that:

---

57. Lincoln, *Ephesians*, 153.

58. Calvin, *Institutes of the Christian Religion*, 4.3.4. See also Dana and Sipes, *Manual of Ecclesiology*, 88.

59. Hooker, "Seventh Book," 7.4.4. Of course, forced by his own theological tradition, Hooker ends by muddying the waters: "And yet the Apostles have now their successors upon earth, their true successors, *if not in the largeness*, surely in the kind of that Episcopal function, whereby they had power to sit as spiritual ordinary Judges, both over Laity and over Clergy where Churches Christian were established" (ibid., emphasis mine).

60. In contradistinction to the claims of Roman Catholic, Anglican, and Swedish Lutheran churches, apostolic succession should once and for all be recognized as human invention and not biblical teaching.

61. Hammett, *Biblical Foundations*, 159.

62. Saucy, *Church in God's Program*, 109.

> *Apostolic succession*, in the dogmatic sense of that ambiguous term, is the *legal fiction* required by the legal mind to connect the growing conceptions of the authority of the clergy with the earlier days of Christianity... A legal fiction has generally some historical basis to start from... The apostles had founded many of the churches, and their first converts or others suitable had become the first office-bearers. There had been a succession of leaders, the characteristics of leadership, as has been explained, undergoing some striking changes in the course of the second century. All these successions of office-bearers could be traced back to the foundation of the churches in which they existed, and therefore to the missionaries, whether apostles or apostolic men, who had founded them. *This was the historical thread on which, in the end, was strung the gigantic figment called apostolic succession—a strange compound of minimum of fact and maximum of theory.*[63]

Nineteenth-century Baptist theologian J. L. Reynolds, having put forth a number of reasons why apostolic succession cannot be supported, is persuasive in his conclusion:

> A fatal objection to the notion of apostolic succession, and the consequences derived from it, consists in the fact, that no such succession can be established by historical evidence. The links of the chain are broken, and lost beyond the possibility of recovery. The transmission of apostolic grace is no longer practicable; for the wires of the mystic telegraph are disconnected, tangled, and, along a portion of the pretended line, nowhere to be found.[64]

Even Joseph Ratzinger, who would later become Pope Benedict XVI, the Bishop of Rome, and whose church is the most adamant in its support of apostolic succession, admits "that there is no explicit statement regarding the Petrine succession in the New Testament."[65]

Instead of the fiction of apostolic succession, the apostles and prophets set up a leadership structure that was to be reproduced, as 1 Cor 3:6, 10 and Eph 2:19–22 relate and as the pastoral epistles evidence. Proper understanding of this principle will enable churches to accurately apply some of

---

63. Lindsay, *Church and the Ministry*, 279, emphasis mine. Lindsay insists on the identity of purpose between apostolic succession and a form of legal fiction that assisted a pagan civilian in tracing the roots of the government of the emperors from Augustus to Diocletian all the way back to the old republican constitution.

64. Reynolds, "Church Polity," 348. Additional arguments against apostolic succession may be found in Kern, *Christianity as Organized*, 274–314.

65. Ratzinger, *Called to Communion*, 48–65.

Theological Considerations for Polity Models (Continued)

the leadership structures listed in the early days of the church, especially those in the book of Acts. Therefore, our patterning of church organization and offices is not to be set after that of the apostles themselves, but after that which they set up for us to duplicate. Hence, we may not hold the example of the Jerusalem Council (Acts 15) meeting to be a depiction of "general assembly," as Presbyterians do, because we recognize the unique, unshared, and unrepeatable nature of the event. The account of the council proceedings was meant to be informational in nature and describe the challenges met in the accomplishment of this mystery of Jews and Gentiles fusing together to form a church.

Otherwise, what we are doing, in essence, is duplicating that system of church government of which the apostles were a part, while using the terminology from the system that they set up for our emulation. Philip Ryken's words provide a good synopsis of this section: "The apostles' [and prophets'] ministry was once and for all because a building has only one foundation, and once it is laid, no other foundation can be established."[66] The foundational role of the apostles is further underscored by a passage like Rev 21, in which their names appear on the twelve *foundations* of the heavenly Jerusalem (21:14). White is absolutely right when he states that Christ does not *refound* his church by starting from scratch with each passing generation:[67]

> Thus the New Testament is unanimous that the apostle in the narrower sense acquires a unique position because of his meeting with the risen —or exalted—Lord (in whatever different ways that position may be understood), and because of the charge given him. To him (perhaps to others too) there is entrusted the fundamental preaching by which the later preaching is to be measured. We can speak of the apostles' pupils, but not of their successors in office.[68]

Therefore, rather than implementing a straight application of what we see in the New Testament, it is necessary for us to interpret what we see, picking out the permanent components of timeless principles without canonizing first-century culture.[69] This will be the focus of the sixth point. For now, however, our attention should shift from those offices that were

---

66. Phillips, Ryken, and Dever, *Church*, 105. See also Schweizer, *Church Order*, 194.
67. White, "Plural-Elder-Led Church," 258, emphasis mine.
68. Schweizer, *Church Order*, 197. See also Davidson, *Ecclesiastical Polity*, 114.
69. Fee, *Gospel and Spirit*, 2.

instrumental in setting up the church to the church leadership offices proposed in the New Testament.

Fifth Principle: The Interchangeability of the Offices of Pastor, Elder, and Overseer

The fifth principle examines the New Testament terminology for church leadership and concludes that the three offices in question—namely those of elder, overseer, and pastor—are interchangeable in nature and function. A short overview of the New Testament terminology for church leadership may be especially helpful at this point. We will start with "elder," or *presbuteros*. *Presbuteros* is used in both the Old and New Testaments. Of the many occurrences of this term, we find "two titular uses common to the papyri, Septuagint, and New Testament."[70] In the first place, this term designated village officials who governed and controlled community affairs.[71] Secondly, *presbuteroi* was used titularly for members of a religious council, such as a council of priests in the papyri, special elders of Israel in the Septuagint, and members of the Sanhedrin and leaders of a local Christian assembly in the New Testament.[72] In the Septuagint it is used to relate various Hebrew terms, among which are: "firstborn," "great," "aged, old," "former, first, chief," and others. The two primary meanings carried by this term in the Old Testament were in descriptions of individuals who have entered old age, and as a leader or group of leaders who performed various functions.[73]

In the New Testament, *presbuteros* and its cognate forms appear sixty-six times.[74] The religious leaders of the Jews were called *presbuteroi*, so the church evidently borrowed this term from them.[75] However, it should be pointed out that there is also a "great deal of difference between Jewish elders and Christian elders. The function and prerogatives of the former

---

70. Mayer, "Exegetical Study," 28.

71. Ibid.

72. Ibid.

73. Mappes, "'Elder' in the Old and New Testaments," 81. Mappes found that the establishing of elders, as a distinct group of leaders, most likely originated in the patriarchal tribal settings of the Semitic peoples, where the family was the basic social unit.

74. For a detailed list of its occurrences in the New Testament, see Arndt et al., *Greek-English Lexicon*, 706.

75. Mayer, "New Testament Elder," 29.

Theological Considerations for Polity Models (Continued)

differ greatly from the latter, so that polity was not directly transferred. Only a current name was borrowed."[76] When referring to a local church, then, the term functions as a title for its spiritual leaders.[77]

The next term is "overseer," or *episkopos*. The word *episkopos* is derived from *epi* ("over") and *skopeō* ("to watch or look"). The *skopos* is a "watcher," and an *episkopos* is an "overseer," one who is attentive to things or people.[78] Previous to the New Testament, the term found "frequent titular employment, but there is no group of *overseers* charged with the spiritual supervision of a religious group."[79]

In the Septuagint, *episkopos* depicts priestly oversight (Num 4:16), military leaders (31:14), stewards (Judg 9:28), and superintendents of those who repaired the temple (2 Chr 34:12, 17). It is even once used of God as the judge of mankind (Job 20:29). In studying the term, Mayer finds, "Thus we find *governors* of cities in the classical period, communal officials in the papyri, and city *supervisors* or *administrators* in the Septuagint. Also of significance are the *officers* in a religious society, found in the papyri."[80]

Based on the pre-New Testament sources, then, *episkopos* implies general or specific oversight by political, religious, communal, military, or municipal individuals.[81] Perhaps one of the main differences between *presbuteros* and *episkopoi* is their cultural usage. As *presbuteros* had basically Jewish antecedents, so Christian *episkopos* seems to have had basically Gentile antecedents.[82] In the context of church leadership, much like in the case of *presbuteros*, *overseer* is "an old term again that seems to be used with an entirely new application."[83] In the church context, *episkopos* designates those who are recognized officials in providing spiritual oversight to members entrusted to them.[84]

The third term for review is "pastor" (*poimēn*). The metaphorical use of *poimēn* for a *leader* of people can be traced through the Septuagint to the

---

76. Ibid. A more in-depth discussion of this subject will be offered in chapter 6 under the section entitled "Addressing the Objections to the Plurality of Elders."
77. Mappes, "'Elder' in the Old and New Testaments," 86.
78. Coenen, "DEπι'σκοπος," 1:188.
79. Mayer, "New Testament Elder," 30.
80. Ibid., 31, emphasis Mayer's.
81. Mappes, "'Elder' in the Old and New Testaments," 163–64.
82. Mayer, "New Testament Elder," 31.
83. Ibid.
84. Mappes, "New Testament Elder," 164.

classics, but it does not occur in this sense in the papyri.[85] As such, it was never used as a title and is instead a functional designation for religious leaders only in the Septuagint.[86] Therefore, the closest antecedent to its use in Eph 4:11, outside the New Testament, is found in the *Shepherds of Israel*.[87] Although this term, when referring to an officer in the New Testament, is used only once in Eph 4:11, it is used seven times elsewhere to describe Christ as the great shepherd (John 10:2, 11, 12, 14, 16; Heb 13:20; 1 Pet 2:25). "Pastor" emphasizes the pastoral role of caring and feeding, although the concept of leadership is also inherent in the picture of a shepherd.[88] The verb *poimanō* occurs four times in describing the activity of elders, who are to feed the church (John 21:26; Acts 20:28; 1 Cor 9:7; 1 Pet 5:2).[89] Knight reiterates and further expounds the interrelation between "pastors" and "elders," writing,

> The solution to the question of what group is in view in the term "pastors" is to be found by recognizing that the shepherding or pasturing responsibility is given to all the elders/bishops in Acts 20:28: "Be on guard for yourselves and for all the flock (*poimniō*), among which the Holy Spirit has made you overseers, to shepherd [to feed, KJV] (*poimainein*) the church of God which he purchased with his own blood" (NASB). The verb used in Acts 20:28 "to shepherd," "to pastor" (*poimainein*, also translated "to feed") is the verbal form of the concept and term we are considering in Eph 4:11, that is, "pastors" (*poimenas*).[90]

85. Mayer, "New Testament Elder," 32.

86. Ibid.

87. Mappes, "New Testament Elder," 164. See also Arndt et al., *Greek-English Lexicon*, 690. It may be of interest that "pastor" is linked in this passage with "teacher," and in fact, the nouns "pastors" and "teachers" are governed by only one Greek article (*tous de poimenas kai didaskalous*). As a result, some interpreters have understood the phrase *pastors and teachers* to refer to one and the same group, calling them "pastor-teachers." This would mean that all pastors are teachers and that all teachers are pastors. But because the nouns are plural, it is extremely unlikely that they refer to the same group, but only that the author is linking them closely together. It is better to regard the pastors as a subset of teachers. In other words, all pastors are teachers, but not all teachers are pastors (syntactic note from the NET Bible). For a helpful treatment of this term and its derivatives in the New Testament, see Cowen, *Who Rules the Church?* 5–7.

88. MacArthur, *Master's Plan for the Church*, 185.

89. Mappes, "New Testament Elder," 164. See also Arndt et al., *Greek-English Lexicon*, 690.

90. Knight, "Two Offices," 9–10.

Theological Considerations for Polity Models (Continued)

Biblical data originating from the New Testament is reasonably straightforward regarding the interchangeableness of *episkopos* ("overseer"), *presbuteros* ("elder"), and *poimēn* ("pastor").[91] In Acts 20:17, 28, Paul charges the Ephesian elders (*presbuterous*), "Be on guard for yourselves and for all the flock, among which the Holy Spirit has made you overseers [*episkopous*], to shepherd/pastor [*poimainein*] the church of God which He purchased with His own blood." Again, in the pastoral letter to his friend and fellow-laborer, Titus, in 1:5, 7, Paul writes, "For this reason I left you in

---

91. In writings dated before the New Testament, *episkops* and *presbuteros* are not used together, see Mappes, "The New Testament Elder," 163. On a different note, some reject the view that *poimēn* ("pastor") is interchangeable with the other two terms. According to their understanding, scriptural evidence does not seem to support the popular practice of properly addressing a single elder as "pastor." The following is their argument: While it is true that the work of the elder as a shepherd is pastoral work in accordance with Acts 20:28 and 1 Pet 5:2, it is interesting to note that "the title that has become most common in our churches today, namely, pastor was not used in conjunction with a church in the New Testament" (Radmacher, *Question of Elders*, 5). "Pastor" is not an office, but a spiritual gift. "One can have the gift of pastor," says Wallace, "without being an elder; and one can hold the office of elder without having the gift of pastor" (Wallace, "Who Should Run the Church?"). Daughters adds that if we call a man by this name, we are calling him by his spiritual gift (Daughters, *New TestameNew Testament Church Government*, 39). Ryrie argues similarly, stating, "nowhere does Paul suggest that gifts are to be attached to a designated place. For instance, Paul does not equate the gift of pastor with the pastorate (as is commonly done today)" (Ryrie, "Pauline Doctrine of the Church" 64). Furthermore, "the definite article is never used with the term 'pastor' except when referring to Jesus Christ" (Radmacher, *Question of Elders*, 7). Interestingly enough, this is conceded even by Baptist theologian Gerald P. Cowen, who states, "although the term *pastor* is commonly used today as the title for the spiritual overseer of a congregation, it was probably not intended in Scripture to be a title but to be descriptive of what an elder does" (Cowen, *Who Rules the Church?* 13).

While they make some good points about spiritual gifts, these theologians must not forget that apostleship, for example, was both a gift and an office. Harold W. Hoehner postulates that "the apostles include the Twelve, who had the office of apostleship by virtue of being with Christ (Acts 1:21–22) and having been appointed by Him (which would also include Paul; 1 Cor 15:8–9; Gal 1:1; 2:6–9). But "apostles" also included others who were recognized as apostles, such as James (1 Cor 15:7; Gal 1:19), Barnabas (Acts 14:4, 14; 1 Cor 9:6), Andronicus and Junias (Rom 16:7), possibly Silas and Timothy (1 Thess 1:1; 2:7), and Apollos (1 Cor 4:6, 9). This latter group had the gift of apostleship but not the apostolic "office" as did the Twelve and Paul" (Hoehner, "Ephesians," 2:634). If that is so, then it is possible that *pastor* could be considered a gift and an office. In either case, Daughters' admonition is extremely appropriate: "We should expect to find a number of persons in our local churches who have been given the spiritual gift of 'pastor-teacher.' Most of them will not be professional clergymen. We need to encourage them to exercise their gifts properly within the body. If we confuse gift with office, we are likely to stifle their freedom to minister" (Daughters, *New Testament Church Government*, 40).

Crete, that you would set in order what remains and appoint elders [*presbuterous*] in every city as I directed you, namely, if any man is above reproach . . . For the overseer [*episkopos*] must be above reproach." Apostle Peter writes along the same lines in his first letter (5:2), "Therefore, I exhort the elders [*presbuterous*] among you, . . . shepherd [*poimanate*] the flock of God among you, exercising oversight [*episkopountes*]."

The passage that, in my view, offers the clearest culmination of this idea of interchangeability of terms is recorded in the same epistle—1 Pet 2:25. Here, Peter describes Jesus Christ as shepherd/pastor and overseer: "For you were continually straying like sheep, but now you have returned to the Shepherd [*poimena*] and Guardian [*episkopon*] of your souls." Commenting on the etymology of *episkopos*, Coenen states:

> As a title of the exalted Christ, it sums up everything expressed by the term in the OT, Jud., and Gk. religious thought. It is no accident, but the expression of a conscious insight, that *episkopos* is here linked with *poimēn*. The two thoughts are already connected in the OT (Num. 27:17) and again in the NT (Acts 20:28). Oversight means loving care and concern, a responsibility willingly shouldered; it must never be used for personal aggrandisement. Its meaning is to be seen in Christ's selfless service, which was moved by concern for the salvation of men.[92]

If Christ himself, as our supreme example, is described as the Shepherd/Pastor and Guardian/Overseer, then it seems to be perfectly acceptable to view these as different terms for what was essentially the same office.[93]

The support for interchangeableness of the two terms, bishop/overseer and presbyter/elder can also be found in the earliest sub-apostolic literature.[94] In terms of how these words related to each other, Mappes postulates that "the context suggests that *episkopos* is a title of *office* synonymous with elder (*presbuteros*), and the present infinitive *poimainein* describes a *function* of the office."[95] Each of the terms, according to Newton, "provides a clearer picture of the dignity and function of elders in church life: *elder* emphasizes the spiritual maturity required for this office; *overseer* implies

---

92. Coenen, "*Episkopos*," 191.

93. In addition to Mappes' and Knight's articles defending the interchangeability of terms, see Mappes, "New Testament Elder" and Knight, "Two Offices." Another detailed demonstration of the interchangeability of terms was produced by Benjamin L. Merkle in his valuable dissertation, "Elder and Overseer."

94. Saint Clement, "First Epistle of Clement," 44.

95. Mappes, "New Testament Elder," 165, emphasis Mappes'.

Theological Considerations for Polity Models (Continued)

the leadership and direction given to the church; *pastor* suggests feeding, nurturing, and protecting the flock."[96] Or, in other words, all the elders/bishops have a shepherding or pastoral responsibility and may be designated as pastors.[97] Considering the interchangeableness of terms defined above, in churches with a plural-elder setting, the pastor/overseer is often understood as an elder in office.[98]

Despite the strong evidence for the interchangeable nature of these three terms for one office, beginning early in the second century, there was a movement toward the development of what is called the monarchical bishop, as an office separate from and higher than the office of elder.[99] Since Scripture does not warrant such a development, a host of reasons has been given for it, all of which can be attributed to organizational expediency in the wake of attempts to combat numerous theological discrepancies throughout early days of the church's existence. Or, as Coenen puts it, "the reason for the triumph of monepiscopacy in the second and third centuries was partly because of individuals with outstanding gifts, and partly because of the need for tighter organization."[100]

That pattern continued until the Reformation, when Calvin became one of the first Reformers to recognize that Scripture uses the terms "elder" and "overseer/bishop" interchangeably.[101] The importance of this principle for our study can be seen when we consider the unwarranted multi-layered organizational pattern of the episcopal model. The support for episcopal polity may have been historically expedient, but it is biblically unsustainable. We now turn to the examination of the proper way of applying biblical commands to contemporary usage.

---

96. Newton, *Elders in Congregational Life*, 36, emphasis Newton's.

97. Knight, "Two Offices," 10. He continues, "When we ask of the Eph 4:11 passage, who are the pastors, we may answer from Acts 20:28 and context that they are the elders/bishops. This answer is borne out also by the passage in 1 Pet 5:1–4 which speaks of the task of elders . . . So we may deduce, from the Apostle Peter as well as from the Apostle Paul in Luke's account in Acts, that pastors equal elders/bishops" (ibid.).

98. White, "Plural-Elder-Led Church," 271. John A. Kern proposes that the word "elder" is used as a title in passages where elders and bishops are mentioned interchangeably, and the word "bishop" as a common term descriptive of the work that a presbyter must do (Kern, *Christianity as Organized*, 259).

99. Hammett, *Biblical Foundations*, 161. In light of biblical evidence such as 1 Pet 2:25; 5 and Acts 20, Schweizer is quite rightly adamant that the ministries of bishop and pastor are one and the same (Schweizer, *Church Order*, 200).

100. Coenen, "Επισκοπος," 192.

101. Calvin, *Institutes of the Christian Religion*, 4.3.8.

Sixth Principle: Application Must Be Preceded by Interpretation

In the conclusion to his detailed study of the origin, position, and import of elders within the sociological setting of the early church, Campbell warns the reader against feeling bound to model present day church structures after those of the first century. In admitting to belonging to a tradition that has not historically utilized elders in church government, Campbell recognizes the difficulty of "straightforward" application of his findings to contemporary practice. The reason? In Campbell's own words:

> The role of the elders in early Christianity was of a piece with their role in society as a whole. We cannot reconstruct the first-century house-church unless we first reconstruct the Graeco-Roman world of which it was a part.[102]

While Campbell may be wrong in his conclusion, he is right in advocating, perhaps implicitly, the need for accurate interpretation of the biblical data before any thoughts of application can take place. Roy B. Zuck, in commenting on the importance of interpretation, believes it to be the most difficult and time-consuming of the three steps of hermeneutics—namely, observation, interpretation, and application. "Yet cutting Bible study short in this area," he writes, "can lead to serious errors and faulty results."[103]

Interpretation should build on observation and *then* lead into application.[104] Interpretation is foundational to application. In the words of Zuck, "If we do not interpret properly, we may end up applying the Bible wrongly."[105]

Therefore, in considering the scriptural evidence related to church polity, careful interpretation must precede any application. As the passages are weighed, only that which is proven to be supra-cultural may be applied into contemporary practice. Or as Powers puts it, "The mere fact that we are able to establish what the early church did in relation to a particular matter does not automatically require that the church today must do the same thing. We must rightly divide the Word of Truth."[106] Bernard Ramm concurs, stating that it is "mandatory for a preacher to realize that interpre-

---

102. Campbell, *Elders*, 254.
103. Zuck, "Why of Interpretation," 14.
104. Ibid., 16.
105. Ibid., 17.
106. Powers, "Patterns of New Testament Ministry," 167. See also Zuck, "Why of Interpretation," 14–18.

tation of the meaning of the text is one thing, and the range of application is another, and that he must always keep these two matters separate."[107]

In interpreting biblical data, we come across three types of commands (and/or precedents) in the Scripture.[108] The first type is the universal instruction. According to Alan F. Johnson, "when God reveals theological truth about himself, about man, or the world then this truth, though expressed in culturally laden human language, is not relative to any particular culture. Neither are the moral universals and general moral principles found in Scripture."[109] Among these may be included "such condemned practices as homosexual sexual acts, extramarital sexual relations, hatred, lying, incest, love of the world, idolatry, racism, the neglect of the poor, revenge, and a host of other biblical teaching."[110] The moral law expressed in the Ten Commandments, which was stated clearly in the Old Testament and restated by Jesus in the New Testament, is another example of this type of instruction.

The second type is a command that, although it may not be directly applicable today, contains a principle that can be put into practice. "Principlizing" is a term employed by Virkler to denote an attempt to discover the spiritual, moral, or theological principles in a narrative that have relevance for the contemporary believer.[111] Unlike allegorizing, which gives a story new meaning by assigning it symbolic significance not intended by the original author, principlizing recognizes the validity of both the historical details of narrative and the principles those details attempt to teach.[112] "Methodologically," Virkler goes on,

> the approach is the same as in the exegesis of any biblical passage. The historical circumstances and the cultural customs that illuminate the significance of various actions and commands are carefully observed. The purpose of the book within which the narrative occurs is studied, as well as the narrower context of the passages immediately preceding and following the section under examination. The state of theological knowledge and commitment is also surveyed.[113]

107. Ramm, *Protestant Biblical Interpretation*, 113.

108. This correlates with the arguments in Virkler, "Proposal for the Transcultural Problem," 239–43; Kraft, "Interpreting in Cultural Context."

109. Johnson, "Problems of Normativeness in Scripture," 263.

110. Ibid.

111. Virkler, "Proposal for the Transcultural Problem," 232.

112. Ibid.

113. Ibid.

Paul's instruction for married women in the Corinthian church to wear a head covering as a sign of their submission to their husbands is an example of the second type of command. The head covering is a culturally-specific command that does not literally apply today. It is rather a meaningful symbol in the ancient world that needs some sort of corresponding symbol today, but not necessarily in the form of a head covering.[114]

The third type is the instruction that was specifically designated for the time and the locale of the intended readership. It was culturally conditioned and thus not normative for believers today. These are the commands that are, in the words of Johnson, "so highly particular to a given historical situation or specific cultural expression that for the modern reader the injunction is irrelevant,"[115] because there is no cultural parallel, at least in the Western hemisphere. Among the examples of this type of command are instructions that deal with eating food sacrificed to idols, as recorded in 1 Cor 8 and elsewhere. Jesus' command to his disciples instructing them to wash one another's feet in John 13:14 is another example. The changing cultures and times have lessened the need and significance of the practice.[116] "We all recognize," states Grant R. Osborne, "that portions of Scripture are not meant to be followed today, such as historical narrative or purely cultural commands."[117]

To claim that some scriptural commands are culturally limited while others are not necessitates the development of criteria for distinguishing between those commands that apply literally and those that do not.[118] In discerning whether principles are transcultural or culture-bound, Virkler recommends first that we determine the reason given for the principle. If the reason for a principle is culture-bound, then the principle may be also.[119] If the reason has its basis in God's unchanging nature (his grace, his love, his moral nature, or his created order), then the principle itself should probably not be changed.[120] Osborne similarly suggests that if the scriptural teaching

---

114. For a full argument, see Wallace, "What Is the Head Covering." See also Knight, "Response to Problems of Normativeness," 247.

115. Johnson, "Problems of Normativeness in Scripture," 262.

116. Virkler, "Proposal for the Transcultural Problem," 239.

117. Osborne, *Hermeneutical Spiral*, 453.

118. Virkler, "Proposal for the Transcultural Problem," 239.

119. Ibid., 241.

120. Ibid. Virkler provides some suggested steps in translating biblical commands from one culture and time to another; see Virkler, "Proposal for the Transcultural Problem," 242–43. Kraft argues along the same lines, perhaps from a bit of a different perspective; see Kraft, "Interpreting in Cultural Context," 251–52.

Theological Considerations for Polity Models (Continued)

transcends the norms of the society of the original recipients, it will provide a clear signpost for the supra-cultural relevance of the command.[121] To implement it practically, we would have to distance ourselves from the "biblical text by a thorough examination of the Bible's literary, cultural, historical, and theological context."[122] This distancing, according to Johnson, needs to be followed by a "serious reflection on our own contemporary cultural predisposition, values, practices, etc."[123] Only then, Johnson correctly postulates, "can we fuse the two horizons, the biblical and ours."[124]

At the risk of belaboring the point, the following helpful principles, provided by Johnson, are included here to aid the interpreter in determining the normativeness of any biblical instructive teaching,

1. How does my specific social-cultural and psychological background aid and distort my reading of the scriptural matter?
2. Is the matter theological (affecting our relationship to God) or moral (affecting our relationship to others)?
3. Does the immediate context limit the recipient or the application?
4. Does subsequent revelation limit the recipient or the application?
5. Is the specific teaching in conflict with other biblical teaching?
6. Is the exhortation a general moral principle, or is it a particular cultural directive?
7. If the exhortation is a particular cultural directive, does the immediate context or the larger biblical context or the biblical author's cultural context help to identify the author's intent or the general moral principle behind the particular directive?
8. Are there cultural conditions mentioned in the biblical context or assumed in the author's larger cultural context?
9. Is the particular cultural *form* present today? If so, does it have the same semantic symbol value as in the ancient culture? Is a more appropriate form available to express the same symbol value of the form in the ancient culture?

---

121. Osborne, *Hermeneutical Spiral*, 453.
122. Johnson, "Problems of Normativeness in Scripture," 267.
123. Ibid.
124. Ibid.

10. If the teaching is found in poetry, story, apocalyptic symbolism or historical narrative, what is the author's intent in the material? The matter may be normative if the larger biblical context affirms it.

11. Is the exhortation related to a social institution? Have subsequent cultural changes affected the way people relate to each other in the institution?[125]

What is the import of the foregoing discussion to the topic of this work? Careful interpretation can help us to determine whether a passage was intended only for the people to whom it was initially addressed or whether it was intended for ensuing generations. The findings of the biblical precedent of church polity must be demonstrated to be relevant outside of the culture of the original audience alone (i.e., of the first or second type of command above). Only that type of scriptural evidence can be endorsed for modern application.

Perhaps a few illustrations will be helpful at this point. Since this section began with the discussion of elders, let us continue along the same lines. As Campbell noted above, before we adopt the New Testament idea of eldership at the helm of a local church into contemporary ecclesiastical practice, we must provide sufficient proof for the supra-cultural nature of biblical instructions. Since a number of scholars insists that the New Testament Eldership was simply an adaptation of a practice present within Judaism that was carried over from the Old Testament and implemented in the time of Christ within a local synagogue, then in order to prove cultural transcendence of early Christian eldership, a careful exegete must demonstrate the uniqueness of the scriptural eldership—if not as a new office, then at least as a newly defined one, and a certain level of independence from the dominant religious and political forms of the day. Only by proving that neither culture, nor religious background, nor political pressure can adequately account for the formation of the eldership in the New Testament can we establish that "God ordained this governmental structure because it best suits the nature of His Church."[126] Then, and only then, can the claim for application be considered valid.

---

125. Johnson, "Problems of Normativeness in Scripture," 280, emphasis Johnson's.
126. Daughters, *New Testament Church Government*, 30–31.

5

Multiple-Elder Congregationalism
The Most Biblically Defensible Model

FRESH ANALYSIS OF THE BIBLICAL DATA ON POLITY

The goal of this chapter is to assimilate the biblical data on polity in view of the six theological principles discussed in chapters 3 and 4.[1] This will be accomplished through a review of each polity style in light of its scriptural foundation in order to endorse a structure that most closely mirrors the precedent of the New Testament. To reiterate here, this research was conducted with no presuppositions at the outset as to what lay at the end. There was no sense of feeling bound or determined to reach a certain goal, or of putting together whatever arguments were necessary. As the Lord is my witness, my mind was open and my heart's only desire was to search his word for a better way to understand his teaching regarding the structure of his body on this earth. In this chapter, armed with the sword of the Spirit and assisted by the established theological perimeters, we will discover what the Bible teaches regarding polity.

In chapter 2, we examined three different styles of church government. Evaluatory comments on each have so far been purposefully kept to a minimum in order to lead the reader through the entire process. Now is the time to evaluate these three styles of church government and endorse the most biblically sound candidate.

---

1. These theological principles themselves are a derivation of the scriptural teaching plainly read and sensibly interpreted.

Church Government According to the Bible

The Bible Does Not Support Episcopal Polity

The first reason why episcopal polity cannot be upheld as the most biblically defensible model in this work is because the key office around which this polity structure is based cannot be found in the New Testament as distinct from presbyters.[2] Or, as Hammett puts it, "the distinction between *episcopos* and *presbyteros* inherent in episcopalianism is not sustained by New Testament usage."[3] Jürgen Roloff echoes this sentiment in his entry on church government in *The Encyclopedia of Christianity*: "Neither the post-Pauline congregations nor any other writing in the New Testament envisions a threefold pattern of ministry (bishop, presbyter, and deacon)."[4]

Second, the New Testament's use of *episkopos* does not center on a single bishop, but rather on a plurality of bishops who serve together, not to supervise the leaders of other congregations, but to lead a single congregation.[5] Therefore, the second theological principle—literal hermeneutic—would prevent us from adopting the office of the bishop in the same manner in which it is used within episcopal structure.[6] Third, the episcopal model leaves the local congregation passive, while the New Testament reveals very active self-governed churches.[7] Fourth, the idea of apostolic succession, which is popular within this view, is nowhere found in the Bible. In addition to the evidence against apostolic succession presented in the previous chapter, the following argument put forth by Saucy serves as yet more proof that the concept of the apostolic succession is nothing short of fallacy:

> 1. The absence of instruction for succession. In the original commission of the apostles there is no provision for any successors

---

2. "Presbyters" is a synonym for "elders." Michael Harper recognizes that when he says that "there is no office in the New Testament that approximates to the modern bishop" (Harper, "Duplicating the New Testament Church" 24).

3. Hammett, *Biblical Foundations*, 139.

4. Roloff, "Church Government," 1.2.3.

5. Hammett, *Biblical Foundations*, 140.

6. Harper states, "If we were to follow the New Testament slavishly we should be looking ... askance at our bishops" (Harper, "Duplicating the New Testament Church," 24). Harper's point is that we should discriminate between the portions of the New Testament that were meant to be exemplary and those that were meant to be mandatory. But who is to be the final authority on which is which? And what are the criteria to establish which is exemplary and which is mandatory? The answer, of course, comes back to one's theological presuppositions.

7. Hammett, *Biblical Foundations*, 140.

(Mark 3:14ff.), nor are any instructions given subsequently to that end.

2. The absence of early historical succession. In agreement with the absence of instruction is the lack of any mention of the transfer of the apostolic office in the New Testament record. When Paul charges the elders for the care of the church in Ephesus, there is no hint of a transfer of any authority of office (Acts 20:17, 28). The same is true in the case of Timothy and Titus, where succession could most logically be expected to appear. There is no evidence that the apostle ordained them as successors to his office. The New Testament shows the elders and bishops taking the place of the apostles, but precisely as elders and bishops and not apostles. They succeed apostles, but in a fundamentally different position . . . Historically the doctrine of succession by ordination does not appear for some time after the New Testament church. Although Ignatius writes very early recognizing the episcopate, he has nothing to say about succession . . . Monarchical succession is first found in Irenaeus' writings at the end of the second century. But even here there is no doctrine of the *transmission* of grace or authority by ordination, only a sequence of ministry. It is not until the third century that the doctrine of succession through ordination comes into being, and that, according to Lindsay, by lawyers of the Latin Church who sought to connect the growing authority of the church with the apostolic authority in much the same way that the government of the emperors from Augustus to Diocletian was said to be the prolongation of the old Republican constitution.

3. The uniqueness of the apostolic office . . . necessitates qualifications only found in the apostles of Christ's time. . . .

4. The priesthood of all believers. The imposition of an essential ministry for the conveyance of grace to the church does serious harm to the doctrine of the priesthood of the believers according to which all members of the church have the same direct access to God and His grace.[8]

Some scholars, such as Peter Toon, are quite frank in stating that "the Anglican form of church government is an attempt to conform in general terms to the pattern in place in the early church in the third, fourth, and fifth centuries," thus admitting their reliance on tradition more so than on

---

8. Saucy, *Church in God's Program*, 109–112. More discussion of the apostolic succession may be found in chapter 4's fourth theological principle.

the word of God.⁹ The reliance that this system places on church tradition for the support of apostolic succession, despite its glaring absence from Scripture, violates theological principles number one, two, and four.¹⁰

Also, in upholding apostolic succession, advocates of the episcopal form of church government give insufficient attention to Christ's direct exercise of lordship over the church.¹¹ It was Christ himself who installed Paul without any intermediary; no other apostle was involved.¹² Paul makes much of this point in justifying his apostleship (Gal 1:15–17).¹³ The conclusion Erickson arrives at in pursuing this line of logic should certainly be pondered. If Paul received his office directly from God, rather than resting upon previous apostolic authority, might not others as well?¹⁴ On these grounds, apostolic succession must be rejected unequivocally.

The fifth reason why the episcopal system of church government is not biblically defensible is because the New Testament church, according to the understanding of the advocates of episcopal polity, takes its root during the life of Christ, which the Scripture does not support. As such, the timing of the origin of the church, according to the episcopal tradition, runs against the third theological principle.¹⁵

All in all, that the episcopal model seemed to be useful in the early centuries of the church is certainly a strong point, but it lacks the forcefulness of biblical basis. In light of this evaluation, Hammett's conclusion is fitting: "Despite its early appearance and widespread usage in church history, episcopalianism has the weakest biblical support of any of the three major views on church government."¹⁶

The Bible Does Not Support Presbyterian Polity

Similarly, there are several reasons why presbyterian polity cannot be endorsed here. First, while the office of elder can certainly find plentiful support in Scripture, the distinction between teaching and ruling elders

9. Toon, "Episcopalianism," 24.
10. See chapters 3 and 4.
11. Erickson, *Christian Theology*, 1074.
12. Ibid.
13. Ibid.
14. Ibid.
15. See chapter 3.
16. Hammett, *Biblical Foundations*, 140.

advocated by theologians of this tradition is contrived. It hinges on a single verse found in 1 Tim 5:17, a verse that does not explicitly warrant this distinction, especially in light of the 1 Tim 3:2 requirement that all elders be "able to teach." It was not until Calvin, in fact, that the two classes of eldership were first promulgated.[17] Second, there is the idea that the elders *rule* the congregation. Such notion, however, is questionable at best.[18] It too is primarily based on 1 Tim 5:17. But *proistēmi*, the word translated as "rule," can carry a number of meanings from ruling to directing to helping or giving aid. Furthermore, the "elder rule" practice, according to Radmacher, "is a violation of the priesthood of each individual believer."[19] The teaching of the New Testament as a whole on the role of elders would suggest that, rather than ruling, they "lead the church into spiritually minded consensus."[20]

The third distinctive feature of presbyterian polity that has no solid scriptural foundation is the system of hierarchical governing bodies. Though the proponents of this model may point back to the Jerusalem Council of Acts 15 as the basis for authoritative representative bodies above the local church, such a foundation is weak and inconclusive. I agree with Saucy, who states, "while the Jerusalem council does present an example of an inter-church discussion and agreement, it does not clearly establish an authoritative organizational structure over the local church."[21]

In order to argue for hierarchy from Acts 13 and 15, we would have to make a number of assumptions. It must be assumed that there were many congregations in Antioch, that they formed a presbytery, that the presbytery sent Paul and Barnabas to Jerusalem, that those present in Acts 15 from Jerusalem represent the presbytery of the Jerusalem church, that the letter they sent out was church law, that all churches were obligated to obey, and that Acts 15 is not a unique occurrence, but a divinely given pattern.[22] "All these assumptions," in the words of Hammett, "are simply that: assumptions that are not mentioned, much less proven in Scripture."[23]

17. As a nineteenth-century Baptist scholar, William Williams articulates that ruling elders "were never known until Calvin invented them" (Williams, "Apostolical Church Polity," 534).

18. Hammett, *Biblical Foundations*, 142.

19. Radmacher, *Question of Elders*, 12.

20. Carson, "Church, Authority in," 230. A helpful discussion of 1 Tim 5:17 and the whole issue of ruling elders is found in Williams, "Apostolical Church Polity," 533–35.

21. Saucy, *Church in God's Program*, 113.

22. Hammett, *Biblical Foundations*, 142.

23. Ibid.

Presbyterianism elevates what is a possible inference from Scripture to a normative principle.[24] In light of the second and fifth theological principles, therefore, such a church government structure must be rejected.

Congregational Is the Most Biblically Defensible Model of Church Polity

Norman is right in stating, "Congregationalism is the form of polity most faithful to Christ and His Word."[25] Consistent application of the six theological principles defended in the previous chapter yields congregationalism as the most biblically defensible model of church polity. Lindsay calls the early local churches established in the New Testament "little self-governing republics," each "with an active, eager, enthusiastic life of its own."[26]

Many of the biblical, theological, and practical reasons for preferring the congregational model over the others have been laid out in the section entitled "Main Polity Models," in chapter 2.[27] To these four arguments in favor of congregationalism, more will be added here. First, an examination of the dominant images of the church offers support for congregationalism. As Hammett observes, none of the images is hierarchical; instead, all are "interdependent and breath the spirit of mutuality. For example, kingdom is not a major biblical motif for the church, but body and family are."[28]

Second, an observation of the addressees of most of the letters in the New Testament yields an indirect support for congregationalism. An overwhelming majority of these letters are written to churches and not just to individual leaders. Hammett explains,

> Peter, Paul, James, and John seemed to expect churches to take responsibility for their own doctrine. Paul tells the churches of Galatia to reject heretical teaching, even if it comes from an angel or apostle (Gal 1:8–9). Apparently, he saw doctrinal purity as a congregational responsibility.[29]

---

24. Carson, "Church, Authority in," 230.
25. Norman, "Together We Grow," 106.
26. Lindsay, *Church and the Ministry*, 57.
27. In addition to reviewing the appropriate portion of chapter 2, the inquisitive reader is invited to examine Sutton, "Congregational Polity," 113–19, for an interesting historical trace of the usage of congregational polity.
28. Hammett, *Biblical Foundations*, 147.
29. Ibid.

Third, from a more practical perspective, congregationalism is better able than any other form of church government to counter the tendency of churches to drift doctrinally, which causes them to suffer spiritually.[30] Mark Dever offers the following historical outlook: "Friends, the verdict of history is in. While it is clear that no certain polity prevents churches from error, from declension, and from sterility, the more centralized polities seem to have a worse track record than does congregationalism in maintaining a faithful, vital, evangelical witness." He adds, "Could it be that the gospel is so simple and clear, and the relationship that we have with God by the Holy Spirit's action in giving us the new birth is so real, that the collection of those who believe the gospel and who know God are simply the best guardians of that gospel?"[31]

A recent conservative resurgence within the Southern Baptist Convention is a great case in point of the validity of Dever's assertion. According to Hammett, "the change in the Southern Baptist Convention could not have occurred had it not preserved in its constitution some of the elements of the congregationalism of its churches. The power that changed the course of the Southern Baptist Convention was the power of thousands of grassroots Baptists."[32] No denomination, advocating different type of polity, ever experienced a similar return to theological conservatism in the history of Christianity.

Fourth, there is another practical benefit of congregationalism, namely, that it provides for what is a practical inevitability.[33] Dever argues that every church is congregational in nature:

> Every local church in Christendom, from Greek Orthodox to Pentecostal, from Roman Catholic to Baptist, from Episcopalian to Lutheran, from Presbyterian to Methodist, is congregational in nature. They exist only as the people continue to participate in their activities. When the people vote—whether at a congregational meeting or (where that's not allowed) with their funds or their feet—the leaders of the congregation must listen. They don't have to agree, but they must listen. The congregation will have their say. That's a simple fact. It is like gravity. It is just a matter of the way things work.[34]

30. Ibid., 150.
31. Dever, *God's Glory*, 38–39.
32. Hammett, *Biblical Foundations*, 150.
33. Ibid.
34. Dever, *Nine Marks*, 211; ibid., *God's Glory*, 37.

In light of this fact, Hammett's recommendation is quite appropriate:

> Rather than merely acknowledging that a degree of congregational involvement is inevitable and seeking to minimize it, a wiser course is heartily adopting a full congregationalism and accepting the challenge of developing a congregation that can responsibly and fully participate in governing itself, rather than a congregation that passively accepts whatever the leadership hands down.[35]

Fifth, in the words of Dagg, congregationalism is biblically superior to any other form of government because: "The independence of the churches, and the democratic form of church government [two of the key features of congregationalism], appeal strongly to individual responsibility, and have, therefore, a powerful tendency to promote holiness among the lay members."[36] Garrett echoes Dagg's sentiment, writing that congregational polity is "more capable than other polities of developing loyalty to and support of the congregation" and it is "very likely to produce stronger, more mature Christians than other polities."[37]

Because there are several different branches within the congregational structure, our next goal is to determine which one comes closest to the precedent set by the New Testament examples. In view of the principles outlined in chapters 3 and 4, an examination of the relevant New Testament texts reveals that the type of church government that most closely resembles biblical precedent cannot be single-elder-led.

Single-Elder-Led Form Is Not Biblically Defensible[38]

The reason that the single-elder-led form of congregational polity is not biblically defensible is because its foundation is logically derived and

---

35. Hammett, *Biblical Foundations*, 150–51.

36. Dagg, *Church Order*, 276. R. Stanton Norman, a modern Baptist theologian, wrote a whole chapter dedicated to examining how congregational polity is the best form of church government in its ability to facilitate corporate sanctification. For his excellent discussion of this issue, see Norman, "Together We Grow," 95–110.

37. Garrett, "Congregation-Led Church," 193.

38. Gerald P. Cowen calls this "Pastoral Leadership-Congregational Rule" (Cowen, *Who Rules the Church?* 3). Rather than dealing with the democratic congregationalism in general, I chose to be more specific and examine two of the most popular forms of democratic congregationalism, namely single-elder-led model and deacon-board-led model. However, the observations made under this and the next section apply equally to a trustee-led model. Aside from the fact that there is no scriptural warrant for it, what

supported more by tradition rather than explicitly stated biblical texts. Single-elder congregationalism is subject to the same critique that Luther applied to Roman Catholic Scholasticism; it is a foreign imposition on Scripture rather than a paradigm derived from Scripture.[39] Daughters puts it simply: "There is no Biblical warrant for having only one elder in a local church."[40]

As a short digression, let us examine the origins of the single-elder model of church government. Perhaps it was the strong sense of individualism Baptists were known for that contributed to the rise of this system. According to Kern, in the early twentieth century it was "carried to a further extreme among the Baptists than among the present-day Congregationalists."[41] Thus the Baptist emphasis on congregationalism, combined with the early American emphasis on individualism, likely resulted in the decline of churches governed through elder plurality.[42] Three nineteenth-century historical developments probably further contributed to the development of single-elder government. First was the westward movement of the American population.[43] With the opening of the American frontier, people started moving west. When it came to church leadership, however, the decision to move or stay was made on an individual basis, sometimes resulting in relocation by only one elder. This man would arrive in a town of his choosing, along with family, and start a church. He would be the sole elder, pastor, and overseer of this new congregation. Moreover, his leadership would not be limited only to the congregation, but extend to any groups of believers that he could establish in the nearby vicinity, making him not only a sole elder, but also a circuit-riding preacher. In the words of Paul Burleson, "while circuit riding ministry was an assist to little towns and little churches as they moved west, it did cause us to lose the understanding of a plurality of leaders in a local congregation."[44]

---

would be the qualification for choosing trustees for a congregation? If their qualifications are those from 1 Tim 3:2–7, then why not just call them elders? If they are from 1 Tim 3:8–13, why not call them deacons?

39. Yarnell, *Formation of Christian Doctrine*, 64.
40. Daughters, *New Testament Church Government*, 24.
41. Kern, *Christianity as Organized*, 387.
42. Newton, *Elders in Congregational Life*, 96.
43. Dever, *Nine Marks*, 20.
44. Burleson, "Case for Elders."

Second was the rise and increasing influence of landmarkism. One of the five points of what constitutes a New Testament church was democratic rule, effectively setting aside plural-eldership. Third was the birth of Campbellism. Campbellites, otherwise known as the Church of Christ or the Disciples of Christ, were the followers of Thomas Campbell and his son, Alexander Campbell, former Irish Presbyterian ministers. Desiring to get back to the basics of the "New Testament only" church polity, they broke away from the Presbyterian denominations and established their own churches and associations. In its description of church officers, the Church of Christ used the word "elder" almost exclusively. Perhaps partly as a reaction to this separatist movement, Baptists threw the word "elder" out of their nomenclature and chose the word "pastor" instead.[45]

When frank, even Baptist theologians will recognize that the foundation of single-elder congregationalism stems more from their traditions than from scriptural testimony. A case in point is the following statement by a well-known nineteenth-century Baptist ecclesiologist, Edwin C. Dargan, who, in comparing the conformity of the Baptist polity of his day to the model of New Testament, freely admitted: "Our churches have discarded the plurality of elders."[46] "It is our custom now," he continued, "even in very large churches, to have only one active pastor, or elder, while it seems clear that in the New Testament churches, certainly the larger ones, there were several or even many elders."[47] Incidentally, a previous library patron who had taken out Dargan's tome before me, wrote "Why?" in the margin next to Dargan's statement. Why, indeed?

Unfortunately, however, rather than attempting to correct such glaring neglect of clear New Testament precedent, Dargan instead comforts himself and his readers with the following words: "as compared to the resemblances [to the model of the New Testament] before pointed out, these differences [between the New Testament model and the current Baptist practice] are few and not vital."[48] From Dargan's own argument, such deviation from the scriptural pattern should alarm, rather than comfort, all Bible-believing individuals, because a few paragraphs later, he declares that "the departures written in history from the scriptural mode of government have certainly been no improvement upon it, but have the rather wrought

---

45. Graves, "'Landmark' Our Fathers Set," 48.
46. Dargan, *Ecclesiology*, 115.
47. Ibid.
48. Ibid.

much evil."⁴⁹ Only in this case, Dargan is speaking of the evils committed by the papacy, not realizing that on a smaller scale, the same critique can perhaps be made against his own tradition in the area of church leadership.

The usual way of defending single-elder-leadership of the church is by citing a passage like Acts 20:17-18, 28: "From Miletus he [Paul] sent to Ephesus and called to him the elders of the church. And when they had come to him, he said to them . . . 'Be on guard for yourselves and for all the flock, among which the Holy Spirit has made you overseers, to shepherd the church of God which He purchased with His own blood,'" where the terms "elder" and "overseer" are used synonymously and are both entrusted with the authority to "shepherd/pastor" the church. An elder, according to this argument, is the same as an overseer and a pastor. Therefore, it is acceptable to have a church led by a pastor/elder.

Such argumentation would be quite satisfactory, had it not been for the fact that in the New Testament the term "elder" is never used in the singular; it is always in the plural.[50] It is usually at this point that proponents of the single-elder/pastor-led model introduce logical derivations rather than explicit biblical data into the argument. Their contention is that, since the early church, like the church in Jerusalem, was most likely comprised of a number of smaller groups that would gather in households with an elder presiding over each, the combined leadership strata of the Jerusalem church was that of elders, but on a local level there was only one leader for each household congregation.[51] The same, they say, may have been true of the church in Ephesus, Philippi, and other cities.[52] Therefore, in light of the evidence that there was only one church in each city in the New Testa-

---

49. Ibid., 117.

50. To list a few examples: Acts 14:23; 16:4; 20:17; 21:18; 1 Tim 5:17; Titus 1:5; Jas 5:14; 1 Pet 5:1.

51. For examples of this kind of argument, see Cowen, *Who Rules the Church?* 14–16; Yarnell, "Article VI," 63. In this line of argument, we know from Scripture that the group of believers in a city was usually addressed as one church. We also know that some of these congregations were quite large in number (as in Jerusalem). Finally, the Bible points out that in some cases there were believers meeting in the houses. The facts above are documented in Scripture. What is not clearly spelled out is whether the believers in each city would necessarily meet in their smaller units in homes, or whether in some cities there were venues capable of housing the whole church. Further, an additional assumption is made when the advocates of single-elder model postulate that each smaller unit was led by a single elder.

52. For a helpful discussion of the early church's utilization of private homes, see White, *Building God's House*, 103–111.

ment period, and the different ways things are done now, single-elder-led church proponents argue that the plural-eldership of the early church was a plurality for a different context than the one in which churches function today. Unfortunately, in addition to making an argument from silence, such logic is wrought with weaknesses and inconsistencies, a few of which will be listed below.

First, would a model like the one proposed in this argument be called multiple-elder-led church or single-elder-led church? The answer is easy for the local church level, but what of the city church level—the church of Jerusalem in this example? Was the Jerusalem assembly multiple-elder-led or single-elder-led? The answer to this question is fairly straightforward as well: multiple-elder-led. So, while the advocates of single-eldership have no problem with the application of household-level leadership in a local church, my question to them is: What would be today's equivalent of the Jerusalem church-level? Furthermore, what does such thinking do for their scripturally sound commitment to the autonomy of the local church? One cannot apply only those parts of the conclusion from the New Testament that are convenient to traditional views and throw the inconvenient parts away. In other words, if we have no problem applying principles written to the churches on a "city level" in many cases, why should we in this case? Getz is thinking along the same lines when he asserts that although all the believers who comprised household churches "may have met for teaching, fellowship, and worship at different locations throughout a particular city, they were still considered *one church* led by a *single body of elders*."[53] Daughters similarly states, "It is crucial for us to remember, however, that the New Testament picture is not of single elders overseeing individual housechurches, but of plurality of elders guiding the church in a particular city."[54]

Moreover, the Bible tells of various public places used for worship by the first Christians. From the early church in Jerusalem that gathered in both temple courts and believers' homes (Acts 2:42–47) to other Jewish converts meeting in synagogues (Acts 26:10–11; James 2:1) to Ephesian converts assembling in the "lecture hall of Tyrannus," there were venues where a whole city church could convene in one place. "Even the church at Jerusalem," writes Hammett, "which numbered several thousand from Acts 2 onward, is reported as gathering and acting together (Acts 11:22;

53. Getz, *Elders and Leaders*, 211, emphasis Getz's.
54. Daughters, *New Testament Church Government*, 46.

12:5)."⁵⁵ Additionally, some of the latest archaeological discoveries of private homes in Jerusalem, which date from first century a.d., have revealed that some of them measured in excess of six thousand square feet, with up to twenty rooms.⁵⁶ So although the Bible is silent concerning how exactly these household units were governed,

> . . . if a home was large enough to house hundreds of people, it would certainly take more than one elder/overseer to shepherd these believers effectively. Archaeologists have discovered residences in some locations in the Roman Empire that could actually seat up to five hundred people in the garden room alone. This may describe a family complex owned by a well-to-do man like Cornelius in Caesarea or Philemon in Colossae.⁵⁷

Second, consider a passage like Phil 1:1, "Paul and Timothy, bondservants of Christ Jesus, to all the *saints* in Christ Jesus who are in Philippi, including the *overseers* and *deacons*" (emphasis mine). It is clear from this greeting that the letter to follow is addressed to all the saints in Philippi (a church), which was governed by the overseers/bishops (*episkopois*) and served by the deacons. All three terms ("saints," "overseers," and "deacons") are in the plural here, meaning that one church consisted of many saints governed by multiple elders and served by several deacons. Applying the logic of the city church, which was made up of many house churches led by a single elder, to this case would result in single-elder-led and single-deacon-served churches today. For why should a supposition regarding the leadership structure of a house church be limited to the office of the overseer only? Why could it not also be extended to the office of a deacon? Acts 6 provides no relief either, for although a number of deacons were elected there (seven to be exact), who is to say that these seven original deacons were not to serve individually in various smaller parts of the Jerusalem church? When it comes to deacons, however, that is not the way these instructions are interpreted and implemented in the churches of the defenders of the single-elder-led model.⁵⁸ And rightly so! Therefore, there

---

55. Hammett, *Biblical Foundations*, 30.
56. Getz, *Elders and Leaders*, 212.
57. Ibid., 215.
58. Getz weighs in here by declaring that nowhere in the Bible is there any "reference to the appointment of '*one*' elder or '*one*' deacon for any given church. Obviously, no *one* individual was ever asked to serve alone" (Getz, *Sharpening the Focus*, 110, emphasis mine).

is no warrant for interpreting the "elder" passages with a prejudice that taints a clear testimony of Scripture.

Third, as Grudem points out, it seems inconsistent to argue that the New Testament falls short of giving a clear command that all churches should have a plurality of elders, when the passages on qualifications of elders in 1 Tim 3:1–7 and Titus 1:5–7 are used as scriptural requirements for church officers today.[59] For how can churches say that the qualifications for elders found in these verses are commanded for us today while the system of plural elders found in these very same verses is not commanded, but was required only in that time and in that society?[60] Grudem is absolutely right in stating that it seems unwise to ignore a clear New Testament pattern that existed throughout all the churches for which we have evidence at the time the New Testament was written:

> When the New Testament shows us that *no* church was seen to have a single elder ("in *every* church," Acts 14:23; "in every town," Titus 1:5; "let him call for the *elders*," James 5:14; "I exhort the *elders* among you," 1 Pet 5:1), then it seems unpersuasive to say that smaller churches would have only had one elder. Even when Paul had just founded churches on his first missionary journey, there were *elders* appointed "in every church" (Acts 14:23). And "every town" on the island of Crete was to have elders, no matter how large or small the church was.[61]

Moreover, the church of the Thessalonians was commanded "to respect those who work hard among you, who are over you in the Lord" (1 Thess 5:12).[62] Their leadership was clearly referred to as a group and not as individual.

Fourth, while James may have acted as a presiding officer in the church in Jerusalem, this does not imply that he was the pastor of the congregation in a single-elder format.[63] As Acts 15:2 makes clear, there were *elders* (plural) in the church in Jerusalem, and James himself was probably numbered among the apostles (see Gal 1:19), rather than the elders.[64] Fifth, the

---

59. Grudem, *Systematic Theology*, 929.
60. Ibid.
61. Ibid., 930, emphasis Grudem's.
62. Hammett, *Biblical Foundations*, 178.
63. Grudem, *Systematic Theology*, 930.
64. Ibid. The church in Jerusalem, in fact, is spoken of eight times in the book of Acts as having elders—11:30; 15:2, 4, 6, 22–23; 16:4; 21:18.

churches to which James wrote had elders (James 5:14), as did the churches to which Peter wrote (1 Pet 5:1).[65]

Sixth, whereas passages like 1 Tim 3:2 and Titus 1:7 may have *episkopos* in the singular and *diakonous* in the plural, the Greek definite article modifying *episkopos* simply shows that Paul is speaking of general qualifications as they applied to any one example.[66] Furthermore, it is indisputably clear from other passages that both in Ephesus, where Timothy was serving, and on Crete, where Titus ministered, there was a plurality of elders (cf. Acts 20:17 and Titus 1:5). Seventh, there is no verse in the whole New Testament describing anyone as *the* elder of a church.[67] Eighth, except for the three times Paul used the term *overseer* "generically" as the term for a church officer in 1 Tim 3:1–2 and Titus 1:7, its only other occurrence is in the plural in Phil 1:1. Ninth, the only place where *pastor* is used for a church office, it is given in the plural, though not referring to a specific church (Eph 4:11).[68]

Tenth, the "elder" of 2 John 1 and 3 John 1 cannot be the lone elder at the church for several reasons. First, as Wallace points out, "the author is writing to two different people at apparently two different churches. Would he be their elder?"[69] If so, then we have "an anomalous situation unparalleled in the rest of the New Testament."[70] If not, and John is one of the elders at a church in Ephesus, for example, "what business does he have meddling in other churches' affairs."[71] Second, there is a very slim chance that John is actually writing these two letters to one and the same church, whose elder he is. Such a view would produce a problem insofar as John would have been an "absentee elder who gives no certain evidence that he will even visit the church, let alone teach there (2 John 12; 3 John 10)!"[72] Third, the apparent meaning of "the elder" in these two little letters seems to be the equivalent of "the old man."[73] Wallace correctly points out that "the term used, in fact, can only be given a technical nuance in contexts that seem to

---

65. Hammett, *Biblical Foundations*, 178.
66. Grudem, *Systematic Theology*, 930; Kelly, *Pastoral Epistles*, 74.
67. Hammett, *Biblical Foundations*, 178, emphasis Hammett's.
68. Ibid.
69. Wallace, "Who Should Run the Church?"
70. Ibid.
71. Ibid.
72. Ibid.
73. Ibid.

demand it."[74] As in Acts 2:17 and 1 Tim 5:1, *presbuteros* is a word that frequently meant simply "old man." This designation of *presbuteros* seems to fit better the context of 2 and 3 John, because by the time John had settled in Asia Minor as the last living apostle, it would have been quite appropriate for him to take on a term of endearment and affection: "This letter is from the old man."[75]

Eleventh, the author of the Epistle to the Hebrews refers to a plural leadership three times in the thirteenth chapter. He exhorts his readers to "Remember *those* who led [*ēgoumenōn*, plural masculine] you , who [*oitines*, plural masculine] spoke [*elalēsan*, aorist active indicative verb, third-person plural] the word of God to you; and considering the result of *their* conduct, imitate *their* faith" (13:7). A bit later he writes, "Obey your leaders [*tois ēgoumenois*, plural masculine] and submit *to them* [*autoi*, plural masculine], for *they* keep watch [*agrupnousin*, plural masculine] over your souls as those who will give an account [*apodosōntes*, plural masculine]" (13:17). And finally, he closes with "Greet all of your leaders [*pantas tous ēgoumenous*, plural masculine] and all the saints" (13:24).[76]

Twelfth, the evidence from the seven churches in Rev 2–3 has been under so much debate that it cannot be used as a conclusive proof for any form of church government. That, in any case, was certainly not the intent of the passage. Daniel Wallace advances the following exegetical argument against equating the "messengers" of Rev 2–3 with pastors. First, the Greek word *aggelō* (*aggelos*) is used sixty-seven times in Revelation. If we exclude the references in chapters two and three for the sake of argument, we see a remarkable thing: Every instance of *aggelō* (*aggelos*) refers to an angel.[77] Second, even if Rev 2–3 were an exception, "messenger" is hardly an appropriate term for a pastor, modern Baptist nomenclature notwithstanding. In New Testament times, pastors were geographically restricted to a certain locale. But a messenger is one who moves about. Third, the genre of the Revelation fits what is called "apocalyptic" writings. In apocalyptic literature we find a strong emphasis on angels. Among other duties, angels are responsible before heaven for groups of godly people.

74. Ibid.

75. Ibid.

76. Daughters, *New Testament Church Government*, 42. Daughters continues, "Although the specific term for 'elder' or 'overseer' was not used in this passage, from the context we can determine with reasonable accuracy that the people the author is referring to were elders" (ibid.).

77. Wallace, "Who Should Run the Church?"

Thus, when the Lord says, "to the angel of the church at ___, write" we see apocalyptic symbolism and imagery. Angels are evidently in view, not pastors.[78] In light of the evidence presented above, for example, "the angel of the church in Ephesus" from Rev 2:1 can hardly refer to a single-elder-type pastor in the church of that city, for we know from other Bible passages that there were plural elders leading that congregation. Therefore, if "angel" does not warrant a single-elder-type pastor in Rev 2:1, neither should it be used that way with the other six churches!

The final two reasons why a single-elder-led church is biblically indefensible are more pragmatic. The thirteenth reason is because it is not wise from a practical standpoint. Having been privileged to serve as a staff member and leader of churches that were governed both by a single elder and by multiple elders, I had the opportunity to make some practical observations over time. In my experience, it becomes especially difficult for a pastor within the single-elder-led system in the area of church discipline. When the majority of the deacons in place lack the necessary biblical knowledge and spiritual qualifications to assist the pastor in exercising church discipline, he may find himself unable and unwilling to do it alone. As a result, there is no exercise of church discipline, and thus both the church and the community may begin to think that there are no consequences for belligerent public rebellion. In the end, it is the pastor himself who is at the main disadvantage within such a system: He loses respect from both the congregation and the community at large; he lowers the bar for holiness and righteousness in the lives of the members; and, in effect, he dishonors the Lord and his instructions regarding the importance of holy and righteous living that are to be enforced via church discipline.[79]

On the other hand, when the pastor can count on the support of biblically astute and spiritually qualified men, a totally different picture emerges. He does not have to be a lone ranger who may be misunderstood by the congregation. Nor does he have to refrain from exercising his biblical responsibility. Not only can sinners be properly dealt with in such a system, but the pastor also often finds joy and fulfillment in his obedience to the Scripture when he practices church discipline. He finds joy, rather than the discouragement and despair too often seen in the lives of his peers within the single-elder-led environment. White concurs, seeing a plurality

---

78. Ibid.

79. For a more in-depth study of the importance of church discipline, see Goncharenko, *Wounds That Heal*.

Church Government According to the Bible

of elders as extremely helpful in the exercise of discipline in addition to providing a check for the errors of any one leader and better providing for the full spectrum of needs in a congregation.[80]

Fourteenth, a single-elder system can produce either an excessive concentration of power in one person or an excessive number of demands lain upon him,[81] or in many cases, both. As Grudem points out, in either case, the temptations to sin are great and the lessened degree of accountability makes yielding to temptation more likely. To borrow the words of Radmacher, "Multiple leaders, therefore, will serve as a 'check and balance' on each other and serve as a safeguard against the very human tendency to play God over other people (cf. Mark 10:42–44)."[82] In the New Testament, however, it was never the pattern, even with the apostles, to concentrate ruling power in the hands of any one person.[83] Besides, in Dever's experience, plural leadership would seem to offer many practical advantages:

> Probably the single most helpful thing to my pastoral ministry among my church has been the recognition of the other elders. The service of the other elders along with me has had immense benefits. A plurality of elders should aid a church by rounding out a pastor's gifts, making up for some of his defects, supplementing his judgment, and creating support in the congregation for decisions, leaving leaders less exposed to unjust criticism. Such a plurality also makes leadership more rooted and permanent, and allows for more mature continuity. It encourages the church to take more responsibility for the spiritual growth of its own members and helps make the church less dependent on its employees.[84]

In summary, Grudem accurately and precisely articulates why the single-elder-led church model is more traditional than biblical:

> It should be noted that the "single elder" view of church government really has no more New Testament support than the "single bishop" (episcopalian) view. Both seem to be attempts to justify what has already happened in the history of the church, not

---

80. White, "Plural-Elder-Led Church," 282–83.
81. Grudem, *Systematic Theology*, 931.
82. Radmacher, *Question of Elders*, 7.
83. Grudem, *Systematic Theology*, 931.
84. Dever, *God's Glory*, 24.

conclusions that have grown out of an inductive examination of the New Testament itself.[85]

In light of the overwhelming biblical evidence contrary to the single-elder congregationalism, read plainly and interpreted literally (see the second theological principle presented above), this polity model must be declared scripturally unsupportable, and as such, rejected outright.

Deacon-Board-Led Form Is Not Biblically Defensible

The same principles applied to the study of the biblical data on polity reveal that the church that desires to pattern itself after the New Testament precedent may not be deacon-board-led. Why? Because nowhere in Scripture are deacons entrusted with the spiritual *oversight* of the congregation. From the very inception of their office, which is recorded in Acts 6, their duties mainly concerned the physical side of matters in order to free up the apostles to care for the spiritual needs of the people. Dana and Sipes are clear and concise in their conclusion: "When that which is said of the office in the New Testament is compared with the root meaning of the word, it becomes probable that the deacon was the special personal helper to the elder, and the one whose duty it was to attend to the material side of the church life."[86]

Having said that, however, a measure of caution is in order here. In light of the list of qualifications given for the diaconate in 1 Tim 3:8–10, it would be improper to state that their *sole* responsibility was to care for the "administrative" issues of the church. Ryrie elaborates further:

> The qualifications for deacons (1 Tim 3:8–10) indicate that they performed a spiritual ministry, so that one would conclude that the distinction between elders and deacons was not that the former performed the spiritual ministry while the latter concerned themselves with material things (cf. Acts 11:30). Rather the distinction was that the deacons constituted the subordinate office performing their duties under the general direction and oversight of the elders. They were the helpers of the elders.[87]

---

85. Grudem, *Systematic Theology*, 931.
86. Dana and Sipes, *Manual of Ecclesiology*, 89.
87. Ryrie, "Pauline Doctrine of the Church," 66.

Church Government According to the Bible

Daughters provides another helpful observation relative to the type of spiritual gifts that seems to be required of the deacons:

> The spiritual gifts required to function properly as a deacon are different than those required of an elder. An elder must be able to teach; a deacon does not. The deacon ought to have the gift of helps, since his job description is to help the elders. The elder does not need to be gifted in that way. The consequence of this realization will lead to the understanding that the diaconate is not necessarily intended to be a stepping stone into the eldership. The kind of man God equips to be a deacon may not be the same kind of man called and equipped to be an elder.[88]

Thus, although the responsibilities of the deacons include spiritual matters, they are never described as providing oversight or overall direction for the spiritual maturity of the church. As such, to place responsibility for the spiritual direction of a church on the shoulders of the deacon board is tantamount to reversing the course set by the apostles themselves in Acts 6.

In summary, Grudem is right to ask why we should adopt as the norm those patterns of church government that are *nowhere* found in the New Testament, even as we reject a pattern *everywhere* found in the New Testament.[89] It is to the closer inspection of the latter pattern that we must now turn.

Multiple-Elder Congregationalism Is the Most Biblically Defensible Model

If the church is the body of Christ, which it is, and if Christ's body is important to God, which it is, then it stands to reason that the Lord would make sure to leave us clear instructions for organizing the church, which he does. "The household of God" is one of the numerous images of the church that is left for us in the pages of the New Testament (1 Tim 3:14–15). Therefore, just as it would be outrageous to enter another person's home and, without permission, begin to rearrange their furniture or discipline

---

88. Daughters, *New Testament Church Government*, 56. For another helpful resource regarding the office of the deacon, see Cowen, *Who Rules the Church?* 101–116.

89. Grudem, *Systematic Theology*, 930, emphasis Grudem's. As Powers states, "The one occasion in the New Testament where reference is made to one individual who is giving himself the preeminence in this way, it is to condemn him (3 John 9, 10)" (Powers, "Patterns of New Testament Ministry," 171).

their children, how much more outrageous to think that we have the right to reorganize the specially arranged government of God's holy, glorious, and unique house![90]

What is that government left for us in the New Testament? A careful analysis of the New Testament evidence under the previously established principles reveals that the church that desires to pattern itself after the early church must include a plurality of elders[91] within a congregational form of government.[92] Why is this so? The case for plural-eldership can be made on biblical, pragmatic/theological, and historical grounds.

Because the Support for It Is Biblically Impenetrable

More than any other model, church government by a plurality of elders enjoys the overwhelming support of Scripture. Sometimes it is hard to appreciate the full force of the New Testament teaching concerning the plurality of eldership in a local church unless those passages that comprise it are listed. The sheer number of passages in the New Testament that relate plural-eldership in the context of church government provides quite a convincing case. With that in mind, the following is a chronological listing of the New Testament data regarding church leadership, compiled in consultation with Getz's work, *Elders and Leaders*:

- The *elders* in Jerusalem (Acts 11:30).
- "He should call the *elders* of the church" (Jas 5:14).
- "Paul and Barnabas appointed *elders* for them in each church" (Acts 14:23).
- The apostles and *elders* in Jerusalem (Acts 15:2, 4, 6, 22, 23; 16:4).
- "*Those* who work hard among you, *who are over you* in the Lord . . . hold them in the highest regard" (1 Thess 5:12–13).
- "Paul sent to Ephesus for the *elders* of the church" (Acts 20:17).
- "Keep watch over *yourselves* and all the flock of which the Holy Spirit has made you *overseers*" (Acts 20:28a).

---

90. Waldron, "Plural-Elder Congregationalism," 204.

91. With plurality of elders, the church must necessarily differ from democratic or single-elder-led congregationalism.

92. As such, this church will be distinct from those that are governed by representation within elder-ruled-Presbyterian model.

- "Be *shepherds* of the church of God" (Acts 20:28b).
- "All the *elders* [in Jerusalem] were present" (Acts 21:18).
- "To all the saints in Christ Jesus who are in Philippi, including the *overseers* and deacons" (Phil 1:1).
- "If anyone sets his heart on being an *overseer,* he desires a noble task" (1 Tim 3:1).
- "Now the *overseer* must be above reproach" (1 Tim 3:2).
- "The *elders* who direct the affairs of the church well are worthy of double honor" (1 Tim 5:17).
- "Do not entertain an accusation against an *elder* unless it is brought by two or three witnesses. *Those* who sin are to be rebuked publicly, so that the *others* may take warning" (1 Tim 5:19–20).
- "To the *elders* among you, I appeal as a fellow elder . . . Be *shepherds* of God's flock that is under your care, serving as *overseers*" (1 Pet 5:1–2).
- "Appoint *elders* in every town . . . An *elder* must be blameless" (Titus 1:5–6).
- "Since an *overseer* is entrusted with God's work, he must be blameless" (Titus 1:7).
- "Remember *those* who led you, who spoke the word of God to you; and considering the result of *their* conduct, imitate *their* faith . . . Obey your *leaders* and submit to *them* . . ." (Heb 13:7, 17).
- The elders in Heaven are plural (Rev 5:14; 11:16; 19:4).[93]

To the list of passages above may be added the fact that, when they are mentioned in the rest of the Bible, the elders seem to be overwhelmingly referred to in the plural. Such is the case with the elders of Israel, every reference to whom throughout the pages of the Gospels and Acts is made in the plural. Thus it is clear, even from the short biblical survey cited above, that although the Bible never specifies a precise number of elders for a local congregation, plurality is always assumed when they are mentioned in the context of a leading body. Or, as Getz puts it, "In this unfolding set of references to local church leaders, the overall profile demonstrates that God's ideal plan was that every local church should be led by

---

93. Getz, *Elders and Leaders*, 209–210, emphasis Getz's.

Multiple-Elder Congregationalism

more than one elder/overseer."[94] It is impossible to ignore that the type of church leadership that is most extensively endorsed by the Bible is that of multiple-eldership. Powers concurs, stating, "On the basis . . . of this very consistent, repeated testimony [of Scripture] it would seem beyond dispute that a congregation which is patterned on the New Testament basis would have a number of elders."[95] To argue for anything else would require either some serious exegetical acrobatics or misrepresentation of the biblical data.

Also, we must consider the fourteen arguments against single-elder-led church government furnished above. While my original intent was to show why the case for single-elder-led church is both biblically and practically inferior to the argument for plural-elder-led church, the "unsatisfactory" verdict for the former system was automatically a "satisfactory" verdict for the latter. Rather than repeating them here, therefore, I will just point the reader to the few paragraphs immediately preceding this one for a recapitulation of the clear biblical and practical advantages of government by plural-eldership in a local congregation. Interestingly enough, when tasked with the job of defending the traditional Baptist single-elder-led church model, well-known Baptist theologian Daniel Akin, who happens to be the president of one of seven Southern Baptist Seminaries, admits that this model does not have as much scriptural warrant as is popularly thought in Southern Baptist life.[96] I could not agree more. Notwithstanding his traditional background, as a true student of the Word, Dr. Akin is to be admired for his loyalty to Scripture when he adds that based upon biblical evidence, the argument for a plurality of elders is easier to make than that for a single-elder-government.[97]

To sum up the biblical evidence, since it is overwhelmingly on the side of multiple elders, the few passages that might be interpreted to support single-eldership certainly do not have to be interpreted as such, and in fact, most likely should not be.[98] This would certainly be in line with the hermeneutical principle of letting clearer passages, or those that are less ambiguous, influence the interpretation of those that are less clear or more ambiguous.

---

94. Ibid., 211.
95. Powers, "Patterns of New Testament Ministry," 170.
96. Akin, "Single-Elder-Led Church," 64.
97. Ibid.
98. Wallace, "Who Should Run the Church?"

Church Government According to the Bible

Because This Model Is Pragmatically/Theologically Sound

First, as Hay puts it, the reason that several elders are needed in a congregation is because "No one Elder has all the varieties of the gifts for Eldership that are needed for a complete ministry."[99] Therefore, in the words of Radmacher, "if the church is going to have the advantage of all of the gifts manifested in its leadership, then it must have multiple leadership so that the leaders' gifts and talents complement one another and there is a mutuality of ministry."[100] Second, in Grudem's words, the strength of this system of government is seen in the fact that the pastor does not have authority over the congregation on his own, but instead that authority belongs collectively to the entire group of elders.[101] Even the pastor himself, like every other elder, is subject to the authority of the elder board as a whole.[102] In the day-to-day operation of the church, this can be a great benefit in keeping a pastor from making mistakes and in supporting the pastor in adversity and protecting him from attacks and opposition.[103] I personally experienced the tremendous support that a member of a pastoral staff finds in an elder-led church, as well as the paralyzing void that can be felt in the context of single-elder-led system when, aside from the pastor, there is a genuine lack of biblically literate and spiritually mature leaders.

The third reason why it is wise, from a practical perspective, to have multiple elders is that it provides better insight into decision-making. Daughters accurately points out that since "No one has the perfect picture of God's revelation, a greater number of godly men contribute greater insight when various decisions need to be made."[104] He further relates:

---

99. Hay, *New Testament Order*, 183. Or, as Newton puts it, "Here is precisely the wisdom of the New Testament pattern of plural eldership. No one man possesses all the gifts necessary for leading a congregation. Some men are endowed with strong pulpit gifts, but lack pastoral skills. Others excel in pastoral work of visiting and counseling, but are not strong when it comes to pulpit exposition. Some have unusual abilities in organizing and administrating the ministries of the church, but fail in pulpit and counseling skills. Some, to be sure, are multigifted and capable of enormous work at different levels. But the strain of tending to the entire ministry needs of the church can quickly deplete even the most gifted man" (Newton, *Elders in Congregational Life*, 38).

100. Radmacher, *Question of Elders*, 7.

101. Grudem, *Systematic Theology*, 933.

102. Ibid.

103. Ibid.

104. Daughters, *New Testament Church Government*, 76.

The job of the leadership is to interpret as best as possible what Christ's leading is in the matter. It is much safer to have more than one man making this interpretation. One man is likely to have a personal bias which can be weeded out in a group decision.[105]

Finally, according to M. James Sawyer, a church historian at Western Conservative Baptist Seminary, there is another reason why having a plurality of eldership is beneficial. Sawyer found that churches that have a pastor as an authority above others (thus, in function, a monarchical episcopate) have a disproportionately high number of moral failures at the top level of leadership.[106] In other words, it is less likely for a pastor to fall into sin if he is *primus inter parus* (first among equals in the sense of his visibility and training, not spirituality) than if he is elevated above the rest of the church leadership.[107]

Because This Model Is Historically Proven

Perhaps one of the strongest testimonies for a plurality of eldership from a historical perspective can be drawn from the example of the Metropolitan Tabernacle of London, England. This was the well-known church pastured by one of the premiere Baptist preachers of history, Charles Haddon Spurgeon. Spurgeon's church, obviously a blessed and successful ministry even by the modern standards, had an order of elders who did not preach, but instead assisted the pastor in attending to the spiritual concerns of the congregation, leaving the deacons to look after the poor and the finances.[108] Spurgeon was not alone, however, in his practice of plural-eldership. The Devonshire Square Church in London, led by William Kiffin, was another congregation practicing plural-eldership. Other well-known pastor-theologians like Benjamin Keach, Nehemiah Coxe, and Hanserd Knollys led their churches in a similar practice.[109]

Though Spurgeon's example may be one of the brightest stars in the sky of the history of plural-eldership, as is already evidenced, it is not the only one. Going as far back as the Apostolic Fathers, we find indications of the early church practicing plural-eldership/presbyterate in a local

---

105. Ibid.
106. Quoted in Wallace, "Who Should Run the Church?"
107. Ibid.
108. Dargan, *Ecclesiology*, 120–21.
109. Newton, *Elders in Congregational Life*, 25–28.

congregation. Take, for example, Saint Ignatius, who in his *Epistle to the Magnesians*, writes the following:

> Since, then, I have had the privilege of seeing you, through Damas your most worthy bishop, and through your worthy presbyters Bassus and Apollonius, and through my fellow-servant the deacon Sotio, whose friendship may I ever enjoy, inasmuch as he is subject to the bishop as to the grace of God, and to the presbytery as to the law of Jesus Christ, [I now write to you].[110]

Ignatius here assumes that in the local church at Magnesia there was a single bishop, several presbyters (or elders), and several deacons.[111] Likewise, Clement, in his letter to the Corinthian church, writes:

> Who then among you is noble-minded? Who compassionate? Who full of love? Let him declare, "If on my account sedition and disagreement and schisms have arisen, I will depart, I will go away whithersoever ye desire, and I will do whatever the majority commands; only let the flock of Christ live on terms of peace with the presbyters set over it." He that acts thus shall procure to himself great glory in the Lord; and every place will welcome him. For "the earth is the Lord's, and the fullness thereof." These things they who live a godly life, that is never to be repented of, both have done and always will do.[112]

Therefore, although single-bishop rule would later hold universal sway in the ante-Nicene church, that was not the case during the time of the Apostolic Fathers. During their time, the model of government practiced in their churches seemed consistent with plural-elder congregationalism.[113] Waldron points out that "it is certainly true that the Apostolic Fathers manifest a church in transition to episcopacy. All the evidence, however, is consistent with the idea that the starting point of that transition and development was plural-elder congregationalism."[114]

The practice of plural-eldership common among the Puritan Congregationalists of England and its American colonies, including the Particular Baptists, is another example from history. Since the Particular Baptists declared themselves in favor of a plurality of elders, it is not surprising to

---

110. Saint Ignatius, "Epistle of Ignatius to the Magnesians," II.I.
111. Waldron, "Plural-Elder Congregationalism," 195.
112. Saint Clement, "First Epistle of Clement," 54.
113. Waldron, "Plural-Elder Congregationalism," 197.
114. Ibid., 199.

Multiple-Elder Congregationalism

discover that the 1689 Baptist Confession suggests that each church should have a plurality of elders:

> A particular church, gathered and completely organized according to the mind of Christ, consists of officers and members; and the officers appointed by Christ to be chosen and set apart by the church (so called and gathered), for the peculiar administration of ordinances, and execution of power or duty, which he entrusts them with, or calls them to, to be continued to the end of the world, are bishops or elders, and deacons.[115]

Additionally, there was a considerable number of nineteenth-century American Baptists who had voiced their support for plural-eldership.[116] Edwin Dargan concedes that "it appears to be well-nigh certain that in the apostolic churches generally there was a plurality of elders."[117] Samuel Jones, in his "Treatise of Church Discipline" noted several of the advantages of plurality in leadership.[118] As the first president of the Southern Baptist Convention, W. B. Johnson argued for a plurality of elders in each church on the basis of Scripture and practical benefits.[119] Today, John Hammett, Mark Dever, James R. White, Samuel Waldron, Wayne Barber, and Phil A. Newton are just a few among many of the better-known Baptist leaders who join Akin in his endorsement of multiple-eldership.[120]

---

115. *Baptist Confession of Faith*, http://www.vor.org/truth/1689/1689bc26.html.

116. Predating even them were the early English separatists from whose ranks some of the early Baptists arose, including Henry Barrowe. Barrowe believed that the congregation should elect elders as its rulers, and thus govern itself not directly but rather through representatives. Still it must stand independent of all ecclesiastical government except its own—and so it cannot become Presbyterian—but notwithstanding its ruling eldership will remain congregational (Kern, *Christianity as Organized*, 379).

117. Dargan, *Ecclesiology*, 57.

118. Jones, "Treatise of Church Discipline," 146.

119. Johnson, "Gospel Developed," 190–95. In addition, Benjamin Griffith allows for multiple elders in a local church, although his understanding can be described as a mix between Presbyterianism and congregationalism (Griffith, "True and Orderly Gospel Church," 98). J. L. Reynolds recognizes the biblical precedent for the plurality of elders and deacons (Reynolds, "Church Polity," 349). Likewise, P. H. Mell mentions someone within his church by the title "Elder" (Mell, "Corrective Church Discipline," 451).

120. See Hammett, *Biblical Foundations*, 159–89; Dever, *God's Glory*; White, "Plural-Elder-Led Church"; Waldron, "Plural-Elder Congregationalism," 185–221. Paige Patterson, while defending single-elder congregationalism, also recognizes biblical precedent for plural-eldership and allows for its modern practice where necessary (Patterson, "Single-Elder Congregationalism," 133–52). Phil A. Newton adds another Baptist voice in defense of plural-eldership (Newton, *Elders in Congregational Life*).

As we discuss the advantages of the government by multiple elders, it is important to remember that this particular form of church government still falls under the larger umbrella of congregationalism. As such, while the elder board is empowered by the congregation to handle many of the day-to-day operations of the church, some large decisions have to be brought to the whole church for approval. Scripturally, such is the requirement in cases dealing with church discipline and excommunication, according to Matt 18:17 and 1 Cor 5:4. Additionally, such decisions as calling pastors, major changes in the ministry direction, annual budget approval, and any other large financial steps are generally best left to the approval of the congregation as a whole. Based on personal experience, however, I believe that churches governed by a plurality of elders need to make bigger strides in involving the congregation in the government of the church. In doing so, they will reap many different benefits, not the least of which include a greater sense of ownership on the part of the congregation as to what goes on in the life of the church, an increase in the spiritual maturity of those who actively participate in decision-making, and growth in the faith of the congregation at large as they watch God's hand lead his body.

Having ardently argued for the "distinctly biblical" precedent of plural-eldership in a local congregation, I will now attempt to provide a short synopsis of the early church's understanding of elders. In the New Testament, the first mention of "elders" occurs in Acts 11:30 in connection with the Christian community in Jerusalem.[121] The title was transferred from the Old Testament, where it serves to identify a community leader who makes religious, social, and administrative decisions.[122] In his study of the eldership phenomenon in the Old and New Testaments, as well as the surrounding societies, Campbell notes:

> Among the Jews [as well as the Greeks] the term 'elders' usually connoted respect rather than office. 'Elders' serves as a collective title for those with most honour in the community, among whom the holders of various offices would be included, so that 'elders' is an imprecise term in comparison to terms denoting the holders of definite office . . . In short 'the elders' is not so much a defined office or rank, but more a way of referring quite generally to those

---

121. Davidson, *Ecclesiastical Polity*, 117.
122. Swanson, *Dictionary of Biblical Languages*.

who held office or possessed rank and to whom respect was due on account of their seniority.[123]

Based on the wide usage of the concept of eldership at the time of the foundation of the early church, it is not surprising to see its somewhat casual and fairly seamless introduction into the structure of the body of Christ. Yet within the New Testament church, the office of elder receives a new definition that effectually distinguishes it from the culture at large. It is to this key office in the leadership of the church, its distinction from the cultural usage, and the responsibilities that it entails that our focus will turn in the next chapter.

---

123. Campbell, *Elders*, 160.

6

Addressing Objections and Providing Practical Recommendations

OPENING CONFESSION

Much like Marvin E. Mayer, who set out to study the New Testament teaching on the local pastor in his doctoral dissertation only to have his focus changed by the biblical testimony, which "knows nothing of a one-man ministry," my views were greatly affected by the findings of this research.[1] I too found the lack of biblical data on single-elder congregationalism quite shocking, especially in view of its wide popularity within my own denomination. This chapter, therefore, came about as a result of the widespread neglect of the clear biblical precedent for church government among Southern Baptists. Multiple-elder leadership is being neglected in many churches today for the sake of traditional ways of doing things. Much like the Anabaptists, who carried the process of reformation to its logical and biblical conclusion, I am captivated by the word of God and can do nothing else but carry the process of polity examination under the theological principles set out in chapters 3 and 4 to its logical and biblical conclusion.

The nature and quantity of biblical evidence unearthed during my investigation was so compelling and overwhelming that it propelled me to launch an in-depth inquiry into the area of plural-eldership. If the Bible is this explicit regarding the leadership structure of the church, so my reasoning went, why is it so blatantly disregarded within my own Baptist

---

1. Mayer, "New Testament Elder," 1.

tradition? It was with this type of thinking, in addition to a conviction that theology was never meant for the scholar's study or the classroom alone, but mainly for the church,[2] that I began to pursue my findings from chapter 5 more deeply. Therefore, in elaborating further on the subject of plural-eldership and responding to those who attack it, my main intent in this chapter is to work out the implications of the findings of the last chapter for the community of Christ on a local level.

NUTS AND BOLTS OF PLURAL-ELDERSHIP[3]

Having discussed the necessity for the plural-eldership at the helm of the local church, now is the time to put it all together. In this section some practical questions regarding the plurality of elders in a local church will be addressed. Among these are the following: a list of responsibilities of a body of elders within a congregation, suggestions pertaining to the number of elders that a church should have, scriptural observations regarding a primary leader of the team, and a word regarding financial obligation that a congregation has towards its elders.

What does plural-eldership look like? Do all the elders share the teaching/preaching load? Should they all be on the payroll of the church? These questions may be designated the nuts and bolts of plural-eldership because without the specifics to which they direct attention, no amount of commitment to the idea of plural-elder-led church can actuate implementation.

The Responsibilities of Elders

Of the scattered references to the tasks, or responsibilities, of elders throughout the New Testament, perhaps the most important texts may be found in Acts 20:28–31; Rom 12:8; Eph 4:11–16; 1 Thess 5:12; 1 Tim 3:1–7; 5:17; Titus 1:5–9; Heb 13:7, 17; and 1 Pet 5:1–4.[4] These passages document four primary responsibilities assigned to elders. The first responsibility is

---

2. Osborne, *Hermeneutical Spiral*, 409.

3. In an attempt to stay true to the original focus of this work, I purposefully do not include a lengthy discussion of the office of the deacon. For those interested in studying this very important leadership office in the context of the local congregation, please see Dever, "Doctrine of the Church," 798–800; Hammett, *Biblical Foundations*, 191–215; Kern, *Christianity as Organized*, 148–67.

4. Hammett, *Biblical Foundations*, 163.

elders' duty to teach.[5] Acts 20:31 and Titus 1:9 reflect the charge laid on elders to preserve sound doctrine; Eph 4:11 links the office of pastor with that of teacher; 1 Tim 3:2 gives "able to teach" as one of the elders' qualifications; certain elders who work at "preaching and teaching" are described in 1 Tim 5:17; and Heb 13:7 identifies leaders as those "who spoke the word of God to you."[6] Whether it is called preaching, teaching, prophecy, or exhortation, the ministry of the elder is emphatically a ministry that includes the communication of God's Word.[7] In elaborating on this requirement for eldership, Dever postulates, "Anyone serving as an elder should have a better-than-average grasp of the basics of the gospel as well as the great truths of Scripture, especially those that are under assault in one's own day."[8] Teaching is the primary means by which elders exert the influence of leadership in the congregation.[9]

Elders' second responsibility is commonly termed "pastoral ministry." This is derived from the charge laid on elders in Acts 20:28 and 1 Pet 5:2 to shepherd/pastor the church. Analyzing the range of duties of the New Testament shepherd, the following responsibilities fall within the purview of his assignment: (1) feed the flock the word of God (1 Pet 2:2; Matt 4:4); (2) protect the sheep (John 10:11–13) from the dangers of false doctrine (Acts 20:29–31); (3) watch over the flock (Heb 13:17), which includes but is not limited to pastoral visitation, personal counseling, and ministry in times of sickness (Jas 5:14) and grief.[10]

---

5. Getz, *Elders and Leaders*, 266–67. In quoting Getz so extensively in this work, I need to clarify one thing. While in agreement with him on a number of issues when it comes to plurality of eldership, I disagree with Getz on one main point. He sees hardly any warrant in Scripture for congregational government, advocating instead the representative form. This is where his understanding of polity, from the perspective of this work, may be considered more in line with the Presbyterian form of church government.

6. Hammett, *Biblical Foundations*, 163.

7. Ibid.

8. Dever, "Doctrine of the Church," 802.

9. Hammett, *Biblical Foundations*, 163.

10. Ibid., 163–64. John Murray offers a fourfold challenge on what it means to "shepherd the church of God: (1) A shepherd keeps his flock from going astray. In practice this means instruction and warning ... (2) A shepherd goes after his sheep when they go astray. In practice this means reproof and correction, in many cases the exercise of ecclesiastical discipline ... (3) A shepherd protects his sheep from their enemies ... Perhaps there is no more ominous feature of members of the church than the lack of discernment; ... here the elders in tending the flock must cultivate for themselves and inculcate in the members of the church, that sensitivity to truth and right, so that they and the people will be able to detect the voice of the enemy ... (4) A shepherd leads his flock to the fold;

Addressing Objections and Providing Practical Recommendations

Feeding the flock the word of God is self-explanatory. Protecting the sheep in doctrinal purity takes place when elders make sure members in the church are not promoting false teachings.[11] Watching over the flock may include a front-line role in administering church discipline. Scriptural patterns involve the congregation as a whole in the final stages of the discipline process,[12] but with the help of elders, attempts can be made to assure that the discipline process never reaches the final stages. The elders will do all of that, mindful of the fact that according to Heb 13:17, they must give an account to God for their proper care of the congregation entrusted to them.

Oversight or leadership is the third duty reserved for the elders. It is significant that even the term "oversight" is derived from the office of overseer (*episkopos*). The idea of leadership can be further clarified by three other biblical terms. In Titus 1:7, the elder is called to be an *oikonomos*, or "steward," of God.[13] An entry in *Harper's Bible Dictionary* defines steward as someone who does the "overseeing" of the possessions, business affairs, property, servants, the training of children, etc., of an owner or master.[14] Because it is a position of considerable trust, the key requirement of a good steward is faithfulness to the master according to 1 Cor 4:2.[15] A second term *ēgeomai*, found in Heb 13:7, 17, and 24, means "to guide, lead, rule."

---

he pours oil into their wounds and gives them pure water to quench their thirst. I would like to press home the necessity and the blessing of the ministry of consolation" (Murray, *Claims of Truth*, 265–66).

11. Getz, *Elders and Leaders*, 268.

12. Getz, like many other representative government advocates, misses it here. The clear guidelines set up in passages like 1 Cor 5:4 and Matt 18:17, among others, address and involve the entire congregation in the discipline process. While it may be right and necessary to involve elders at the initial stages of the process, they are not to be the final link in the chain of biblical discipline. If they failed, their duty is to bring the matter before the whole church (thus, "when you [*umōn*, second-person plural pronoun; i.e., the church and not the elders] "are assembled . . ." and "If he refuses to listen to them, tell it to the church") the practice that was not ever mentioned by Getz in relating his own experiences with administering church discipline.

13. Hammett, *Biblical Foundations*, 164.

14. R. H. S., "Steward." A steward is one who is placed "over the house" (Gen 43:19; 44:1, 4; 1 Kgs 16:9; 18:3; etc.). That "house" can be a private household and its function (Gen 44:1; Luke 12:42; Gal 4:2), a specific task (1 Chron 29:6), a palace (Esther 1:8; 1 Kgs 18:3; Isa 36:3; Luke 8:3), business affairs (Matt 20:8; Luke 16:1–8), a city treasury (Rom 16:23), and in the New Testament in a metaphorical sense of the divine mysteries, i.e., the gospel Rev (1 Cor 4:1), a divine commission (1 Cor 9:17), or a divine gift (1 Pet 4:10).

15. Hammett, *Biblical Foundations*, 164.

Its occurrence in these verses seems to connote a measure of authority, especially when the instruction of verse 17 is considered: "Obey your leaders and submit to them."[16]

The third term is *proistēmi*, and it is used six times in reference to church leaders.[17] The "generic" nature of this Greek word makes it difficult to derive a precise angle of meaning when it comes to church leaders.[18] Due to the generalized nature of the key terms that identify church leadership, the issue of the nature and extent of pastoral authority cannot be decided on purely lexical evidence.[19] Hammett's correct solution is to look to the larger context of overall biblical teaching:

> On that topic, we find a delicate tension. On the one hand, church members are called upon to recognize their leaders' authority, submit to them, and obey them (see 1 Thess 5:12; Heb 13:17) . . . On the other hand, the way leaders exercise their authority in the New Testament is never dictatorial, but with a humble spirit, open to the input of others and seeking to lead the church into spiritually minded consensus.[20]

"This pattern," Hammett opines, "fits congregational government with elder leadership."[21] Elders' fourth duty, in keeping with 1 Pet 5:3, is to serve as an example to the flock.[22] Again Hammett weighs in, "Leaders are to be set apart, not just to honor them but to recognize them as setting forth the

---

16. Ibid., 165.

17. Rom 12:8 does not specifically link it to an office, but speaks of how those who lead should do so. 1 Thess 5:12 is also a general reference. 1 Tim 3:4–5 gives the ability to lead or manage one's family as a qualification for an overseer; 1 Tim 3:12 uses it in the same way as a qualification for a deacon. First Tim 5:17 speaks of leading as an activity of the elders (Hammett, *Biblical Foundations*, 164).

18. *Proistēmi* can be used in a variety of senses, from the authoritative leadership one would exercise in an army to the idea of assisting or helping, and even to the idea of leadership in a family (Hammett, *Biblical Foundations*, 164). For more information on this Greek term, see Reicke, "Προΐστημι," 700–703.

19. Hammett, *Biblical Foundations*, 165.

20. Ibid.

21. Ibid.

22. This is in line with the qualifications for elders/overseers set in 1 Tim 3 and Titus 1. In trying to maintain the single focus of this work, I will purposely not cover the qualifications for elders/overseers set out in 1 Tim 3 and Titus 1. For some excellent sources providing useful discussion of this topic, see Hammett, *Biblical Foundations*, 166–74; Getz, *Elders and Leaders*, 294–97; Kelly, *Pastoral Epistles*, 75–80; Fee, *1 and 2 Timothy*, 41–47; Guthrie, *Pastoral Epistles*, 79–82; Knight, *Pastoral Epistles*, 150–66.

Addressing Objections and Providing Practical Recommendations

pattern of faith and life that the congregation is to emulate (Heb 13:7)."[23] Getz puts it similarly, "If we are to 'teach the word of God' effectively, we must simultaneously 'live the word of God.'"[24]

The Number of Elders?

As to the number of elders that a church should have, there is no set figure anywhere in Scripture. The number of elders should depend on how many people the church possesses who are qualified and willing to serve in that capacity. That number will obviously increase proportionately to the growth of the church membership, in keeping with a ratio that enables the elders to shepherd the flock effectively.[25]

Primary Leader of the Team

In leading the congregation, just as it is clear that government by a plurality of elders enjoys unrivaled biblical support, it is equally understood from Scripture that someone needs to function as the primary leader of the team.[26] Jesus himself modeled this idea with great clarity. While on earth, he served as the primary leader of the twelve apostles who followed him. Meanwhile, as Christ was preparing all of them to carry out the Great Commission, he focused his efforts on equipping Peter to be the main spokesman for the rest of the apostles once he returned to the Father.[27] Getz illustrates this point well:

> When Matthew, Mark, and John recorded their Gospels, and Luke recorded his Gospel and the book of Acts, they mentioned Peter's name dozens of times more than the other apostles [189 times, as compared to fifty times for John, the next closest]. And when they recorded the "events" involving Peter, these episodes *far exceed* the number of events involving any other apostle. For example, Peter is mentioned specifically in fifty-seven events compared with his

---

23. Hammett, *Biblical Foundations*, 166.
24. Getz, *Elders and Leaders*, 267. Some add to this list overseeing the finances of the church (ibid., 270).
25. Hammett, *Biblical Foundations*, 186. See also Powers, "Patterns of New Testament Ministry," 169.
26. Getz, *Elders and Leaders*, 217. See also Patterson, "Single-Elder Congregationalism."
27. Getz, *Elders and Leaders*, 218.

brother Andrew, who is mentioned in only eight events. Of course, many more events could have been recorded about Jesus and His association with these men (John 21:25), but we can assume that what has been recorded represents what actually happened in the larger setting. Clearly, Jesus focused on equipping Peter to be the primary leader.[28]

This he certainly became, for when the apostles returned to Jerusalem following Christ's ascension and entered the Upper Room, the Scripture says that it was Peter who "stood up among the believers" (Acts 1:15), and led them in making a decision to replace Judas.[29] As Getz correctly points out, "Jesus had prepared him for this moment, and everyone among the one hundred and twenty in that room knew that Peter was their leader."[30]

The same relational dynamic can be seen in the pages of Scripture when the apostles consider an early outreach effort to the Gentiles. At first, these efforts were led by Barnabas and Saul (Paul) with John Mark as their assistant.[31] Initially, Barnabas was in the driver's seat, but starting with Acts 13:13, the picture changed such that Barnabas, recognizing Paul's unique apostolic calling, voluntarily became second in command.[32] From this point forward, the order in which their names appeared in Scripture reflected that change. Starting with the next missionary journey, Paul became the primary leader of the missionary enterprise among the Gentiles.

In the Jerusalem church, it was James, the half brother of Christ, who quickly emerged as the primary leader. When Peter was released from prison in Acts 12:17 and went to Mary's house, he definitely acknowledged James' leadership role.[33] Furthermore, during the council meeting when they were resolving the law/grace controversy, Peter represented the apostles (Acts

---

28. Ibid., emphasis Getz's.

29. Ibid., 220.

30. Ibid. Getz continues, "Though Jesus' ultimate purpose in calling these twelve men was not clear in their minds until He had ascended and sent the Holy Spirit, all of them were ready to respond to Peter's leadership. When he stood up on the Day of Pentecost and explained from the prophet Joel what was happening, not one of the apostles hesitated to follow him. Even James and John had a new perspective. They never again tried to do an 'end-run' around Peter, trying to maneuver themselves into a position of power ... Peter was continually the primary spokesman, and John stood by his side affirming and confirming the message of Christ's death and resurrection" (ibid.).

31. Ibid., 221.

32. Ibid., 67.

33. Ibid., 221.

Addressing Objections and Providing Practical Recommendations

15:7–11) while James represented the Jerusalem elders (Acts 15:13–21).[34] Many years later, when Paul returned to Jerusalem, he went first "to see James, and all the elders" (Acts 21:18).[35] Thus, whether James, Timothy, and Titus served as the apostolic representatives or presiding elders, two things are clear: (1) They seemed to be the primary leaders wherever they lived, and (2) they did not do their jobs alone, for in the New Testament, "the elders . . . clearly exercised their oversight jointly in a congregation."[36]

Based on the evidence above, it seems reasonable to set aside at least one person from among the elders who is given the primary teaching responsibility in the church and is supported by it.[37] Hence, a plurality of elders with one of them functioning as the primary leader seems to be the biblically mandated model for imitation.[38] It needs to be remembered, however, that the pastor is just one of the elders of his congregation.[39]

Paid or Unpaid?

Practically, what does this look like?[40] The pastor of the church is usually paid and thus able to devote his full time to pastoral ministry.[41] This is in accord with the witness of Scripture. In 1 Tim 5:17, Paul states that "the elders who rule well are to be considered worthy of double honor." The Greek word for "honor," *timē*, usually means respect or reverence, but it can also have the sense of compensation, as in honorarium.[42] The context supports the latter meaning in this text.

In the verse that follows, Paul quotes from Deut 25:4 for scriptural support in honoring faithful elders: "You shall not muzzle the ox while he

34. Ibid.
35. Ibid.
36. Powers, "Patterns of New Testament Ministry," 171.
37. For further argumentation of this point, see Dever, *God's Glory*, 24.
38. Any type of co-leadership scenario where either all or several elders equally share the leadership load has neither biblical precedent nor practical wisdom. For further discussion on the benefits of primary leadership within a system of multiple elders, see Getz, *Elders and Leaders*, 252–59.
39. Dever, *God's Glory*, 24.
40. From a purely pragmatic perspective, Dever offers some helpful recommendations for clearing the confusion regarding the relationship between elders and church staff; see ibid., 21.
41. Hammett, *Biblical Foundations*, 185.
42. Arndt et al., *Greek-English Lexicon*, 825.

is threshing." Since he uses this same passage in 1 Cor 9:9 to support his argument that he and Barnabas should benefit financially from those whom they benefited spiritually, it should have the same intent here, namely, that of urging financial remuneration for the elders.[43] Earlier in this same chapter Paul makes a similar connection; widows should be honored in the local church with material support (vv. 3, 4, 8, 16).[44] Similarly, in Christ's understanding of the fifth commandment, he too tied financial support with honoring one's parents (Matt 15:1–9).[45] Furthermore, in Gal 6:6, Paul urged those who have been taught the Word to share their material blessings with those who did the teaching.[46]

The evidence presented thus far offers substantial proof that "honor" in 1 Tim 5:17 refers to financial remuneration—a salary.[47] The rest of the elders do not have to be financially supported by the church. The pastor sees himself as one of the elders, accountable to them and under their corporate authority, even as they as a whole are under the ultimate authority of the congregation.[48]

ADDRESSING THE OBJECTIONS TO THE PLURALITY OF ELDERS

A number of the objections to plural-eldership have already been addressed in the arguments set forth for government by multiple elders. To these, a few more may be added here. Listed below, therefore, are some of the most popular objections, at least within the Baptist circles, to the plurality of elders in a local congregation.

Multiple-Eldership—Merely a Cultural Adaptation

The first objection to plural-eldership often concerns the idea of eldership in general. Those who raise this concern usually believe that the New

---

43. Wasser, "Pastor-Elder-Overseer," 70–71.
44. Ibid., 71.
45. Ibid.
46. Powers, "Patterns of New Testament Ministry," 178.
47. In view of this evidence, the Plymouth Brethren are wrong in rejecting paid pastors.
48. Ibid.

Addressing Objections and Providing Practical Recommendations

Testament church merely adopted a previously existing model of eldership, either from Hellenistic societies or Jewish organizations.[49] They declare eldership to be a cultural adaption, and therefore not binding on today's churches.

David Miller argues against such notions. His examination of Greco-Roman civic life yielded evidence that reveals quite a few differences between the eldership of the New Testament church and that utilized by the society around it. In consulting the *Theological Dictionary of the New Testament*, Miller notes that although the Alexandrian guild of six millers called *presbuteroi* had an *iereus*, or "priest," at its head,[50] the New Testament eldership had no such *iereus*.[51] The Constitution of Sparta denotes a *presbus* as a political title for the president of a college.[52] This single *presbus* is in contrast to the strong evidence for a plurality of elders in each New Testament church (Acts 15:4; 20:17; 21:18; Phil 1:1; and James 5:14).[53] Miller's analysis of the relevant data causes him to conclude:

> With the exception of two Egyptian documents (the presbyter-priests of Socnopaios and a local government officer), the Hellenistic understanding of the term *presbuteroi* is a reference to "older men," not to an office.[54] The term *presbuteros* does not become a title for the member of the *gerousia* / 'Council,' of the Hellenistic cities until the middle of the second century a.d. Having considered the evidence, it is safest to place no direct link between the office of elder in the New Testament church and the elder of any Hellenistic civil or religious organization.[55]

The vast majority of scholars regard the New Testament Eldership to be borrowed directly from the Jews.[56] They cite multiple Old Testa-

---

49. Alastair Campbell argues along these lines, suggesting that the New Testament church simply continued in the process of recognizing and utilizing the distinguished older members of the community—a practice that had been in place for many years prior and throughout various surrounding cultures (Campbell, *Elders*, 160).

50. Bornkamm, "Πρεσβύ'τερος," 653.

51. Miller, "Uniqueness of New Testament," 316.

52. Bornkamm, "Πρεσβύ'τερος," 653.

53. Miller, "Uniqueness of New Testament," 316.

54. Interestingly enough, this finding is also confirmed by Campbell's research (Campbell, *Elders*, 160).

55. Miller, "Uniqueness of New Testament," 316.

56. See, for example, Burtchaell, *Synagogue to Church*, 180–271; Powers, "Patterns of New Testament Ministry," 167–69; Lightfoot, *Saint Paul's Epistle*.

ment references to the role of elders in Israelite society and conclude that it was natural for the first Christians, who were ethnically Jewish, to take up similar organizational structures in the newly-established church. As a representative of this perspective, Lightfoot asserts, "the name and office of the presbyter [elder] is essentially Jewish."[57] This is not so, however. The Old Testament Elders were representatives of the whole people, and not only in the sense of mere representation rather than with any initiative or governing power, working along with and under leading figures like Moses and Joshua.[58] In contrast, Miller points out that the New Testament Elders:

> . . . were not mere representatives of the people, answering to the dictates of one man, such as Moses. The elders of Israel who met for decision-making later came to be leading men from the tribes or districts. These elders were so powerful that they were able to demand a king (1 Sam. 8:4). They continued to exert great influence during the reigns of Saul, David, and Solomon. However, the elders continued to be representatives of the people. Their function and qualifications were vastly different from those of the New Testament church elder in a local congregation.[59]

Harvey's conclusion appropriately summarizes the evidence above; there was no "institution in Old Testament times which could be regarded as the forerunner . . . of the Christian presbyterate."[60] The Sanhedrin, a Jewish organization created for adjudicating social matters in every important city that boasted a significant Jewish population during New Testament times, was, in the opinion of some theologians, another possible source for the Christian eldership. This is because the members of the Sanhedrin were sometimes referred to as elders (Matt 15:2; Mark 7:5; Luke 22:66; Acts 4:5–8). A careful comparison between the Sanhedrin and the New Testament Eldership, however, reveals major differences between the two. The Sanhedrin existed for adjudication—judgment of actions. Church discipline, in contradistinction,

> . . . is given to the spiritual (Gal 6:1–2), but such are not specified as elders. In fact, the whole church seems to have some responsibility in discipline (Matt 18:15–17 and 1 Cor 5:1–13). While New Testament Eldership did decide on some doctrinal matters (Acts 15),

---

57. Lightfoot, *Saint Paul's Epistle*, 191.
58. Bornkamm, "Πρεσβυ'τερος," 655–58.
59. Miller, "Uniqueness of New Testament," 317.
60. Harvey, "Elders," 320.

Addressing Objections and Providing Practical Recommendations

the New Testament never gives it the responsibilities of a court by way of example or specified duties.[61]

Miller's conclusion, in light of the evidence, is inevitable: "There are too many major differences between the Sanhedrin eldership and the New Testament local church elder to claim the former provided the pattern for the latter."[62] Harvey echoes the sentiment:

> There would be grave difficulties in regarding the Sanhedrin as a whole as the prototype of the Christian presbyterate. The word "elders," when applied to the Sanhedrin, was either a technical name for a specific class of aristocratic laymen, or was a more general word, with strong Pharisaic overtones, which was used to refer to scribes both inside and outside the Sanhedrin. In neither case is there any easy analogy with Christian presbyters.[63]

Finally, Lightfoot, Morris, and a host of other theologians believe that the New Testament church eldership came directly from the synagogue organization.[64] Yet, according to Campbell's research, "the elders no more occupy an office in the synagogue than do the priests, but, like the priests, they are among the leaders of the local community, men of education and influence and, as such, likely to be called on by the *arkisunagōgos*[65] to teach

---

61. Miller, "Uniqueness of New Testament," 318.
62. Ibid.
63. Harvey, "Elders," 323–24.
64. Lightfoot, *Saint Paul's Epistle*, 192; Morris, *Ecclesiology*, 139–40.
65. "Ruler of the synagogue" referred to the highest officer in the synagogue, whose responsibilities as president were to conduct the worship services and delegate various responsibilities (such as who would read the Scriptures and who would pray). He was also responsible for the construction and maintenance of the building (many sources show he financed the erection and upkeep). For all of his responsibilities, he was highly esteemed (Schrage, "Αρχισυνα'γωγος," 845–46. The synagogue president had a paid assistant (the *arkisunagōgos* was not paid) known as the *hazzan* or "attendant" (*upēretēs*, Luke 4:20). Among his duties were taking care of the furniture, paying special attention to the scrolls, announcing the start and end of the Sabbath by blowing a trumpet, teaching the young in the synagogue school, and carrying out the sentence of punishment passed by the elders. While there have been numerous attempts throughout history to correlate the attendant with a New Testament church official, whether as overseer or deacon, such undertaking is futile because there is no connection between the terms documented anywhere in Scripture. In addition to the president and the attendant, there were three other synagogue officers that are not mentioned in the New Testament: (1) the collector of alms, (2) the messenger, and (3) the herald of Shema (Miller, "Uniqueness of New Testament," 320). See also Cohen, "Sanhedrin," 1642.

and lead when the community meets for prayer and study of the Torah."[66] The Jewish synagogue, with its president, attendant, collector of alms, messenger, and the herald of Shema, is organized quite differently from the pattern established for the New Testament congregation. In fact, there were no clear matches in the church for the synagogue officers listed above. Moreover, unlike their Jewish counterparts, the New Testament church elders are encouraged to lead and to teach, as in 1 Tim 5:17, and must be able to teach in order to qualify for the position according to 1 Tim 3:2.[67]

Campbell succinctly summarizes the evidence, stating that "the ancient synagogues were 'run' on a day-to-day basis by their officers, the *arkisunagōgos* and *theupēretēs*. Men who were recognized as the elders of the community exercised great influence in its life, but they did not, as such, hold office."[68] And later,

> We must wonder how likely it is that those who left synagogues to join the church, and Gentiles who had never belonged to them, would have wanted to reproduce their structures when they decisively rejected their whole basis of membership and initiation. The dependence of the churches on the synagogue is a large assumption for which little hard evidence can be produced.[69]

Lindsay's comments should finally drive out all doubt from the minds of those who may have ever wondered whether the New Testament church eldership was just an adoption of the Jewish concept:

> When we find "elders" in charge of the community in Jerusalem, ready to receive the contributions for the relief of those who were suffering from the famine which overtook them in the reign of Claudius, it is impossible to doubt that the name came from their Jewish surroundings. At the same time it must always be remembered that Christian "elders" had functions *entirely different* from the Jewish, that the vitality of the infant Christian Communities made them work out for themselves that organization which they found to be most suitable, and that in this case *nothing but the name was borrowed*.[70]

---

66. Campbell, *Elders*, 53–54. See also Harvey, "Elders," 324; Sobosan, "Role of the Presbyter," 129–46.

67. Miller, "Uniqueness of New Testament," 321.

68. Campbell, *Elders*, 54.

69. Ibid., 119.

70. Lindsay, *Church and the Ministry*, 153, emphasis mine. Having researched the occurrence of the "elder" in the Old and New Testaments, Mappes's conclusion shares

Addressing Objections and Providing Practical Recommendations

Although the defense of the uniqueness of the organization of the New Testament church eldership has overtaken much space, the import of this issue to the subject of the present work cannot be overstated. Because the New Testament idea of church eldership is unparalleled within the organizational structures of either Greco-Roman society or Jewish institutions, and because of the critical importance of the government of the institution that is often called "the body of Christ" to God himself, it can be assumed that the carefully outlined precedent left on the pages of the New Testament was designed for us to emulate in setting up the structure of today's churches.[71] Miller's conclusion needs no clarification: "Our Lord's church should be organized the way he has designed it in his word."[72]

No Biblical Mandate to Implement Multiple-Eldership

Paige Patterson's opinion regarding the plurality of elders may be reviewed as the second major objection to this form of church government.[73] Patterson argues strongly that a plurality of elders cannot be mandated because there is no commandment relating to the number of elders in the New Testament.[74] Leonard Hillstrom similarly notes, "While Scripture indicates a multiple eldership in the apostolic church, there is no injunction absolutely requiring it."[75] In the absence of such a command, Patterson believes we should decide the issue of plurality based on leadership patterns we see

---

the spirit of Lindsay's, though it is not as dogmatic: "while the synagogal eldership did influence church eldership, the influence was of a general nature" (Mappes, "'Elder' in the Old and New Testaments," 91–92). Among the similarities between the synagogue elders and the early church elders, Mappes includes "the plurality of the eldership, the responsibility of the elders for the well-being of the people; the authority of the elders within the community, the desired moral qualities of the elders, and the elders' responsibility to communicate and take care of the Scriptures" (ibid.).

71. This is in accordance with the sixth theological principle detailed in chapter 4.

72. Miller, "Uniqueness of New Testament," 327.

73. Interestingly enough, Patterson defends a system that he calls "single-elder congregationalism," but in Waldron's opinion, with which Patterson agrees, it could be more accurately called "primary-elder congregationalism" (Waldron, "Plural-Elder Congregationalist's Response," 171).

74. Patterson, "Single-Elder Congregationalism," 150–52. To be fair, Patterson admits that neither single-elder congregationalism nor plural-elder congregationalism has explicit biblical mandate in the New Testament (ibid., 150).

75. Hillstrom, "New Testament Teaching," 180.

elsewhere in Scripture. He writes, "the general pattern that emerges in the Bible is that God calls a leader from among the people."[76]

In response to this objection, Waldron's curiosity is befitting: If, in Patterson's words, "there are simply no 'commandments' [in Scripture] on this issue," why is singe-elder congregationalism so important to Patterson?[77] Could it be because this is the traditionally "Baptist" way of doing ecclesiology? Granted, my question is further fueled by an occasion when one of my former pastors, a graduate of the institution once led by Dr. Patterson, concluded our discussion of New Testament ecclesiology one Wednesday night with the following words: "The Bible seems to lean more towards plural-eldership as the model for church government, but we cannot do that because we are Baptists." This sort of logic begs the question of whether we are critiquing contemporary practice in light of the New Testament, or interpreting the New Testament in light of contemporary practice?[78]

Second, in implying that the primary biblical evidence is not clear on this issue, Patterson resorts to "observing leadership practice throughout the Scriptures."[79] He begins this observation in the Old Testament. Does it not seem odd to be calling on the Old Testament to support leadership practice in the church, which according to Patterson's own emphatic pronouncement is a distinctly New Testament organization?[80] Furthermore, Waldron is correct to counter Patterson's claim with the following words: "Perhaps it is not that the New Testament is unclear, but rather that Patterson is not inclined to look too closely at what it actually says."[81]

Third, using Patterson's methodology of seeking out general patterns in Scripture, when it comes to church leadership it is impossible to come up with a pattern different from the plurality of elders. Fourth, neither the individuals who argue for plural elders nor the churches that practice it usually have a problem with "the primary leader" or "preacher-teacher of the flock."[82] Therefore, arguing "for" such a point man in no way diminishes arguments for plural-eldership. Patterson's findings in no way establish that

---

76. Patterson, "Single-Elder Congregationalism," 150.
77. Patterson, qtd. in Waldron, "Plural-Elder Congregationalist's Response," 171.
78. Ibid., 177.
79. Patterson, "Single-Elder Congregationalism," 152.
80. Ibid., "Single-Elder Congregationalist's Response," 109–110.
81. Waldron, "Plural-Elder Congregationalist's Response," 171.
82. See, for example, Getz, *Elders and Leaders*, 252–59.

Addressing Objections and Providing Practical Recommendations

there ought to be a primary elder with an office or authority that the rest of the elders do not possess.[83]

Fifth, Patterson's logic reveals some inconsistency, for the very "pattern" against which he seems to speak with regard to the question of plurality of elders is what he would rely on in arguing *for* congregationalism. For example, in his response to the anglican polity, Patterson states, "when the Bible speaks either by mandate or by precedent, it represents not only truth but also sufficient guidance for the ordering of life and church."[84] In response to presbyterian polity, Patterson continues, "the church is not free to deviate from the apostolic patterns observable in Holy Scripture."[85] In the case of congregational government, in the absence of explicit biblical commandment, we are left to depend on the precedent, or biblical pattern.[86] Thus, in the same way that we handle biblical precedent, in the absence of an explicit mandate to advocate congregationalism, multiple-eldership can be advanced. In other words, if biblical precedent for congregationalism constitutes sufficient evidence for Patterson to adhere to it today, then in the absence of mandate, similar scriptural precedent for multiple-eldership ought to be equally sufficient.[87]

On the contrary, would it not stand to reason that if the Lord wanted us to use the single-elder-led church model, he would have left numerous examples and illustrations of the advantages of such a system throughout the pages of Scripture? Baptist theologian Augustus Hopkins Strong seems to agree with this idea of biblical precedent when he writes that "a proper theory of development does not exclude the idea of a church organization already complete in all essential particulars before the close of the inspired canon, so that the record of it may constitute a providential example of

---

83. Waldron, "Plural-Elder Congregationalist's Response," 172.

84. Patterson, "Single-Elder Congregationalist's Response," 55.

85. Ibid., 111.

86. Not to say anything about the fact that "a leader from among the people" logic would go really well with the Episcopal model.

87. Gordon Fee offers another possible approach to this when he writes, "if the New Testament is one's 'sole authority' and that authority does not in fact teach anything directly about church order at the local level, then one might rightly ask whether there is a normative church order. If the best one has is paradigm, then it is certainly arguable that whatever paradigm one goes with it should minimize the potentiality of individual overlordship or authoritarianism and maximize accountability and servanthood" (Fee, "Reflections on Church Order," 149–50). A singe-elder system can be hardly described as such paradigm!

binding authority upon all subsequent ages."[88] B. W. Powers similarly states that "when in the New Testament we find patterns of ministry being tried, being found successful in the church, and being specifically commended and commanded for other churches to adopt, then the onus of proof lies with those who would advocate that the church does not need to use such patterns of ministry today."[89]

Sixth, as mentioned in chapter 5, Grudem points out the inconsistency of arguing that the New Testament falls short of giving a clear command that all churches should have a plurality of elders when the passages on qualifications of elders in 1 Timothy 3:1–7 and Titus 1:5–7 are used as scriptural requirements for church officers today.[90]

Multiple-Eldership Will Eliminate Congregationalism

Third, some fear that plural-eldership may eliminate congregationalism, pointing to presbyterian polity as an example. While it is true that in the presbyterian structure of church government, plural-eldership can effectively bypass the congregation, it need not be so. Careful study of Scripture shows that in the early church, the congregation was involved in all decisions to some degree.

On the other hand, however, not all decisions made in the early church were executed by congregational vote. Some, like the decision regarding the church's position towards the Judaizers (Acts 15), were handled primarily by the apostles and elders and involved the congregation only at a later stage by means of informing them. Thus, in the words of Newton, "Congregationalism certainly existed, but not to such a degree that the public assembly literally ran the church."[91]

Multiple-Eldership Is Un-Baptist and Un-biblical

The fourth objection to plural-elder congregationalism is represented by the writings of Malcolm B. Yarnell III. Yarnell ventures to speak for all Southern Baptists in America in his advancement of "Article VI: The Church" of

  88. Strong, *Systematic Theology*, 896.
  89. Powers, "Patterns of New Testament Ministry," 167.
  90. Grudem, *Systematic Theology*, 929. For a more in-depth discussion on this matter, see the third argument against the single-elder-led-church in chapter 5.
  91. Newton, *Elders in Congregational Life*, 58.

Addressing Objections and Providing Practical Recommendations

Baptist Faith and Message 2000. Claiming the deep commitment of Baptists to strict biblicism,[92] Yarnell proceeds to declare that practicing any form of church government other than democratic congregationalism is un-Baptist,[93] and implicitly unbiblical. Providing a scant and cursory representation of multiple-elder congregationalism, Yarnell attempts to dismantle that position by appealing to a linguistic detail called the distributive plural in Greek. This allows him to assume that in a large church, like Jerusalem, each smaller sub-group that met in local homes was led by a single elder.

In response to Yarnell's first objection, it must be pointed out that his argument is not supported by the biblical testimony, historical data, or modern practice. Scripturally, the overwhelming biblical support for plural-elder congregationalism has already been illustrated here at great lengths. Unfortunately, the same cannot be said of a single-elder system. There is just not much, if any, New Testament precedent for this particular structure.[94]

Historically, a number of Baptists, including some well-known Southern Baptists, have been adherents to multiple-elder congregationalism.[95] One cannot rewrite history and call these people, among whom we can count the first president of Southern Baptist Convention (SBC), un-Baptist. When it comes to modern practice, as has already been pointed out, there is a good and growing number of Southern Baptist theologians practicing plurality of eldership in their churches.[96] Added to their number is a list of Baptist statesmen that includes the presidents of two SBC seminaries—Paige Patterson and Daniel Akin—who recognize the biblical precedent for and allow the use of plural-eldership when and where necessary.[97] Therefore, instead of speaking on behalf of the whole Convention, past and present, Yarnell may find himself representing a smaller minority with regard to church government.

---

92. Yarnell, "Article VI," 55.

93. Ibid., 61, and in personal correspondence.

94. A further distinction needs to be made that arguing for congregationalism is not the same as arguing for democratic congregationalism. Yarnell presents quite a forceful biblical case for congregationalism with which I could not agree more (ibid). The same, however, could not be said of his case for single-elder/democratic congregationalism.

95. W. B. Johnson, P. H. Mell, J. L. Reynolds, and Benjamin Griffith, to name a few.

96. Among the better known are Mark Dever, Samuel Waldron, Phil Newton, and John Piper.

97. Akin, "Single-Elder-Led Church," 64; Patterson, "Single-Elder Congregationalism," 150.

In invoking the distributive plural, Yarnell is correct in noting that it is a feature present within the New Testament.[98] He runs into problems, however, in defending his reasons for using it in the passages where the corporate plural could be used just as well and where the corporate plural would yield a simpler meaning. It becomes somewhat arbitrary at that point as to which plural should be used, warranting a departure from purely grammatical to exegetical or theological reasons.

When and where it is impossible to determine a meaning of the text from a purely grammatical standpoint, consideration should be given to the agreement of the text in question with the teaching of several different passages of Scripture on the particular issue. If that is the case, then we are bound to find that the corporate plural offers a much better explanation of the texts and agrees with the overwhelming biblical support of plural-eldership. The choice to use the distributive plural can only be explained by personal presuppositions that assure that the desired result is found in the text. In the area of hermeneutics, we would call that practice eisegesis (from the Greek *eis*, or "into," when one brings meaning *into* the text rather than gathers meaning *out* of the text). If Southern Baptists, as Yarnell writes, "are first, last, and always followers of Jesus Christ, with the full recognition that Scripture is the final authority on all beliefs and doctrinal systems,"[99] then perhaps it is time for us to re-examine our adherence to the Word in the area of church polity.

---

98. Unfortunately this assertion could not be confirmed, as Yarnell does not cite the Greek grammar from which he obtained this understanding, thus the burden of proof for the usage of the "distributive plural" in the particular texts pertaining to the argument lies with him. In other words, in making such a sweeping assertion, Yarnell owes it to the reader to cite the Greek grammarians discussing the idea of distributive plural and citing polity passages as examples, his logic for using it in a particular passage—especially when corporate plural could also be used—and the list of the specific passages out of all the "elder" references in the New Testament to which he applies this practice. My examination of the following sample of New Testament Greek grammar texts found that only two of them discussed distributive plural (making it a very rare occurrence in the New Testament), and none mentioned any connection between this Greek form and polity passages: Moulton, *Grammar of New Testament Greek*; Winer, *Grammar of New Testament Greek*; Robertson, *Grammar of the Greek New Testament*; Stevens, *New Testament Greek*; Mounce, *Basics of Biblical*; Dana and Mantey, *Manual of Grammar*; Blass and Debrunner, *Greek Grammar*.

99. Yarnell, "TULIP of Calvinism."

The More in Charge, the Harder to Get Along and More Difficult to Support

As a different kind of objection, in his tome on ecclesiology, Baptist theologian Edwin C. Dargan admits to a certain deviation within his tradition from the New Testament model of leadership by plural elders. His reasons are twofold: Dargan wonders whether the pastors/elders could get along and how a congregation could afford to support them adequately.[100] This is a trivial pretext for not following the leadership pattern set up by God for his church in accordance with his Word. In response to Dargan's first fear, I would like to consider it in theory and in practice. Theoretically, looking to the Bible, there is a certain measure of expectation that the leadership of the church will operate under the guidance and direction of the Holy Spirit rather than in the flesh. Practically speaking, there are countless examples, including from my own experience, of the flawless and beautiful way in which the unity of the Spirit is displayed through the decisions made by such a group of elders. In terms of supporting these leaders financially, an earlier section of this chapter already dealt with that issue.

Behind Most Objections . . .

Speaking from a wealth of pastoral experience within the Southern Baptist Convention, Newton is right to point out that "at the root of much opposition to plural-eldership are pastors who fear the loss of their authority in the church."[101] Although many Baptist churches claim to exercise congregationalism, their actual structure is monarchical episcopacy—the solitary rule of one person over the congregation.[102] Incidentally, monarchical episcopacy in the Church of Rome and Church of England, with all its practical abuses of power, was one of the very reasons for the birth of Baptists.

---

100. Dargan, *Ecclesiology*, 121.
101. Newton, *Elders in Congregational Life*, 59.
102. Ibid.

THE DANGERS OF ABANDONING THE PATTERN OF PLURAL-ELDERSHIP

Though some of this material has already been stated in this work in a different context, it would be beneficial to reiterate it here as a list of real dangers associated with knowingly or unknowingly abandoning the scriptural pattern of plural-eldership.

It Would Be Unscriptural

The first danger associated with abandoning the distinct biblical pattern of plurality of elders at the helm of the local church is that it is unscriptural. One would be hard-pressed to provide an equal amount of biblical support for *any* other form of church government. Therefore, adopting a structure that is neither commanded nor warranted in Scripture may result in hindrance rather than advancement of the proper function of the body of Christ.[103]

It Would Ignore the Principle of the Priesthood of Believers

The second danger of abandoning the multiple-elder-led model is that it does great damage to the principle of the priesthood of believers.[104] The priesthood of the Old Testament was especially separated by God to stand as mediators between God and the people. The death of Christ on the cross, accompanied by the tearing of the veil in the temple (Matt 27:51), brought a new era in which all believers are priests, with all the privileges and

---

103. Daughters, *New Testament Church Government*, 77.
104. Ibid.

responsibilities that go with priesthood.¹⁰⁵ Yet, in many cases, the single pastor will usurp the rights and privileges that belong to every believer.¹⁰⁶

It Would Retard the Body's Development

The third danger of ignoring the multiple-elder-led model is that it tends to retard the development of the body of Christ by discouraging the exercise of many God-given gifts.¹⁰⁷ Daughters correctly argues:

> According to Eph 4:11–13, the leadership was given to the church by God to equip the saints to do the work of the ministry so that the body could mature. But the idea of a single professional pastor is not as effective as multiple leadership in achieving this. Too many saints avoid taking part in the work of the ministry because they think that is what they are paying the pastor to do.¹⁰⁸

How much better it would be to spread the responsibility for leading the church over a greater number of people!

---

105. Ibid. Priesthood of all believers—the assertion that the gift of grace is bestowed on *every* church member, and that therefore *every* member is called to service—is constant in the New Testament, just as it is understood that every church member can baptize, distribute the Lord's Supper, and speak in any assembly of the church (Schweizer, *Church Order*, 156). Or, as Daughters puts it, "As believer-priests, there is no ministry that is performed by the elders from which a regular church member should be excluded (1 Pet 2:5–9; Rev 1:5, 6; 5:10). Preaching from the pulpit, performing baptisms, and distributing the elements at communion are not privileges reserved only for professional clergy" (Daughters, *New Testament Church Government*, 77).

106. Ibid. Carson notes similarly that "some forms of congregationalism elevate the pastor, once he has been voted in, to near papal authority, in practice if not in theory" (Carson, "Church, Authority in," 1:230). I personally witnessed this phenomenon occur in one of the churches I served, where the pastor wielded his power masterfully, leaving the congregation feeling powerless to oppose him, his ideas, his choices, or his direction. In his quest for control, the pastor left the congregation selectively educated—presenting them with only the side of things that was most beneficial for his purposes and making them feel that to disagree with him was equivalent to promoting disunity. These were the very words expressed to me by several members of the congregation.

107. Daughters, *New Testament Church Government*, 78.

108. Ibid.

It Would Place Too Much Reliance on One Man

Fourth, in the single-elder-led environment, the spiritual state of the church depends too much on one man.[109] If he lags spiritually, the whole church will tend to follow.[110] Such unhealthy reliance has neither the support of Scripture nor common wisdom behind it.

It Would Be More Open to Human Manipulations

Fifth, a professional pastor is more likely to be amenable to human will because he is dependent on others for his paycheck. Daughters adds that in a single-elder-led church the pastor's performance may be evaluated "by the number of people added to the church roll during the year."[111] This type of evaluation creates a strong temptation to lower the standards of reception for new members in order to look better.[112]

These pressures are not as likely to fall on a group of elders. Judging the success of the ministry, and ultimately, the pastor, by the congregation's numbers is perhaps one of the most debilitating and discouraging factors to those churches whose growth may be other than numerical.[113] This practice is especially proliferated within the Southern Baptist Convention, whose annual meetings still laud those pastors who have performed most baptisms in the previous year.

THE WAY FORWARD: PRACTICAL SUGGESTIONS FOR APPLICATION

Prior to engaging in the provision of any practical suggestions, a word of clarification is in order. Earl Radmacher makes an excellent distinction in his short work, *The Question of Elders*, between congregational government and congregational authority. "The congregation has the authority," states Radmacher, "to conduct *all* of its business in session, if it chooses, but this would make meaningless the choosing of elders and deacons."[114] What is

---

109. Ibid., 79.
110. Ibid.
111. Ibid.
112. Ibid.
113. Ibid.
114. Radmacher, *Question of Elders*, 13.

Addressing Objections and Providing Practical Recommendations

the solution? Radmacher recommends that the congregation should be "careful not to destroy their own efficiency and effectiveness by becoming immersed in the managing or governing for which they have elected spiritually-qualified leaders, and the leaders must be careful not to usurp authority for themselves which rightfully belongs to the congregation as a whole."[115] The only way that such balance can be achieved is "when the leaders lead by love, teach by example, and when the congregation exercises proper submission to those whom they have chosen in submission to the word of God and the Spirit of God."[116] For a biblical example of such a balance, Radmacher rightly points to Heb 13:7 and 17.

For those churches that find themselves outside of the biblical model of church leadership, in his work *Biblical Foundations for Baptist Churches: A Contemporary Ecclesiology*, Hammett provides some practical recommendations for making a transition to the plurality of elders. He informs the pastors that transitions of this type can take anywhere from two to four years, citing a few illustrations from the related experiences of Piper and Dever.[117] It would begin with a careful evaluation of the church's present state of affairs, including identifying the real power brokers within the congregation. The second step in the transition to multiple-eldership would involve educating the congregation about the biblical teaching on leadership through every means possible. Especially beneficial at this point might be creating various opportunities for congregational interaction with the leadership and the pastor. At the same time, as Daughters points out,

> The pastor should avoid actions which encourage a clergy-laity gap. He should avoid the use of professional titles which tend to separate him from the general layman. In the Biblical pattern, all believers are priests. If he allows members of his congregation to call him "Pastor," he is feeding the notion that only full-time professionals can be pastors. Instead, he should communicate the fact that "pastor" is a spiritual gift, not an office. He should point out others in the congregation who have the gift. He should not allow any to call him "Reverend." No one is to be revered, except God. If he has earned a doctorate, he ought to consider whether or not the use of that title is causing some to feel they cannot minister

---

115. Ibid.

116. Ibid.

117. Newton, a thirty-year veteran in the pastorate within the Southern Baptist Convention, provides a helpful guide for those desiring to transition to plural-eldership (Newton, *Elders in Congregational Life*, 113–54).

because of lack of formal training. He should not allow anyone to refer to him as "the minister," implying that he is the only one who ministers. He must communicate to his flock in all that he says and does that every believer is a priest and all should minister.[118]

Despite his experience and particular education, the pastor must communicate with his every word and action that he is just another believer-priest like they are, and the only difference is that he has been called to shepherd them.[119]

By a way of practical recommendation, an interesting point was made to me recently by James Schupp, the pastor who oversaw the transition to multiple-elder government at a well-known Southern Baptist mega-church in San Antonio, Texas. According to Schupp, time was the biggest factor in contributing to a smooth transition. Even though his was a well-established congregation, the older members initially had many questions and objections. Taking the necessary time to answer these questions and address objections instead of rushing the vote through made for an almost unanimous consensus in the end. While the entire process lasted almost five years, when the vote was finally set, it did not divide or destroy the body. Interestingly enough, this particular congregation happens to host the San Antonio extension of the Southwestern Baptist Theological Seminary led by Paige Patterson.

When it comes to the step of actually selecting elders, both the congregation and the present leadership of the church should be involved in the process.[120] Daughters is right in his estimation that in regard to leadership selection process, "Acts 6:3 shows a proper balance between the selection of the congregation and the appointment by the leadership."[121] Acts 6:3 says: "Therefore, brethren, select from among you seven men of good reputation, full of the Spirit and of wisdom, whom we may put in charge of this task." The congregation was instructed to select (*episkepsasthe*, or "carefully choose based on diligent investigation") those whom the apostles would appoint (*katastēsomen*, or "put in charge, designate"). Thus, both groups

---

118. Daughters, *New Testament Church Government*, 82–83.

119. Ibid., 83.

120. Hammett devotes some attention to the process of selection, providing detailed step-by-step directions in Hammett, *Biblical Foundations*, 186–88. Getz combines scriptural principles with personal experience of pasturing elder-led churches, yielding some helpful principles for selecting new elders in Getz, *Elders and Leaders*, 237–59.

121. Daughters, *New Testament Church Government*, 48.

worked together to agree on the proper choice: The congregation submitted to the approval of the Twelve, and the Twelve submitted to the selection of the congregation.[122] In the absence of apostles in this day and age, the process of leadership selection, while involving both the congregation and existing leadership, will have to rely heavily on the guidance and direction of the Holy Spirit—the same one, incidentally, that moved the apostles to their decisions in the first place.

CONCLUDING REMARKS

Having illustrated that the most biblically defensible model of church government is multiple-elder congregationalism, I must now make some concluding remarks. For those who believe in congregationalism but practice one of the other forms of church government within this model, I admit along with Davidson that elders are not essential to the *esse*,[123] but to the *bene esse*[124] of churches.[125] As someone who is now convinced of the biblical and practical superiority of the plurality of eldership in a local church, I understand, however, that there may be cases where no more than one qualified elder may be found in a congregation. In such a scenario, I will be quick to admit that a certain degree of freedom does exist in the New Testament, permitting a local congregation to function without disobedience if no body of elders is available.

Davidson's clarification may be especially appropriate to the discussion, for Davidson explains that elders are chosen not because a spiritual community is incompetent to do all *before* that it does *after* obtaining them, but because the ordinances and commandments it is enjoined to observe can be done *better* with than *without* them.[126] The summary of Davidson's argument serves well to communicate the spirit of my position: "That they [elders] should be created in a spiritual corporation is a matter of order and *wise* arrangement, for the purpose of securing the *best* possible *management* of its interest."[127]

---

122. Ibid.
123. Being.
124. Wellbeing.
125. Davidson, *Ecclesiastical Polity*, 113.
126. Ibid.
127. Ibid.

For all readers, I end with this. While biblically I cannot advocate any other than a congregational form of church government with a plurality of elders, history is full of examples of God working in the midst of, and through, other models of church government as well. Should a recognition of this sort embolden anyone in the pursuit of other forms of church government, a warning may be useful: It is dangerous to use history alone in building a case for any one model of polity. Because God's Word transcends history, this work has advocated the model supported by Scripture, namely, plural-elder-led congregationalism.

Daughters' plea makes a fitting conclusion to my argument:

> Let us not be reluctant to follow the scriptural example simply because it is not convenient or because we are used to a different way. Let us not be tempted to force a different interpretation upon the Scripture so that we can have a license to continue our popular practice. Let us boldly choose to follow God's example laid down in the foundation of the Church.[128]

May God help us in doing so!

---

128. Daughters, *New Testament Church Government*, 88.

Appendix

Further Thoughts from Getz and Bar

GENE GETZ' STORY: AN ELDER-LED MODEL

I became involved in church planting while a professor at Dallas Theological Seminary in the early seventies. A number of students were reacting against cultural institutionalism and included the "institutional" church in their concerns and criticisms. Their questions drove me back to the New Testament to take a fresh look at what God intends the church to be. In the process I wrote a book entitled *Sharpening the Focus of the Church*, which led me to conclude that in terms of overall ecclesiology, the Holy Spirit has given us absolutes in function and principles, but sets us free to develop forms and structures that are unique to particular cultures. Little did I realize this research would lead me out of the seminary classroom to plant the first Fellowship Bible Church, which quickly led to multiple churches throughout the Dallas metroplex and beyond.

Regardless of our various viewpoints on how the church should function, most of us would agree that *leadership* and *governance* is at the heart and core of ecclesiology. My research led me to conclude that having more than one highly qualified spiritual leader in each local church is a noble goal. We called them "elders," although Scripture does not dictate "absolute titles"—only absolutes in terms of function and responsibility.

As the churches in the New Testament grew, some of these men served as leaders "worthy of an ample honorarium" (1 Tim 5:17). Some volunteered their time to be good managers and shepherds of the church, and there is no question that these men served together as leaders in what are

Appendix

described as churches in various cities or towns. However, we are never given a detailed description or blueprint of the methods and forms involved in each house church setting within those towns or cities.

In our own church planting efforts, we have given serious attention to the qualifications for spiritual leaders outlined in 1 Timothy and Titus (1 Tim 3:1–7; Titus 1:5–9). We believe these requirements, rightly interpreted, are indeed supracultural requirements and standards.

When we appointed these men to lead the Fellowship Bible Church, we viewed them as "multiple fathers" leading the larger church family, with their wives serving as "multiple mothers." And since this approach worked well, we saw no need to have an official membership requirement for the total congregation—a methodology that has a variety of forms that came into existence long after the New Testament era.

In this sense, we have been "elder led" churches. In terms of accountability, we have taken seriously Paul's charge to the Ephesian elders to maintain accountability among themselves (Acts 20:28–31). Furthermore, our goal has been to be servant leaders and caring shepherds totally committed to the spiritual growth and care of all those who attend and identify with each local fellowship.

However, we do not believe that our practices constitute the only correct model or structure for church governance. As with all forms, there are pragmatic variations even within the "elder led" model. However, we do believe, as Goncheranko does, that churches are to be led by multiple mature leaders. Consequently, we have seen positive results from taking the qualifications of our leaders seriously. When we have violated this principle of mature leadership, we have invariably suffered the consequences. All it takes is one carnal leader misusing his authority to destroy unity at the leadership level as well as unity in the church. However, we have also discovered that mature leaders will confront and discipline immature leaders.

One other observation: Since establishing the first Fellowship Bible Church in the Dallas area, a great many more have been planted in the United States and overseas. Since we chose not to create a central governing organization—also a freedom in form—many of these churches are organized along lines of multiple-elder leadership blended with various forms of traditional congregationalism. I readily admit that this has added an element of more accountability.

In terms of my leadership experience, just prior to passing the baton to my successor as Senior Pastor of Fellowship Bible Church North (now

Chase Oaks Church), I was encouraged to research and write a book on local church leadership. Taking this challenge seriously, I asked my fellow elders at Fellowship Bible Church North to join me in this study. Most were godly businessmen who had served with me in several church planting efforts, some for over twenty-five years. Together we studied the New Testament story, taking an in-depth look at every reference and passage that unfolds the story of church leadership. The result was a book entitled *Elders and Leaders: God's Plan for Leading the Church; A Biblical, Historical, and Cultural Perspective.*

The following is a list of supracultural principles that emerged from this study. Even a cursory look will demonstrate that we believe that these are normative truths and guidelines that can be used in every culture of the world and at any moment in history to develop a system of governance that is both biblical and culturally relevant. You'll note that we have used the term "spiritual leaders" since one of our conclusions is that titles for these leaders are not absolute. However, their "biblical functions" are as follows.

Principle 1: First Official Appointments

When local churches are established, the first official appointments should be spiritual leaders who are able to give overall direction to the church; however, they should not be appointed unless they are qualified.

Principle 2: A Unified Team

The goal of every local church should be to eventually appoint qualified leaders who serve together as a unified team.

Principle 3: Qualifications

All spiritual leaders should be appointed based on the maturity profile outlined by Paul in the Pastoral Epistles.

Appendix

Principle 4: Basic Ethics and Morality

When looking for qualified leaders to serve the church, consider first those men and their families who have grown up in an environment with values shaped by Judeo-Christian ethics and morality.

Principle 5: An Initial Leader

If there are no candidates in the church who are qualified to serve as official spiritual leaders, another qualified leader needs to serve in either a temporary or permanent role until others in the church are sufficiently equipped to serve in such a role.

Principle 6: A Primary Leader

Every group of spiritual leaders needs a primary leader who both leads and serves and who is accountable to his fellow spiritual leaders.

Principle 7: Titles

When determining titles for spiritual leaders in the local church, *how they function* is far more important than *what the local body calls them*.

Principle 8: Multiple Fathers

Spiritual leaders should manage and shepherd the church just as fathers are to care for their families and shepherds are to tend their sheep.

Principle 9: Important Priorities

All spiritual leaders should make sure they manage and shepherd the church well by maintaining six important priorities: teaching the word of God, modeling Christ-like behavior, maintaining doctrinal purity, disciplining unruly believers, overseeing the material needs of the church, and praying for the sick.

Principle 10: Mutual Accountability

Spiritual leaders in the church should hold each other accountable for their spiritual lives as well as the way they carry out their ministries.

Principle 11: Expanded Accountability

To follow the model that unfolds in the New Testament story, every body of local church leaders should have some kind of accountability system that extends beyond themselves—particularly in the case of the primary leader.

Principle 12: Qualified Assistants

In order to maintain their priorities, spiritual leaders should appoint qualified assistants who can help them meet the needs of all believers in the church.

Principle 13: Financial Support

Spiritual leaders are to make sure that those who devote significant amounts of time to the ministry, particularly to teaching the word of God, should be cared for financially and materially.

Principle 14: Adequate Forms

Spiritual leaders are responsible to make sure that adequate forms are developed to carry out the functions required of the biblical principles above.

WAYNE BARBER'S STORY: FROM CONGREGATIONALISM TO ELDERSHIP

I grew up in a Southern Baptist church and spent years in youth and recreation ministry after college, serving several Southern Baptist churches across the South. After about fifteen years, God led me to my first church outside of Frankfort, Kentucky to serve as Senior Pastor in the mid-seventies.

Next, I pastored the First Baptist Church of Lexington, Mississippi. It was there that I was first exposed to "elder leadership" in an independent

Appendix

Bible church. I was intrigued. I became determined to learn more, since I had experienced some recurring problems with congregationalism in the churches I had served.

I left Mississippi in September of 1981 to become Senior Pastor of the Woodland Park Baptist Church in Chattanooga, Tennessee, where I served for the next eighteen years. Dr. Spiros Zodhiates, a noted Greek scholar and author, became a member of the church not too long after I became Senior Pastor. His first question to me when he joined was "Where are your elders?"

This was a turning point. In 1985 we commissioned a group led by Dr. Zodhiates to do a comprehensive study on the subject of elder leadership to present to our congregation. We then spent another year laying the groundwork before we were ready to implement the plan. The faithful of Woodland Park Baptist responded enthusiastically.

After much prayer, we presented a list of trusted men to the church. We listed their names alongside the biblical qualifications for eldership in a letter addressed to the whole congregation.

Over the next thirty days, everyone had a chance to let us know of any concerns about the candidates. In fact, I seriously thought of publishing their names in the local newspaper because an elder must have a good reputation in the community (1 Tim 3:17). The results were affirming and it was a great blessing to watch how God honored our decision to appoint elders to lead our church.

The congregation clearly understood that they no longer had a vote under this new system of governance. I was overwhelmed when, in a church business meeting, the "congregation" voted out "congregationalism" in favor of a new constitution and bylaws.

One of the major challenges we faced was accountability. Obviously, the word of God holds us all accountable. But as the Apostle Paul illustrates in his address to the Ephesian elders, these men needed to hold one another accountable as well. For this reason, we wanted our congregation to have a strong voice in holding our elders accountable for leading the church. Consequently, after presenting what we believe is the Lord's will involving decisions such as the disposal of property and buildings, the calling of a Senior Pastor, choosing elders, etc., we have a time of affirmation. To be more specific, the procedure is that after the elders present what they believe is God's will, we host a thirty-day affirmation period.

During this time, church members can come to the elders to ask any questions that they might have concerning the matter. At the end of the thirty days, we have a stand-up affirmation time in our service. If we perceive that the majority of the congregation is not supportive (at least 75 percent), we then reconsider our decisions and continue to seek the Lord's will.

Whatever forms are developed for elder leadership, we believe that accountability is paramount. In fact, we teach the importance of accountability in our membership classes. As "members of one another" we are accountable to each other both doctrinally and in the way we live.

Consider the matter of restoring a brother or sister in the congregation. This is a huge matter of mutual accountability. It is not only the responsibility of the elders, but also the responsibility of the congregation, which is addressed in all of the "one another" commands in Scripture. This is beautifully illustrated in Gal 6:1.

I left Woodland Park Baptist Church in 2002 to become Senior Pastor at another Southern Baptist church, the Hoffmantown Church in Albuquerque, New Mexico. I immediately began to pursue an elder system of governance. To my delight, some of the leaders had already been studying this concept in Scripture.

To begin with, the church appointed a "transition team." This team was assigned the responsibility of coming alongside the Senior Pastor to help lead the church. They were my "eyes and ears," and although they were very helpful and encouraging, they also understood this was no guarantee that they would be selected as elders when the time finally came a few years later to implement the eldership that still continues to this day.

Lessons Learned

I've learned many important lessons from both of these situations. First, this transition process takes time. We have to curb our tendency to move too quickly. People react against what they perceive as manipulation.

Second, we must make certain that the shift to eldership is not a knee-jerk reaction against power-hungry church leaders or business meetings that demonstrate carnal attitudes and actions.

Third, we must move the congregation with us instead of forcing the process. To do so, we must share with the present leadership and the total congregation what the Bible teaches about eldership.

Appendix

Fourth, choosing leaders for eldership based on the spiritual qualifications in 1 Tim 3 and Titus 1 is imperative. If we do not, the system will have serious flaws and the leadership will lose credibility.

Fifth, elders need to learn that respect is earned, not demanded. We are to be "servant-leaders."

Sixth, elders need to learn that we are not the only ones who can "hear God," but we are nonetheless responsible for making certain that "God is heard."

Seventh, elders must be good listeners—to both God and those they serve.

Eighth, prayer has to be a priority for elders, both individually and collectively.

In terms of a workable form, I've come to believe that it's wise to set up some type of rotation system. In Albuquerque, we set up a plan under which each elder rotates out of the General Council of Elders every six years, but remains an elder who serves as a leader in becoming the eyes and ears of the congregation. Elders are welcome to return after a year's sabbatical, but they must go through the selection process again. This arrangement worked so well that when I came back to Woodland Park Baptist Church to once again serve as Senior Pastor, we included this clause in our constitution and bylaws.

My prayer is that my experiences and insights might be helpful, particularly to my Southern Baptist brothers. After a number of years of experience, I'm convinced that eldership with mutual accountability that is answerable to the congregation far exceeds any governance plan I've ever experienced. In fact, elders have been a part of the Southern Baptist life in years past. I believe the reason is rooted in the New Testament story of the church.

Gene A. Getz
Wayne Barber

Bibliography

Abbot, Walter M. *The Documents of Vatican II*. Angelus Book 31185. New York: Guild, 1966.
Akin, Daniel L. "The Single-Elder-Led Church: The Bible's Witness to a Congregational/Single-Elder-Led Polity." In *Perspectives on Church Government: Five Views on Church Polity*, edited by Chad Owen Brand and R. Stanton Norman, 25–86. Nashville: Broadman & Holman, 2004.
Aquinas, Saint Thomas. *Commentary on Saint Paul's Epistle to the Ephesians*. Aquinas Scripture Series 2. Translated by Matthew L. Lamb. Albany, NY: Magi, 1966.
Arndt, William F., et al. *A Greek-English Lexicon of the New Testament and Other Early Christian Literature*. 4th ed. Chicago: University of Chicago Press, 1957.
Augustine, Aurelius. "Letters of St. Augustine." In vol. 1 of *The Nicene and Post-Nicene Fathers of the Christian Church*, edited by Philip Schaff. Oak Harbor, WA: Logos Research Systems, 1997. Electronic ed.
Barr, James. "The Literal, the Allegorical, and Modern Biblical Scholarship." *Journal for the Study of the Old Testament* 44 (1989) 3–17.
Barth, Karl. *The Doctrine of the Word of God*. Vol. 1 of *Church Dogmatics*. Edited by Geoffrey W. Bromiley and Thomas F. Torrance. Edinburgh: T. & T. Clark, 1956.
Bartholomew, Craig, Colin Greene, and Karl Möller, eds. *After Pentecost: Language and Biblical Interpretation*. Scripture and Hermeneutics 2. Grand Rapids: Zondervan, 2001.
Basil, Saint of Caesarea. "The Book of Saint Basil on the Spirit." In vol. 8 of *The Nicene and Post-Nicene Fathers of the Christian Church*, edited by Philip Schaff and Henry Wace. Second Series. Oak Harbor, WA: Logos Research Systems, 1997. Electronic ed.
Bennetch, John Henry. "Literal Interpretation." *Bibliotheca Sacra* 104 (1947) 350–58.
Berkhof, Louis. *Systematic Theology*. 4th ed. Grand Rapids: Eerdmans, 1941.
Blass, Friedrich, and Albert Debrunner. *A Greek Grammar of the New Testament and Other Early Christian Literature*. Translated by Robert Walter Funk. Chicago: University of Chicago Press, 1961.
Bornkamm, Günther. "Πρεσβυ'τερος." In vol. 6 of *The Theological Dictionary of the New Testament: Pe–R*, edited by Gerhard Friedrich and translated by Geoffrey W. Bromiley, 651–82. Grand Rapids: Eerdmans, 1968.
Brachlow, Stephen. *The Communion of Saints: Radical Puritan and Separatist Ecclesiology, 1570–1625*. Oxford: Oxford University Press, 1988.

Bibliography

Brand, Chad Owen. "Toward a Theology of Cooperation." In *The Mission of Today's Church: Baptist Leaders Look at Modern Faith Issues*, edited by R. Stanton Norman, 155–78. Nashville: Broadman & Holman, 2007.

Brand, Chad Owen, and R. Stanton Norman, eds. Introduction to *Perspectives on Church Government*, 1–25. Nashville: Broadman & Holman, 2004.

Brewster, Paul. "The Perspicuity of Scripture." *Faith and Mission* 22 (2005) 16–34.

Brown, Raymond E. "*EPISCOPĒ and EPISKOPOS*: The New Testament Evidence." *Theological Studies* 41 (1980) 322–38.

Brown, Robert McAfee. *The Spirit of Protestantism*. New York: Oxford University Press, 1961.

Brunner, Emil. *The Mediator: A Study of the Central Doctrine of the Christian Faith*. Translated by Olive Wyon. Philadelphia: Westminster, 1947.

Bultmann, Rudolf. "Is Exegesis without Presuppositions Possible?" In *Existence and Faith: Shorter Writings of Rudolf Bultmann*. Living Age Books 29, edited and translated by Schubert M. Ogden, 289–96. Cleveland: Meridian, 1960.

Burleson, Paul. "The Case for Elders: An Historical Study of Baptist Elders, Peter 5:1–4." Transcript of sermon delivered at Trinity Baptist Church, Norman, OK. *Bruner's Chapel Baptist Church*. http://brunerschapel.com/wp-content/uploads/2010/01/History-of-Eldership.pdf.

Burroughs, Jeremiah. *Gospel-Worship, or, The Right Manner of Sanctifying the Name of God: In General, and Particularly in These Three Great Ordinances: 1. Hearing the Word, 2. Receiving the Lord's Supper, 3. Prayer*. Edited by Don Kistler. 1648. Reprint, Morgan, PA: Soli Deo Gloria, 1990.

Burtchaell, James Tunstead. *From Synagogue to Church: Public Services and Offices in the Earliest Christian Communities*. Cambridge: Cambridge University Press, 1992.

Callahan, James Patrick. "*Claritas Scripturae*: The Role of Perspicuity in Protestant Hermeneutics." *Journal of the Evangelical Theological Society* 39 (1996) 353–72.

Calvin, Jean. *Institutes of the Christian Religion*. Edited by John T. McNeil and translated by Ford Lewis Battles. Library of Christian Classics. 1960. Reprint, Louisville: Westminster John Knox, 2006.

———. "The True Method of Giving Peace to Christendom and of Reforming the Church." In *In Defense of the Reformed Faith*, vol. 3 of *Tracts and Treatises*, edited by Thomas F. Torrance and translated by Henry Beveridge. 1547. Reprint, Grand Rapids: Eerdmans, 1958.

Campbell, R. Alastair. *The Elders: Seniority within Earliest Christianity*. Studies of the New Testament and Its World. Edinburgh: T. & T. Clark, 1994.

Carlson, Leland H. "Archbishop John Whitgift: His Supporters and Opponents." *Anglican and Episcopal History* 56 (1987) 285–301.

Carson, D. A. "Church, Authority in the." In *Evangelical Dictionary of Theology*, edited by Walter A. Elwell, 249–51. Grand Rapids: Baker, 1975.

Childs, B. S. "Critical Reflections on James Barr's Understanding of the Literal and the Allegorical." *Journal for the Study of the Old Testament* 46 (1990) 3–9.

Chisholm, Robert B., Jr. "Does God 'Change His Mind?'" *Bibliotheca Sacra* 152 (1995) 387–99.

———. "Does God Deceive?" *Bibliotheca Sacra* 155 (1998) 11–28.

Chrysostom, Saint John. "Homilies on the First Epistle of St. Paul to the Thessalonians." In vol. 13 of *The Nicene and Post-Nicene Fathers of the Christian Church, First Series*, edited by Philip Schaff. Oak Harbor, WA: Logos Research Systems, 1997. Electronic ed.

Clement, Saint Pope I of Rome. "The First Epistle of Clement to the Corinthians." In vol. 1 of *The Ante-Nicene Fathers: Translations of the Writings of the Fathers down to AD 325*, edited by Alexander Roberts, James Donaldson, and A. Cleveland Coxe. Oak Harbor, WA: Logos Research Systems, 1997. Electronic ed.

Cliffe, J. T. *Puritans in Conflict: The Puritan Gentry during and after the Civil Wars*. London: Routledge, 1988.

Clowney, Edmund P. "Presbyterianism." In *New Dictionary of Theology*, edited by Sinclair Ferguson, David F. Wright, and J. I. Packer. Master Reference Collection. Downers Grove, IL: InterVarsity, 1988.

Coenen, L. "Ἐπίσκοπος." In vol. 2 of *The New International Dictionary of New Testament Theology*. Edited by Colin Brown. Grand Rapids: Zondervan, 1986.

Cohen, Simon. "Sanhedrin." In vol. 2 of *The Wycliffe Bible Encyclopedia*. Edited by Charles F. Pfeiffer, Howard Frederic Vos, and John Rea. Chicago: Moody, 1975.

Collinson, Patrick. *The Elizabethan Puritan Movement*. Berkeley, CA: University of California Press, 1967.

Congar, Yves. *Tradition and Traditions: An Historical and a Theological Essay*. New York: Macmillan, 1967.

Cowen, Gerald P. *Who Rules the Church? Examining Congregational Leadership and Church Government*. Nashville: Broadman & Holman, 2003.

Cox, Geoffrey S. R. "The Emerging Organization of the Church in the New Testament, and the Limitations Imposed Thereon." *The Evangelical Quarterly* 38 (1966) 22–39.

Craik, Henry. *New Testament Church Order: Five Lectures*. Bristol: Mack, 1863.

Cyprian, Saint of Carthage. "The Epistles of Cyprian." In vol. 5 of *The Ante-Nicene Fathers: Translations of the Writings of the Fathers down to AD 325*, edited by Alexander Roberts, James Donaldson, and A. Cleveland Coxe. Oak Harbor, WA: Logos Research Systems, 1997. Electronic ed.

Dagg, John Leadley. *Church Order: A Treatise*. Philadelphia: American Baptist Publication Society, 1871.

Dana, H. E., and Julius R. Mantey. *A Manual of Grammar of the Greek New Testament*. New York: Macmillan, 1957.

Dana, H. E., and L. M. Sipes. *A Manual of Ecclesiology*. 2nd ed. Kansas City: Central Seminary, 1944.

Dargan, Edwin Charles. *Ecclesiology: A Study of the Churches*. Louisville: Dearing, 1897.

Daughters, Kenneth Alan. *New Testament Church Government: The Normative Church Government Structure of the New Testament*. Kansas City: Walterick, 1989.

Davidson, Samuel. *The Ecclesiastical Polity of the New Testament Unfolded; and Its Points of Coincidence or Disagreement with Prevailing Systems Indicated*. London: Jackson & Walford, 1854.

Davies, W. D. *A Normative Pattern of Church Life in the New Testament: Fact or Fancy?* London: Clarke, 1950.

Delivuk, John Allen. "Biblical Authority and the Proof of the Regulative Principle of Worship in *The Westminster Confession*." *Westminster Theological Journal* 58 (1996) 237–56.

Dever, Mark Edward. *A Display of God's Glory: Basics of Church Structure: Deacons, Elders, Congregationalism, and Membership*. Washington, DC: Center for Church Reform, 2001.

Bibliography

———. "The Doctrine of the Church." In *A Theology for the Church*, edited by Daniel L. Akin, 766–857. Nashville: Broadman & Holman, 2007.

———. *Nine Marks of a Healthy Church*. Wheaton, IL: Crossway, 2000.

Dodd, Charles Harold. *The Founder of Christianity*. New York: Macmillan, 1970.

Ellis, Karl C. "The Nature of Biblical Exegesis." *Bibliotheca Sacra* 137 (1980) 151–55.

Eppley, Dan. "Defender of the Peace: John Whitgift's Proactive Defense of the Polity of the Church of England in the Admonition Controversy." *Anglican and Episcopal History* 68 (1999) 312–35.

Erickson, Millard J. *Christian Theology*. 2nd ed. Grand Rapids: Baker, 1998.

———. "Polity." In *The Concise Dictionary of Christian Theology*, 155. Rev. ed. Wheaton, IL: Crossway, 2001.

Fee, Gordon D. *1 and 2 Timothy, Titus*. Vol. 13 of *New International Biblical Commentary*. Peabody, MS: Hendrickson, 1988.

———. *Gospel and Spirit: Issues in New Testament Hermeneutics*. Peabody, MS: Hendrickson, 1991.

———. "Reflections on Church Order in the Pastoral Epistles, with Further Reflection on the Hermeneutics of *ad hoc* Documents." *Journal of the Evangelical Theological Society* 28 (1985) 141–51.

Ferguson, Everett. *The Church of Christ: A Biblical Ecclesiology for Today*. Grand Rapids: Eerdmans, 1996.

Flew, Robert Newton. *Jesus and His Church: A Study of the Idea of the Ecclesia in the New Testament*. London: Epworth, 1938.

Foulkes, Francis. *The Letter of Paul to the Ephesians: An Introduction and Commentary*. Tyndale New Testament Commentaries. Grand Rapids: Eerdmans, 1989.

Frame, John. "Some Questions about the Regulative Principle." *Westminster Theological Journal* 54 (1992) 357–66.

Frost, Herbert. "Church Government: Church History." In *The Encyclopedia of Christianity*, edited by Erwin Fahlbusch et al. and translated by Geoffrey W. Bromiley. Oak Harbor, WA: Logos Research Systems, 1997. Electronic ed.

Fung, Ronald Y. K. "Function or Office? A Survey of the New Testament Evidence." *Evangelical Review of Theology* 8 (1984) 16–39.

Gaebelein, Frank E., et al., eds. *Ephesians-Philemon*. Vol. 11 of *The Expositor's Bible Commentary*. Grand Rapids: Zondervan, 1978.

Gane, Erwin R. "The Exegetical Methods of Some Sixteenth-Century Puritan Preachers: Hooper, Cartwright, and Perkins." *Andrews University Seminary Studies* 19 (1981) 21–36.

Garrett, James Leo, Jr. "The Congregation-Led Church: Congregational Polity." In *Perspectives on Church Government: Five Views on Church Polity*, edited by Chad Owen Brand and R. Stanton Norman, 157–208. Nashville: Broadman & Holman, 2004.

———. *Systematic Theology: Biblical, Historical, and Evangelical*. Vol. 2. Grand Rapids: Eerdmans, 1995.

Getz, Gene A. *Elders and Leaders: God's Plan for Leading the Church: A Biblical, Historical, and Cultural Perspective*. Chicago: Moody, 2003.

———. *Sharpening the Focus of the Church*. Chicago: Moody, 1974.

Goncharenko, Simon Victor. *Wounds That Heal: The Importance of Church Discipline Within Balthasar Hubmaier's Theology*. Eugene, OR: Pickwick, 2012.

Gordon, T. David. "Some Answers about the Regulative Principle." *Westminster Theological Journal* 55 (1993) 321–29.
Gore, Ralph J. "Reviewing the Puritan Regulative Principle of Worship." *Presbyterion* 20 (1994) 41–50.
———. "Reviewing the Regulative Principle Part II." *Presbyterion* 21 (1995) 29–47.
Graves, James Robinson. "A 'Landmark' Our Fathers Set." In *Old Landmarkism: What Is It?*, edited by J. M. Pendleton. 1899. Reprint, Walker, WV: Truth, 1980.
Grayston, K., and G. Herdan. "The Authorship of the Pastorals in the Light of Statistical Linguistics." *New Testament Studies* 6 (1959) 1–15.
Grenz, Stanley J. *The Baptist Congregation: A Guide to Baptist Belief and Practice*. Valley Forge, PA: Judson, 1985.
Griffith, Benjamin. "A Short Treatise Concerning a True and Orderly Gospel Church (1743)." In *Polity: Biblical Arguments on How to Conduct Church Life*, edited by Mark Dever, 95–114. Washington, DC: Center for Church Reform, 2001.
Grudem, Wayne A. *Systematic Theology: An Introduction to Biblical Doctrine*. Grand Rapids: Zondervan, 1994.
Guthrie, Donald. *The Pastoral Epistles: An Introduction and Commentary*. Tyndale New Testament Commentaries 14. Grand Rapids: Eerdmans, 1984.
Haller, William. *The Rise of Puritanism*. New York: Harper, 1957.
Hammett, John S. *Biblical Foundations for Baptist Churches: A Contemporary Ecclesiology*. Grand Rapids: Kregel, 2005.
Hannah, John D. *Our Legacy: The History of Christian Doctrine*. Colorado Springs: NavPress, 2001.
Harper, Michael. "Duplicating the New Testament Church." *Eternity* 29 (1978) 24–27.
Harrison, Percival Neale. *The Problem of the Pastoral Epistles*. London: Oxford University Press, 1921.
Harvey, A. E. "Elders." *Journal of Theological Studies* 25 (1974) 318–32.
Hay, Alexander Rattray. *The New Testament Order for Church and Missionary*. 2nd rev. ed. Dieren, Netherlands: H. H. Blok, 1947.
Hillstrom, Leonard H. "The New Testament Teaching on Church Elders." ThD diss., Grace Theological Seminary, 1980.
Hodge, Charles. *Discussions in Church Polity*. New York: Scribner's Sons, 1878.
———. *Systematic Theology*. Oak Harbor, WA: Logos Research Systems, 1997. Electronic ed.
Hoehner, Harold W. "Ephesians." In vol. 2 of *The Bible Knowledge Commentary: An Exposition of the Scriptures*, edited by John F. Walvoord and Roy B. Zuck. Oak Harbor, WA: Logos Research Systems, 1997. Electronic ed.
Hooker, Richard. "The Seventh Book. Their Sixth Assertion, *That There Ought not to be in the Church, Bishops Indued with Such Authority and Honour as Ours Are*." In *Of the Laws of Ecclesiastical Polity, Books 6–8*, edited by Paul G. Stanwood, 37–55. Folger Library Edition of the Works of Richard Hooker 3. Cambridge, MS: Belknap, 1981.
Ignatius, Saint Bishop of Antioch. "The Epistle of Ignatius to the Magnesians." In vol. 1 of *The Ante-Nicene Fathers: Translations of the Writings of the Fathers down to AD 325*, edited by Alexander Roberts, James Donaldson, and A. Cleveland Coxe. Oak Harbor, WA: Logos Research Systems, 1997. Electronic ed.
Irenaeus, Saint Bishop of Lyon. "Irenaeus: Against Heresies." In vol. 1 of *The Ante-Nicene Fathers: Translations of the Writings of the Fathers down to AD 325*, edited

Bibliography

by Alexander Roberts, James Donaldson, and A. Cleveland Coxe. Oak Harbor, WA: Logos Research Systems, 1997. Electronic ed.

Johnson, Alan F. "A Response to Problems of Normativeness in Scripture: Cultural Versus Permanent." In *Hermeneutics, Inerrancy, and the Bible*, edited by Earl D. Radmacher and Robert D. Preus, 257–82. Grand Rapids: Academie, 1984.

Johnson, Dale. "Time, Scripture and Tradition: A Historical Survey of the Sufficiency of Scripture." In *Written for Our Instruction: The Sufficiency of Scripture for All of Life*, edited by Joseph A. Pipa and J. Andrew Wortman. Taylors, SC: Southern Presbyterian, 2001.

Johnson, Elliott E. "Author's Intention and Biblical Interpretation." In *Hermeneutics, Inerrancy, and the Bible*, edited by Earl D. Radmacher and Robert D. Preus, 409–429. Grand Rapids: Academie, 1984.

———. "What I Mean by Historical-Grammatical Interpretation and How That Differs from Spiritual Interpretation." *Grace Theological Journal* 11 (1990) 157–69.

Johnson, W. B. "The Gospel Developed through the Government and Order of the Churches of Jesus Christ (1846)." In *Polity: Biblical Arguments on How to Conduct Church Life*, edited by Mark Dever, 161–248. Washington, DC: Center for Church Reform, 2001.

Johnston, George. *The Doctrine of the Church in the New Testament*. Cambridge: Cambridge University Press, 1943.

Jones, Hywel R. *Thomas Cartwright, 1535–1603*. Evangelical Library Annual Lecture, 1970. London: Evangelical Library, 1970.

Jones, Samuel. "A Treatise of Church Discipline and a Directory Done by Appointment of the Philadelphia Baptist Association (1798)." In *Polity: Biblical Arguments on How to Conduct Church Life*, edited by Mark Dever, 137–60. Washington, DC: Center for Church Reform, 2001.

Kaiser, Walter C. "A Response to Author's Intention and Biblical Interpretation." In *Hermeneutics, Inerrancy, and the Bible*, edited by Earl D. Radmacher and Robert D. Preus, 441–47. Grand Rapids: Academie, 1984.

———. *Toward an Exegetical Theology: Biblical Exegesis for Preaching and Teaching*. Grand Rapids: Baker, 1981.

Keathley, J. Hampton, III. "The Bible: Understanding Its Message." *Bible.org*. June 3, 2004, accessed November 30, 2007. https://bible.org/seriespage/bible-understanding-its-message.

Kelly, J. N. D. *A Commentary on the Pastoral Epistles: I Timothy, II Timothy, Titus*. Harper's New Testament Commentaries. New York: Harper & Row, 1963.

Kerkham, Andrew. "1689 Baptist Confession of Faith." *Grace Reformed Baptist Church*. http://www.grbc.net/about_us/1689.php.

Kern, John A. *A Study of Christianity as Organized, Its Ideas and Forms*. 3rd ed. Nashville: Cokesbury, 1928.

Kiffin, William. *A Sober Discourse of Right to Church-Communion*. London: Larkin, 1681.

Klein, William W., et al. "Preunderstandings and the Interpreter." In *Rightly Divided: Readings in Biblical Hermeneutics*, edited by Roy B. Zuck, 75–84. Grand Rapids: Kregel, 1996.

Klooster, Fred H. "The Role of the Holy Spirit in the Hermeneutic Process: The Relationship of the Spirit's Illumination to Biblical Interpretation." In *Hermeneutics, Inerrancy, and the Bible*, edited by Earl D. Radmacher and Robert D. Preus, 451–72. Grand Rapids: Academie, 1984.

Bibliography

Knight, George W., III. "Church Government." In *Written for Our Instruction: The Sufficiency of Scripture for All of Life*, edited by Joseph A. Pipa and J. Andrew Wortman. Taylors, SC: Southern Presbyterian, 2001.

———. *The Pastoral Epistles: A Commentary on the Greek Text*. New International Greek Testament Commentaries. Grand Rapids: Eerdmans, 1992.

———. "A Response to Problems of Normativeness in Scripture: Cultural Versus Permanent." In *Hermeneutics, Inerrancy, and the Bible*, edited by Earl D. Radmacher and Robert D. Preus, 243–53. Grand Rapids: Academie, 1984.

———. "The Scriptures Were Written for Our Instruction." *Journal of the Evangelical Theological Society* 39 (1996) 3–13.

———. "Two Offices (Elder/Bishops and Deacons) and Two Orders of Elders (Preaching/Teaching Elders and Ruling Elders) A New Testament Study." *Presbyterion* 11 (1985) 1–12.

Knox, John. *The Early Church and the Coming Great Church*. Hoover Lectures. Nashville: Abingdon, 1955.

Koivisto, Rex A. *One Lord, One Faith*. Wheaton, IL: Victor, 1993.

Kraft, Charles H. "Interpreting in Cultural Context." In *Rightly Divided: Readings in Biblical Hermeneutics*, edited by Roy B. Zuck, 245–57. Grand Rapids: Kregel, 1996.

Küng, Hans. *The Church*. New York: Sheed & Ward, 1967.

Ladd, George Eldon. "Historic Premillennialism." In *The Meaning of the Millennium: Four Views*, edited by Robert C. Clouse, 17–40. Downers Grove, IL: InterVarsity, 1977.

Lambert, J. C. "Church." In vol. 1 of *The International Standard Bible Encyclopedia*, edited by James Orr et al. Chicago: Howard-Severance, 1915.

Lane, A. N. S. "Scripture and Tradition." In *New Dictionary of Theology*, edited by Sinclair B. Ferguson and David F. Wright. Master Reference Collection. Downers Grove, IL: InterVarsity, 1988.

———. "Scripture, Tradition and Church: An Historical Survey." *Vox Evangelica* 9 (1975) 37–55.

Lewis, Edwin. "Constructive Statements: Evangelical." In *The Ministry and the Sacraments: Report of the Theological Commission Appointed by the Continuation Committee of the Faith and Order Movement*, edited by Roderic Dunkerley. New York: Macmillan, 1937.

Liefeld, Walter L. "Leadership and Authority in the Church." In *In God's Community: Essays on the Church and Its Ministry*, edited by David J. Ellis and W. Ward Gasque, 29–39. Wheaton, IL: Shaw, 1978.

Lightfoot, J. B. *Saint Paul's Epistle to the Philippians*. Grand Rapids: Zondervan, 1956.

Lincoln, Andrew T. *Ephesians*. Vol. 42 of *Word Biblical Commentary*. Edited by David A. Hubbard et al. Waco, TX: Word, 1990.

Lindsay, Thomas Martin. *The Church and the Ministry in the Early Centuries: The Eighteenth Series of the Cunningham Lectures*. Minneapolis: James Family, 1977.

Lloyd-Jones, D. Martyn. "Henry Jacob and the First Congregational Church." In vol. 4 of *Puritan Papers, 1965–1967*, edited by J. I. Packer. 1966. Reprint, Phillipsburg, NJ: Presbyterian & Reformed, 2004.

Longman, Tremper, III. "What I Mean by Historical-Grammatical Exegesis—Why I Am not a Literalist." *Grace Theological Journal* 11 (1990) 137–55.

Luther, Martin. "Against the Heavenly Prophets in the Matter of Images and Sacraments." In *Church and Ministry II*, vol. 40 of *Luther's Works*, edited by Conrad Bergendoff

Bibliography

and Helmut T. Lehmann, and translated by Bernhard Erling, 73–223. 1525. Reprint, Philadelphia: Muhlenberg, 1958.

———. *The Babylonian Captivity of the Church*. In *Word and Sacrament II*, vol. 36 of *Luther's Works*, edited by Abdel Ross Wentz and Helmut T. Lehmann, and translated by A. T. W. Steinhäuser, 3–126. 1520. Reprint, Philadelphia: Muhlenberg, 1959.

MacArthur, John F. *The Master's Plan for the Church*. Chicago: Moody, 1991.

———. "Perspicuity of Scripture: The Emergent Approach." *Master's Seminary Journal* 17 (2006) 141–58.

Mackenzie, D. "Views of Modern Churches: Reformed American." In *The Ministry and the Sacraments: Report of the Theological Commission Appointed by the Continuation Committee of the Faith and Order Movement*, edited by Roderic Dunkerley. New York: Macmillan, 1937.

Maddox, Timothy D. F. "Scripture, Perspicuity, and Postmodernity." *Review and Expositor* 100 (2003) 555–85.

Mappes, David. "The 'Elder' in the Old and New Testaments." *Bibliotheca Sacra* 154 (1997) 80–92.

———. "The 'Laying on of Hands' of Elders." *Bibliotheca Sacra* 154 (1997) 473–79.

———. "The New Testament Elder, Overseer, and Pastor." *Bibliotheca Sacra* 154 (1997) 162–74.

Marshall, I. Howard. "The Holy Spirit and the Interpretation of Scripture." In *Rightly Divided: Readings in Biblical Hermeneutics*, edited by Roy B. Zuck, 66–74. Grand Rapids: Kregel, 1996.

Martin, Ralph P. "Authority in the Light of the Apostolate, Tradition and the Canon." *Evangelical Quarterly* 40 (1968) 66–82.

Mason, Arthur James. "Conceptions of the Church in Early Times." In *Essays on the Early History of the Church and the Ministry*, edited by Henry Barclay Swete, 1–56. London: Macmillan, 1918.

Mayer, Marvin Edward. "An Exegetical Study on the New Testament Elder." ThD diss., Dallas Theological Seminary, 1970.

Mell, P. H. "Corrective Church Discipline: With a Development of the Scriptural Principles upon Which It Is Based (1860)." In *Polity: Biblical Arguments on How to Conduct Church Life*, edited by Mark Dever, 409–478. Washington, DC: Center for Church Reform, 2001.

Merkle, Benjamin L. "The Elder and Overseer: One Office in the Early Church." PhD diss., Southern Baptist Theological Seminary, 2000.

Michaels, J. Ramsey. "Scripture, Tradition, and Biblical Scholarship." *The Reformed Journal* 20 (1970) 14–17.

Miller, David W. "The Uniqueness of New Testament Church Eldership." *Grace Theological Journal* 6 (1985) 315–27.

Mitton, C. Leslie. *Ephesians*. Vol. 56 of *New Century Bible Commentary*. Edited by Ronald E. Clements and Matthew Black. Grand Rapids: Eerdmans, 1973.

Moede, Gerald F. *The Office of Bishop in Methodism: Its History and Development*. New York: Abingdon, 1964.

Morris, Edward D. *Ecclesiology: A Treatise on the Church and Kingdom of God on Earth*. New York: Scribner, 1885.

Morris, Leon. *Ministers of God*. Great Doctrines of the Bible. London: InterVarsity, 1964.

Moulton, James Hope. *A Grammar of New Testament Greek*. Edinburg: T. & T. Clark, 1908.

Mounce, William D. *Basics of Biblical Greek Grammar.* 2nd ed. Grand Rapids: Zondervan, 2003.
Murray, John. *The Claims of Truth.* Vol. 1 of *Collected Writings of John Murray: Professor of Systematic Theology, Westminster Theological Seminary, Philadelphia, Pennsylvania, 1937-1966.* Carlisle, PA: Banner of Truth Trust, 1976.
Nelson, J. Robert. *The Realm of Redemption: Studies in the Doctrine of the Nature of the Church in Contemporary Protestant Theology.* London: Epworth, 1951.
New, John F. H. "The Whitgift-Cartwright Controversy." *Archiv für Reformationsgeschichte* 59 (1968) 203-212.
Newton, Phil A. *Elders in Congregational Life: Rediscovering the Biblical Model for Church Leadership.* Grand Rapids: Kregel, 2005.
Norman, R. Stanton. "Together We Grow: Congregational Polity as a Means of Corporate Sanctification." In *The Mission of Today's Church: Baptist Leaders Look at Modern Faith Issues,* edited by R. Stanton Norman, 95-110. Nashville: Broadman & Holman, 2007.
Norton, John. *The Answer to the Whole Set of Questions of the Celebrated Mr. William Apollonius, Pastor of the Church of Middelburg, Looking toward the Resolution of Certain Controversies Concerning Church Government Now Being Agitated in England.* Translated by Douglas Horton. Cambridge, MS: Belknap, 1958.
O'Brien, Peter T. *The Letter to the Ephesians.* Vol. 10 of *The Pillar New Testament Commentary.* Edited by D. A. Carson. Grand Rapids: Eerdmans, 1999.
Orru, Marco. "Anomy and Reason in the English Renaissance." *Journal of the History of Ideas* (1986) 177-96.
Osborne, Grant R. *The Hermeneutical Spiral: A Comprehensive Introduction to Biblical Interpretation.* 2nd rev. ed. Downers Grove, IL: InterVarsity, 2006.
Packer, J. I., ed. *Puritan Papers: 1968-1969.* Vol. 5. Phillipsburg, NJ: Presbyterian & Reformed, 2005.
Pastor of Hermas. "Visions." In vol. 2 of *The Ante-Nicene Fathers: Translations of the Writings of the Fathers down to AD 325,* edited by Alexander Roberts, James Donaldson, and A. Cleveland Coxe. Oak Harbor, WA: Logos Research Systems, 1997. Electronic ed.
Patterson, Paige. "Single-Elder Congregationalism." In *Who Runs the Church? Four Views on Church Government,* edited by Steven B. Cowan, 131-52. Counterpoints. Grand Rapids: Zondervan, 2004.
———. "A Single-Elder Congregationalist's Response." In *Who Runs the Church? Four Views on Church Government,* edited by Steven B. Cowan, 168-84. Counterpoints. Grand Rapids: Zondervan, 2004.
Pendleton, J. M. *Church Manual: Designed for the Use of Baptist Churches.* Philadelphia: Judson, 1958.
———. *An Old Landmark Re-Set.* 1899. Reprint, Walker, WV: Truth Publications, 1980.
Perkins, Pheme. *Ephesians.* Edited by Victor Paul Furnish et al. Abingdon New Testament Commentaries. Nashville: Abingdon, 1997.
Perrott, M. E. C. "Richard Hooker and the Problem of Authority in the Elizabethan Church." *Journal of Ecclesiastical History* 49 (1998) 29-60.
Pettegrew, Larry Dean. "The Perspicuity of Scripture." *Master's Seminary Journal* 15 (2004) 209-225.
Phillips, Richard D., Philip G. Ryken, and Mark E. Dever. *The Church: One, Holy, Catholic, and Apostolic.* Phillipsburg, NJ: Presbyterian & Reformed, 2004.

Bibliography

Pipa, Joseph A., Jr., and J. Andrew Wortman, eds. *Written for Our Instruction: The Sufficiency of Scripture for All of Life*. Taylors, SC: Southern Presbyterian, 2001.

Potter, John. *A Discourse of Church Government*. London: Tegg, 1861.

Powers, Beaumont Ward. "Patterns of New Testament Ministry—Elders." *Churchman* 87 (1973) 166–81.

Quick, O. C. "The Doctrine of the Church of England on Sacraments." In *The Ministry and the Sacraments: Report of the Theological Commission Appointed by the Continuation Committee of the Faith and Order Movement*, edited by Roderic Dunkerley. New York: Macmillan, 1937.

Radmacher, Earl D. *The Nature of the Church*. Portland, OR: Western Baptist, 1972.

———. *The Question of Elders*. Portland, OR: Western Baptist, 1977.

———. "A Response to Author's Intention and Biblical Interpretation." In *Hermeneutics, Inerrancy, and the Bible*, edited by Earl D. Radmacher and Robert D. Preus. Grand Rapids: Academie, 1984.

Ramm, Bernard L. *Protestant Biblical Interpretation: A Textbook of Hermeneutics*. 3rd rev. ed. Grand Rapids: Baker, 1970.

Ratzinger, Joseph. *Called to Communion: Understanding the Church Today*. Translated by Adrian Walker. San Francisco: Ignatius, 1996.

Reicke, B. "Προϊστημι." In vol. 6 of *The Theological Dictionary of the New Testament: Pe–R*, edited by Gerhard Friedrich and translated by Geoffrey W. Bromiley, 700–703. Grand Rapids: Eerdmans, 1968.

Reymond, Robert L. "The Presbytery-Led Church: Presbyterian Church Government." In *Perspectives on Church Government: Five Views on Church Polity*, edited by Chad Owen Brand and R. Stanton Norman, 87–157. Nashville: Broadman & Holman, 2004.

Reynolds, J. L. "Church Polity, or The Kingdom of Christ in Its Internal and External Development (1849)." In *Polity: Biblical Arguments on How to Conduct Church Life*, edited by Mark Dever, 295–408. Washington, DC: Center for Church Reform, 2001.

R. H. S. "Steward." In *Harper's Bible Dictionary*, edited by Paul J. Achtemeier et al. San Francisco: Harper & Row, 1985.

Robertson, A. T. *A Grammar of the Greek New Testament in the Light of Historical Research*. Nashville: Broadman & Holman, 1934.

Roloff, Jürgen. "Church Government: Early Church Tendencies." In *The Encyclopedia of Christianity*, edited by Erwin Fahlbusch et al. and translated by Geoffrey W. Bromiley. Oak Harbor, WA: Logos Research Systems, 1997. Electronic ed.

Ryrie, Charles Caldwell. *Basic Theology*. Wheaton, IL: Victor, 1988.

———. *Biblical Theology of the New Testament*. Chicago: Moody, 1959.

———. *Dispensationalism*. Rev. ed. Chicago: Moody, 2007.

———. "The Pauline Doctrine of the Church." *Bibliotheca Sacra* 115 (1958) 62–67.

Saucy, Robert L. *The Church in God's Program*. Chicago: Moody, 1972.

Schaeffer, Francis A. *The Church at the End of the 20th Century*. Downers Grove, IL: InterVarsity, 1970.

Schnackenburg, Rudolf. *Ephesians: A Commentary*. Translated by Helen Heron. Edinburgh: T. & T. Clark, 1991.

Schneiders, Sandra M. "Faith, Hermeneutics, and the Literal Sense of Scripture." *Theological Studies* 39 (1978) 719–36.

Bibliography

Schrage, W. "Αρχισυνα'γωγος." In vol. 7 of *Theological Dictionary of the New Testament*, edited by Gerhard Friedrich and translated by Geoffrey W. Bromiley, 798–851. Grand Rapids: Eerdmans, 1971.

Schweizer, Eduard. *Church Order in the New Testament*. Studies in Biblical Theology 32. London: SCM, 1959.

Schwöbel, Christoph. "The Creature of the Word: Recovering the Ecclesiology of the Reformers." In *On Being the Church: Essays on the Christian Community*, edited by Colin E. Gunton and Daniel W. Hardy, 110–55. Edinburgh: T. & T. Clark, 1989.

Shedd, William Greenough Thayer. *Dogmatic Theology*. Edited by Alan W. Gomes. 3rd ed. Phillipsburg, NJ: Presbyterian & Reformed, 2003.

Smith, Frank Joseph. "What Is Worship?" In *Worship in the Presence of God*, edited by David C. Lachman and Frank Joseph Smith. Greenville, SC: Greenville Seminary, 1992.

Sobosan, Jeffrey G. "The Role of the Presbyter: An Investigation into the *Adversus Haereses* of Saint Irenaeus." *Scottish Journal of Theology* 27 (1974) 129–46.

Stevens, Gerald L. *New Testament Greek*. 2nd ed. Lanham, MD: University Press of America, 1997.

Stöckhardt, George. *Commentary on St. Paul's Letter to the Ephesians*. Translated by Martin S. Sommer. Concordia Heritage. Saint Louis: Concordia, 1952.

Strauch, Alexander. *Biblical Eldership: An Urgent Call to Restore Biblical Leadership*. Littleton, CO: Lewis & Roth, 1995.

Strong, Augustus Hopkins. *Systematic Theology: A Compendium Designed for the Use of Theological Students*. Valley Forge, PA: Judson, 1907.

Sutton, Jerry. "Congregational Polity and Its Strategic Limitations." In *The Mission of Today's Church: Baptist Leaders Look at Modern Faith Issues*, edited by R. Stanton Norman, 111–26. Nashville: Broadman & Holman, 2007.

Swanson, James. *Dictionary of Biblical Languages with Semantic Domains: Hebrew (Old Testament)*. Oak Harbor, WA: Logos Research Systems, 1997. Electronic ed.

Tan, Randall K. J. "Recent Developments in Redaction Criticism: From Investigation of Textual Prehistory Back to Historical-Grammatical Exegesis?" *Journal of the Evangelical Theological Society* 44 (2001) 599–614.

Tanner, Norman, P., ed. "*Decrees of the First Vatican Council*: Chapter 4. On the Infallible Teaching Authority of the Roman Pontiff." *Papal Encyclicals Online*. January 9, 1998. http://www.papalencyclicals.net/Councils/ecum20.htm.

Taylor, L. Roy. "Presbyterianism." In *Who Runs the Church? Four Views on Church Government*, edited by Steven B. Cowan, 71–98. Counterpoints. Grand Rapids: Zondervan, 2004.

Terry, Milton Spenser. *Biblical Hermeneutics: A Treatise on the Interpretation of the Old and New Testaments*. Grand Rapids: Zondervan, 1974.

Tertullian. "The Chaplet." In vol. 3 of *The Ante-Nicene Fathers: Translations of the Writings of the Fathers down to AD 325*, edited by Alexander Roberts, James Donaldson, and A. Cleveland Coxe. Oak Harbor, WA: Logos Research Systems, 1997. Electronic ed.

———. "The Prescription against Heretics." In vol. 3 of *The Ante-Nicene Fathers: Translations of the Writings of the Fathers down to AD 325*, edited by Alexander Roberts, James Donaldson, and A. Cleveland Coxe. Oak Harbor, WA: Logos Research Systems, 1997. Electronic ed.

Bibliography

Thiselton, Anthony C. *The Two Horizons: New Testament Hermeneutics and Philosophical Description with Special Reference to Heidegger, Bultmann, Gadamer, and Wittgenstein*. Grand Rapids: Eerdmans, 1980.

Thomas, J. Mark. "Worshiping a Place That Isn't God." *Christianity and Crisis* (1982) 26–29.

Thon, Nikolaus. "Church Government: Orthodox Church." In *The Encyclopedia of Christianity*, edited by Erwin Fahlbusch et al. and translated by Geoffrey W. Bromiley. Oak Harbor, WA: Logos Research Systems, 1997. Electronic ed.

Toon, Peter. "Episcopalianism." In *Who Runs the Church? Four Views on Church Government*, edited by Steven B. Cowan, 19–41. Counterpoints. Grand Rapids: Zondervan, 2004.

———. "An Episcopalian's Response." In *Who Runs the Church? Four Views on Church Government*, edited by Steven B. Cowan, 42–48. Counterpoints. Grand Rapids: Zondervan, 2004.

Torrance, Thomas F. *God and Rationality*. New York: Oxford University Press, 1971.

———. "The Israel of God." *Interpretation* 10 (1956) 305–320.

Uprichard, Harry. *A Study Commentary on Ephesians*. Evangelical Press Commentary. Auburn, MA: Evangelical, 2004.

Van Engen, J. "Tradition." In *Evangelical Dictionary of Theology*, edited by Walter A. Elwell, 1211–13. 2nd ed. Baker Reference Library. Grand Rapids: Baker, 2001.

Vanhoozer, Kevin J. *Is There a Meaning in This Text? The Bible, the Reader, and the Morality of Literary Knowledge*. Grand Rapids: Zondervan, 1998.

Vincent, Saint of Lérins. "The Commonitory." In vol. 11 of *The Nicene and Post-Nicene Fathers of the Christian Church*, edited by Philip Schaff and Henry Wace. Second Series. Oak Harbor, WA: Logos Research Systems, 1997. Electronic ed.

Virkler, Henry A. "A Proposal for the Transcultural Problem." In *Rightly Divided: Readings in Biblical Hermeneutics*, edited by Roy B. Zuck, 231–44. Grand Rapids: Kregel, 1996.

Von Schlatter, Adolf. *The Church in the New Testament Period*. Translated by Paul P. Levertoff. London: Society for Promoting Christian Knowledge, 1961.

Von Schmidt, Karl Ludwig. "Die Kirche des Urchristentums." In *Festgabe für Adolf Deissmann: zum 60. Geburtstag 7. November 1926*, edited by Druck von H. Laupp. Tübingen: Mohr, 1927.

Waldron, Samuel E. "Plural-Elder Congregationalism." In *Who Runs the Church? Four Views on Church Government*, edited by Steven B. Cowan, 185–221. Counterpoints. Grand Rapids: Zondervan, 2004.

———. "A Plural-Elder Congregationalist's Response." In *Who Runs the Church? Four Views on Church Government*, edited by Steven B. Cowan, 237–52. Counterpoints. Grand Rapids: Zondervan, 2004.

Wallace, Daniel B. "What Is the Head Covering in 1 Corinthians 11:2–16 and Does It Apply to Us Today?" *Bible.org*. June 26, 2004, accessed November 30, 2007. https://bible.org/article/what-head-covering-1-cor-112-16-and-does-it-apply-us-today.

———. "Who Should Run the Church? A Case for the Plurality of Elders." *Bible.org*. May 25, 2004, accessed November 30, 2007. https://bible.org/article/who-should-run-church-case-plurality-elders.

Walvoord, John F. "The Theological Context of Premillennialism." *Bibliotheca Sacra* 150 (1993) 387–96. 1951.

Ward, Timothy. "Reconstructing the Doctrine of the Sufficiency of Scripture." *Tyndale Bulletin* 52 (2001) 155–59.

Wasser, Greg. "Pastor-Elder-Overseer." *Calvary Baptist Theological Journal* 4 (1988) 61–75.
Waterworth, J., trans. "The Council of Trent: The Fourth Session." In *The Canons and Decrees of the Sacred and Oecumenical Council of Trent*, 17–21. London: Dolman, 1848. Hanover College History Department. 1995, accessed 13 October 2007. http://history.hanover.edu/texts/trent/ct04.html.
Webber, Robert E., ed. *Twenty Centuries of Christian Worship*. Complete Library of Christian Worship 2. Nashville: Star Song, 1994.
Webster, John B. *Holy Scripture: A Dogmatic Sketch*. Current Issues in Theology 1. New York: Cambridge University Press, 2003.
Weeks, Noel. *The Sufficiency of Scripture*. Carlisle, PA: Banner of Truth Trust, 1988.
White, James R. "The Plural-Elder-Led Church: Sufficient as Established—The Plurality of Elders as Christ's Ordained Means of Church Governance." In *Perspectives on Church Government: Five Views on Church Polity*, edited by Chad Owen Brand and R. Stanton Norman, 255–96. Nashville: Broadman & Holman, 2004.
White, L. Michael. *Building God's House in the Roman World: Architectural Adaptation among Pagans, Jews, and Christians*. ASOR Library of Biblical and Near Easter Archaeology. Baltimore: Johns Hopkins University Press, 1990.
Whitgift, John. "The Works of John Whitgift." In *The First Portion Containing the Defence of the Answer to the Admonition, against the Reply of Thomas Cartwright*, vol. 1 of *The Works of John Whitgift*, edited by John Ayre. Parker Society. Cambridge: Cambridge University Press, 1851. http://www.prdl.org/author_view.php?a_id=85.
Whiting, C. E. *Studies in English Puritanism from the Restoration to the Revolution, 1660–1688*. Publications NS 5. New York: Macmillan, 1931.
Whyte, Alexander. *An Exposition on the Shorter Catechism, Includes the Westminster Confession and the Larger Catechism*. Fearn, UK: Christian Focus, 2004.
Williams, Rowan. "The Literal Sense of Scripture." *Modern Theology* 7 (1991) 121–34.
Williams, William. "Apostolical Church Polity (1874)." In *Polity: Biblical Arguments on How to Conduct Church Life*, edited by Mark Dever, 527–52. Washington, DC: Center for Church Reform, 2001.
Winer, Georg Benedikt. *A Treatise on the Grammar of New Testament Greek: Regarded as a Sure Basis for New Testament Exegesis*. Translated by W. F. Moulton. 3rd rev. ed. Edinburg: Clark, 1882.
Yarnell, Malcolm B., III. "Article VI: The Church." In *Baptist Faith and Message 2000: Critical Issues in America's Largest Protestant Denomination*, edited by Douglas K. Blount and Joseph D. Wooddell, 55–70. Lanham, MD: Rowman & Littlefield, 2007.
———. *The Formation of Christian Doctrine*. Nashville: Broadman & Holman, 2007.
———. "On the Priesthood of Believers: Rediscovering the Biblical Doctrine of Royal Priesthood." In *Restoring Integrity in Baptist Churches*, edited by Thomas White, Jason G. Duesing, and Malcolm B. Yarnell, III. Grand Rapids: Kregel, 2008.
———. "The TULIP of Calvinism: In Light of History and the Baptist Faith and Message." *SBC Life* 15. April 2006, accessed January 18, 2008, http://www.sbclife.org/articles/2006/04/sla8.asp.
Zuck, Roy B. *Basic Bible Interpretation: A Practical Guide to Discovering Biblical Truth*. Wheaton, IL: Victor, 1991.
———. "The What and Why of Bible Interpretation." In *Rightly Divided: Readings in Biblical Hermeneutics*, edited by Roy B. Zuck, 13–29. Grand Rapids: Kregel, 1996.

Bibliography

Zwingli, Ulrich, and Martin Luther. *Luther's and Zwingli's Propositions for Debate: The Ninety-five Theses of 31 October, 1517, and the Sixty-seven Articles of 19 January, 1523.* Translated by Carl Stamm Meyer. Textus Minores 30. 1523. Reprint, Leiden: Brill, 1963.

Index

Note: Biblical references are collected under the heading "Scripture references."

Abbott, Walter M., 39n40
accountability, 141, 142
adiaphorist stance, 2–3
Agabus, 65
aggelō, 96
agrupnousin, 96
Akin, Daniel L., 26, 103, 107, 127
Alexandrian guild, 119
allegorical interpretation, 52–53, 54, 77
allegory, 52m118–119
Ambrosiaster, 66n51
American Baptists, 107
American expansion, 89
Ananias, 16
Andronicus, 62, 73n91
Anglican Church
    administration of church discipline, 17
    consecration of Lord's Supper, 17
    episcopal model of polity, 12–17
    justification for episcopal polity, 13n30
    role of bishops, 12–14, 16–17
    role of laity, 15, 16
    view of baptism, 16, 17
apdosōntes, 96
apocalyptic literature, 52, 96
apocrypha, 38n37
Apollos, 73n91
apostles
    Anglican bishops as successors of, 13–14
    authority and responsibilities of, 65n48
    Biblical roles of, 25
    calling of as origin of the church, 56
    criteria for, 63
    defined, 62–63
    as foundation of church, 10, 62–70
    as gift and office, 73n91
    interpretation of Old Testament Scriptures, 53
    Peter as leader of, 115–17
    as prophets, 65
    role in early church, 13n30
    role in episcopal model, 15
    work of, 63
apostolic succession
    appeal to in response to Gnostics, 36n24
    episcopal polity based on, 13–14, 82–84
    historical absence of, 83
    justification for authority of tradition, 38n37
    lack of instruction for, 82–83
    as legal fiction, 67–68
    priesthood of all believers vs., 83
    uniqueness of office, 83
apostolic tradition, 35–36, 42–43
apostolos, 62
application of Scripture, 10, 76–80
Aquinas, Saint Thomas, 66n51
archbishops, 1n2

Index

archdeacons, 1n2
"Article VI: The Church" (Yarnell), 126–27
assistants to church leaders, 1n2, 141
Augustine, Saint, 36
autonomy, 20–21, 24–25, 46, 92

The Babylonian Captivity of the Church (Luther), 38
baptism in Holy Spirit, 56–57, 59–60
baptism in water, 4, 16, 17, 36m29, 131n105
Baptist churches, 24, 89, 126–27
Baptist Union of the USSR, 5n18
Barber, Wayne, 107, 141–44
Barnabas
  as apostle, 62, 62n39, 73n91
  appointment of elders, 13, 101
  gift of prophecy, 65
  ministry to Gentiles, 116
Barrowe, Henry, 24, 107n116
Basil of Caesarea, Saint, 36
Benedict XVI (pope), 68
Bennetch, John Henry, 48
Berkhof, Louis, 20n61, 21n64, 22–23, 63, 64n44
Bible. *See* Scripture; Scripture references
Bible churches, 24
Biblical Foundation for Baptist Churches (Hammett), 133
Binney, Thomas, 24
bishops
  duties and selection of, 1n2
  episcopal model and, 82
  first appearance and development of, 15n38
  methodist concept of, 12n21
  overseer as synonymous with, 74–75, 82
  role in episcopal model, 12–14, 16–17
blasphemy, 34
Blomberg, Craig L., 30
Brachlow, Stephen, 2
Brand, Chad Owen, 8
Brown, Robert McAfee, 30–31
Browne, Robert, 24, 24n82

Bultmann, Rudolf, 10n18, 30n3, 52m118–19
Burleson, Paul, 89
Burroughs, Jeremiah, 46–47

Calvin, John
  on apostles and prophets, 67
  establishment of presbyterian polity, 18, 23
  invention of ruling and teaching elders, 85
  propagation of doctrine of illumination, 41
  on relationship between Scripture and church, 44–46
  on role of the apostles, 63
  on supremacy of Scripture, 38, 39
  view of church polity, 75
Campbell, Alexander, 90
Campbell, R. Alastair, 76, 80, 108–9, 119n49, 121–22
Campbell, Thomas, 90
Campbellism, 90
canonization of Scripture, 35, 37, 43–45, 62
Carson, D. A., 131n106
Cartwright, Thomas, 1–3
checks and balance system, 98
Christ. *See* Jesus Christ
Christocracy, 24
Christology, 44
Chrysostom, Saint John, 42, 66n51
church
  Anglican view of, 12
  apostles and prophets as foundation of, 10, 62–70
  authority of, 43
  coincidence of Scripture, tradition and, 35–36
  as creation of the Word of God, 39–40
  defined, 54
  dependence upon spiritual gifts of members, 20–21, 58–59
  dominant images of supporting congregationalism, 86
  earliest meetings, 61
  emulation of elders, 114–15

160

Index

episcopal view of, 14
episcopal view of origin of, 15–16, 61–62, 84
as household of God, 100–101
interrelationship of parts, 20n61
local autonomy, 20–21, 24–25, 92
meetings in early years, 26, 91–93
ministry of, 1n2
New Testament vs. episcopal model, 82
as offshoot of Israel, 56n3
Pentecost as birth of, 10, 56–62
practices in New Testament, 4
presbyterian view of origin of, 61
Scripture's divinely instituted authority over, 43–44
views of origin of, 55–56
visible unity of, 20, 21n64
church discipline
Anglican administration of, 17
Biblical references, 25n87
Cartwright's view of, 3
in congregational polity, 28, 108
congregationalism based on, 23–24
early church practice, 4
excommunication, 108
in presbyterian polity, 22–23
role of congregation, 113n12
role of elders in, 113
in single-elder-led congregationalism, 97
church doctrine, Scripture's supremacy over, 33–47
Church of Christ, 90
church polity
biblical pattern for, 4, 6
Cartwright's view of, 1n2
congregational model, 23–28, 86–109, 137–41
congregation-led form, 5
danger of abandoning plural-eldership, 130–132
defined, 8
episcopal model, 11–17, 61, 82–84
flexible, expedient form, 4–5
presbyterian model, 5, 17–23, 61, 84–86
primary models, 11

Scriptural instructions for, 100–101
sufficiency of Scripture for, 3–6
See also multiple-elder congregationalism; single-elder led congregationalism
circuit-riding preachers, 89
circumcision, 16
classis, 20, 21n64
Clement, 106
clergy
in congregational polity, 26
in presbyterian polity, 21
See also bishops; elders
Coenen, L., 74, 75
coincidence view, 35
Coivisto, Rex A., 29
communion. *See* Lord's Supper
Congar, Yves, 8, 42n62
Congregational church, 24n82
congregational model of polity
appeal to individual responsibility, 88
biblical defense of, 25, 86–109
church discipline, 28
concept of democracy, 24–25
deacon-board-led, 24, 99–100
decision making by whole body, 108–9
democratic congregationalism, 24, 25–26
doctrinal purity maintained by, 86–87
dominant images of church supporting, 86
effects of multi-elder model on, 126
epistles to churches supporting, 86
function of elders, 27–28
inevitability of, 87–88
no-government-but-the-Holy-Spirit congregationalism, 24n85
origins of, 23–24
prevention of doctrinal drift, 87
priesthood of all believers supporting, 26–27
principle of autonomy, 24, 25
of Russian Baptist churches, 5n18
staff-led congregationalism, 24n85
trustee-led congregationalism, 24, 88–89n38

161

Index

congregational model of polity (*continued*)
  See also multiple-elder congregationalism; single-elder led congregationalism
Constitution of Sparta, 119
context, 50
contradictions, 48n93, 52
corporate worship and life, 61
corporate-board congregationalism, 24n85
Council of Nicaea (325), 62
Council of Trent (1546), 38
courts, 19–20
Cowen, Gerald P., 28, 73n91, 88n38
Coxe, Nehemiah, 5n18, 105
Craik, Henry, 11
culture-bound principles, 77–79
Cyprian, 14

Dagg, John Leadley, 88
Dale, Robert William, 24
Dana, H. E., 25n87, 65n49, 99
Dargan, Edwin Charles, 8, 90–91, 107, 129
Daughters, Kenneth Alan
  discussion of views of polity, 5n18
  pastor as gift, 73n91
  on plurality of elders, 89, 92, 104–5
  qualifications for deacons, 100
  on role of leadership, 131
  on selection of leadership, 136
  on single-elder polity, 132
  suggestions for elders, 133–34
Davidson, Samuel, 64n44, 65n48, 135
Davies, W. D., 5n18
deacon-board-led congregationalism, 24, 99–100
deacons
  duties and qualifications of, 99–100
  job description, 65n49
  plurality of, 93
  role in congregational polity, 26
  role in episcopal model, 16–17
  role in presbyterian polity, 22
decision making, 104, 108–9, 126

Decree Concerning the Edition and the Use of Sacred Books (Council of Trent), 38
definitive understanding, 10n18
democracy, 23, 25
democratic congregationalism, 24–25, 90
Dever, Mark Edward, 87, 98, 107, 112
Devonshire Square Church of London, England, 105
Didache, 36n24
Disciples of Christ, 90
distributive plural in Greek, 127–28
Doddridge, Phillip, 24

Eastern Orthodox Church, 12, 13n29, 37n33
ecumenical councils, 37n33
ēgeomai, 113–14
ēgoumenōn, 96
ēgoumenous, 96
eisegesis, 127
ekklesia, 25, 57–58
elalēan, 96
elder rule practice, 85
elders
  accountability of, 141
  advantages of multiple-elder led congregationalism, 104–5
  appointment of, 13, 139
  argument for separate roles of overseer and pastor, 73n91
  attitude of, 133–34
  care of church as fathers, 140
  in congregational polity, 23, 26–28
  as cultural adaptation, 118–23
  duties and qualifications of, 100, 102, 104–5, 111–15, 139–40
  early church's understanding of, 108–9
  establishment as group of leaders, 70n73
  financial remuneration for, 117–18, 141
  initial and primary, 140
  New Testament role of, 85
  as newly defined office, 80
  number needed, 115

Index

Old Testament model of, 120
overseer and pastor synonymous with, 10, 18, 25–26, 70–75, 82
pastoral ministry of, 112–13
patterned after Exodus 18, 54
plurality of in New Testament churches, 88–99, 102
presbyter as synonymous with, 74–75
primary leader of, 115–17
role in episcopal model, 12–13, 82
role in presbyterian polity, 18–19, 21–22, 23, 84–85
as teachers, 112
titles of, 140
unity of team, 139
use of term in Old and New Testament, 70–71
See also multiple-elder congregationalism; overseer; pastor; single-elder led congregationalism
Elders and Leaders (Getz), 139
The Encyclopedia of Christianity, 82
Ephesian church, 101
episcopacy, 5n18
Episcopal Church, 12
episcopal model of polity
  apostolic succession, 82–84
  failures of leadership, 105
  hierarchical structure of, 12–14, 75, 82
  historical support of, 13
  lack of biblical support for, 82–84
  ordination in, 13–14, 83
  origin of the church, 15–16, 61, 84
  reliance on tradition, 46n80
  role of bishop, 13–17, 82
  role of laity, 15
  roots of, 23
  view of baptism and circumcision, 16
  Whitgift-Cartwright-Harrison debate on, 2
episkopois, 93
episkopos
  antecedent of, 71
  episcopal polity's separation from *presbuteros*, 82
  interchangeability with *presbuteros* and *poimēn*, 25–26, 73–74
  New Testament use of, 82
  reference to elder's qualifications, 95
  role in episcopal polity, 11–15
  as role of elders, 113
  use in term prior to New Testament, 71
  See also overseer
episkopountes, 18n53, 74
episkopous, 73
Epistle to the Magnesians (Ignatius), 106
epistles, 86. See also specific epistle under Scripture references
Erickson, Millard J., 25
evangelists, 64n44, 67
excommunication, 22–23, 108
exegesis, 9, 30–32
exegetical abuse of Scripture, 49–50
experience, Scripture's supremacy over, 33–47
exposition, 9
extrabiblical doctrines, 36n29, 37

Fairbairn, Andrew Martin, 24
faith, relationship to the Word, 40
fasting, 36m29
Fee, Gordon D., 9, 31, 34, 125n87
Fellowship Bible Church, 137–39
Ferguson, Everett, 59, 60–61
First Vatican Ecumenical Council, 38–39
Fitz, Richard, 24n82
Flew, Robert Newton, 56n3
forgiveness in Jesus' name, 61
forms, 141
foundational theological principles. See hermeneutics
Frost, Herbert, 4, 5n18
Fung, Ronald Y. K., 5n18

Garrett, James Leo, Jr., 5n18, 5n20, 13n29, 23, 24, 25, 88
Getz, Gene
  on Barnabus' apostleship, 62n39
  biblical references to plurality of elders, 93n58, 101–3
  on elders as role models, 115
  experience of elder-led model of church polity, 137–41

163

Index

Getz, Gene (*continued*)
  on Peter as primary leader of apostles, 115–16
  on Peter's leadership, 115, 116
  principles for selection of elders, 134n120, 140–141
  representative polity advocated by, 112n5, 113n12
  summary of gift of prophecy, 65
  view of local church polity, 92
Gideons International, 43
gifts
  apostles, prophets, and pastors as, 64–67, 73n91
  church's dependence on, 20–21, 58–59
  for function of the church, 5–6
  of prophecy, 64, 66
  required for deacons, 100
  required for pastoring, 104
  sent following Jesus' ascension, 58–59
  of teaching and ruling, 21, 41
  See also spiritual gifts
Gnostics, 36
God's sovereignty, 18
Goncharenko, Simon Victor, 138
gospel, beginning of preaching of, 60–61
Gospel and Spirit (Fee), 9
governmental connectionalism, 19–21, 85
graded assemblies, 19–20, 85–86
grammatical-historical exposition, 47–53
Griffith, Benjamin, 107n119
Grudem, Wayne, 7, 24n85, 94, 98, 100, 104, 126

Hammett, John S.
  on congregationalism, 86, 88, 92
  distinction between *episkopos* and *presbuteros*, 82
  on duties of elders, 114–15
  endorsement of plurality of elders, 107
  on episcopalianism, 84
  on origin of the church, 57
  on presbyterianism, 85
  recommendations for transition to plurality of elders, 133, 134n120
  on temporality of apostleship, 67
Harper, Michael, 5n18, 82n2, 82n6
Harvey, A. E., 120, 121
Hay, Alexander Rattray, 104
hazzan, 122n65
head covering, 78
hermeneia, 9
hermeneuō, 8–9
hermeneutical circle/spiral, 31
hermeneutics
  apostles and prophets as foundation of church, 10, 62–70, 82–84
  application to congregational polity, 86–109
  application to episcopal polity, 82–84
  application to presbyterian polity, 84–85
  clear passages illuminate ambiguous ones, 103
  defined, 8–9
  genesis of principles, 32
  influence on exegesis, 6
  interchangeability of pastor, elder, and overseer, 10, 70–75, 82, 84–86, 87–88
  interpretation preceding application, 10, 76–80
  literal interpretation of Scripture, 10, 47–54, 82, 85–86
  Pentecost as origin of the church, 10, 55–62, 84
  supremacy of Scripture over tradition and church, 10, 33–47, 83–84, 88–90, 98–99
hierarchical governing bodies, 12–16, 19–20, 85–86
Hillstrom, Leonard, 123
historic episcopate, 13n30
historical context, 50
Hodge, Charles, 43
Hoehner, Harold W., 73n91
Holiness denominations, 12
Holy Spirit
  descent on Pentecost as origin of church, 56–57, 59–60

Index

illumination of believers, 40–42, 44
as leader of congregationalism, 24
Hooker, Richard, 13–14, 67
Hubbard, Robert I., 30

Ignatius, Saint, 83, 105
illumination doctrine, 40–42
illustrations, 52
individualism, 89
indulgences, 37
infant baptism, 36m29, 54
initial leader, 140
Institutes of the Christian Religion (Calvin), 18
Institutes of the Christian Tradition (Calvin), 39, 63
interpretation, application following, 10, 76–80
Irenaeus of Lyons, 13n30, 36, 83
Israel, 54
Israeli religious hierarchy, 12

Jacob, Henry, 24n82
James (half-brother of Jesus)
as apostle, 73n91
expectations for churches, 86
leadership in Jerusalem, 13, 15n38, 27, 94, 116–17
writings to churches, 95
Jay, William, 24
Jerome, 66n51
Jerusalem church
as first New Testament church, 56
James as primary elder of, 13, 15n38, 27, 94, 116–17
meetings of, 92–93
as pattern for single-elder polity, 91–93
plurality of elders in, 101, 102, 108, 122
presbyterian interpretation of leadership of, 20, 85
prophets in, 65
subgroups of, 127
Jerusalem Council, 20, 69, 85
Jesus Christ
appointment of apostles, 63, 64
ascension associated with origin of the church, 56, 58–59, 60
calling of disciples as origin of the church, 56
as chief cornerstone of the church, 15
command to wait for the coming of the Holy Spirit, 57, 59
establishment of church, 13n30
giving of apostles, prophets, and evangelists, 66–67
as Great Shepherd, 72, 74
installation of Paul, 84
as leader of apostles, 115
as lord of congregationalism, 24
prayer for unity of the church, 20
prediction of Peter's leadership, 61–62
proclamation as Messiah, 60
references to church, 57
Jewish elders, 12, 12n27, 21, 70–71
John (apostle), 86
John Mark, 116
Johnson, Alan F., 77, 78, 79
Johnson, Dale, 37, 38–39n37, 43
Johnson, Elliott E., 50, 53n125
Johnson, W. B., 107
Jones, Samuel, 107
Judas, 65
Jude, 65
Junias, 62, 73n91

Keach, Benjamin, 105
Kern, John A., 23–24, 74n98, 89
Kiffin, William, 33–34, 46, 105
Klein, William W., 30
Klooster, Fred H., 31, 32, 42
Knight, George W., III, 21n67, 72, 74n98
Knollys, Hanserd, 105
Knox, John, 5n18

laity
in congregational polity, 28
in presbyterian polity, 21
role in episcopal model, 15, 16
role on presbyterian polity, 22
Lambert, J. C., 5n18
landmarkism, 90

165

Index

Lane, A. N. S., 32, 35n22, 36n28, 37, 38–39n37, 39
Last Supper, as origin of the church, 56
Latin Vulgate, 38n37
Of the Lawes of Ecclesiasticall Politie (Hooker), 13–14
laying on of hands, 14n32
leadership of the church, 113, 139–41. *See also* bishops; elders; multiple-elder congregationalism; overseer; pastor; prophets; single-elder led congregationalism
lexicology, 51
Liefeld, Walter L., 6n23
Lightfoot, J. B., 120, 121
Lincoln, Andrew T., 66–67
Lindsay, Thomas Martin, 67–68, 83, 86, 122
literal interpretation of Scripture
  acknowledgement of progression of revelation, 51–52
  benefits of, 54
  episcopal polity and, 82
  as fundamental hermeneutic principle, 10
  grammatical-historical exposition, 47–54
  in historical context, 50
  negation of episcopal model, 82
  in original languages, 51
  rejection of allegorical interpretations, 52–53
  Scripture interprets Scripture, 51
  single-elder led congregationalism and, 99
Lloyd-Jones, D. Martin, 24n82
local church autonomy, 20–21, 24–25, 92
Longman, Tremper, III, 53n127
Lord's Supper, 4, 17, 131n105
Lucius, 65
Luke, 58, 59, 61, 65. *See also* Luke and Acts under Scripture references
Luther, Martin
  critique of Scholasticism, 89
  on literal interpretation of Scripture, 47, 48n93
  rediscovery of priesthood of all believers, 26
  view of Scripture and tradition, 37–38, 42
Lutheran Church, 12

MacArthur, John F., 28, 57
magisterium, 51
Manaen, 65
Mappes, David, 70n73, 73n91, 74, 122–23n70
Mariology, 37
Mark, 64, 65
Marshall, I. Howard, 42
Martin, Ralph P., 5n18
Matthew, 57
Matthias, 62
Mayer, Marvin Edward, 71, 110
Mell, P. H., 107n119
Methodist Church, 12, 13n29
Metropolitan Tabernacle of London, England, 105
Miller, David, 119, 120, 121, 122
ministers, calling and selection of, 1n2. *See also* apostles; deacons; elders; pastor; prophets
model of primitive church government, 1–3
monarchial bishop, 75, 105
monarchial episcopate, 129
monarchial succession, 83
morphology, 51
Morris, Edward D., 5n18, 121
Moses, 27
multiple-elder congregationalism
  advantages of, 98
  Barber's experience with, 141–44
  biblical defense of, 10, 27, 100–103, 110
  biblical mandate for implementation of, 123–26
  church discipline in, 97–98
  churches employing, 24
  as cultural adaptation, 118–23
  dangers of abandoning, 10, 130–132
  decline of in Baptist churches, 89
  difficulties arising from, 129
  effect on congregationalism, 126

Getz's experience with, 137–41
historical proof of, 105–9
pragmatic and theological soundness of, 104–5
responsibilities of elders, 111–15
role of pastor, 75
root of objections to, 129
suggestions for application, 132–35, 139–41, 143–44
supracultural principles for, 139–41
as un-Baptist and un-biblical, 126–28
Murray, John, 112–13n10

The Nature of the Church (Radmacher), 58
New Testament
canonization of, 35, 43–45, 62
fulfillment of Old Testament prophecies in, 50, 53
occurrences of *presbuteros* and *presbuteroi*, 70
pattern for church structure, 4
prophets of, 64–66
See also Scripture; Scripture references
Newton, Phil A., 74–75, 104n99, 107, 126
no-government-but-the-Holy-Spirit congregationalism, 24n85
Norman, R. Stanton, 8, 86, 88n36
normativeness of biblical instruction, 78–80

officers, 14–15, 23, 26–28. See also bishops; deacons; elders
official appointment of leaders, 139
oikodomēsō, 57n11
oikonomos, 113
oitines, 96
Old Testament
as authority for early church, 35
as pattern for church polity, 12n27, 14, 21, 27, 54, 61, 80, 117–18
prophecies fulfilled in New Testament, 50, 53
prophets of, 66
spiritualizing interpretation of, 52–53

use of *presbuteros* and *presbuteroi*, 70
See also Scripture references
ordination
in episcopal polity, 12n28, 13–15
lack of biblical support for, 83
in presbyterian polity, 19, 21
Osborne, Grant R., 78–79
overseer
argument for separate roles of elders and pastor, 73n91
bishop as synonymous with, 74–75, 82
elder and pastor synonymous with, 10, 18, 25–26, 70–75, 82
use of term in New Testament, 71
See also *episkopos*
oversight of the church, 113
Owen, John, 24

papacy, 36n24, 37n33, 38n37, 39
papyri, 70, 71–72
paradidomi, 34n17
Parker, Joseph, 24
Particular Baptists, 106–7
parts of speech, 51
pastor
argument for separate roles of overseer and elders, 73n91
early church's understanding of, 108–9
in multiple-elder congregationalism, 27
overseer and elders synonymous with, 10, 18, 25–26, 70–75, 82
relationship to teachers, 72n87
role in New Testament church, 96
seven angels of seven churches as, 27, 96–97
in single-elder-led congregationalism, 26–27
as spiritual gift, 73n91
See also elders; overseer; *poimēn*
Pastor of Hermas, 55
Pastoral Leadership-Congregational Rule. See single-elder led congregationalism
pastoral ministry, 112–13
patriarch of Constantinople, 13n29

Index

Patterson, Paige, 56, 107n120, 123–25, 127, 134
Paul (apostle)
  acknowledgement of James as leader, 117
  appointment of, 73n91, 84
  appointment of elders, 13, 101
  arrest and persecution of, 65
  baptism of, 16
  charge to elders, 83
  defense of apostolic authority, 25, 84
  definition of gospel, 61
  directions to Timothy, 64n44
  establishment of Holy See associated with, 36n24
  expectations for churches, 86
  ministry of, 62, 116
  ordination of Titus, 15
  reference to church as mystery, 58
  securing offerings for destitute churches, 25n87
pentarchy, 13n29
Pentecost
  as birth of the church, 10, 56–62
  new events on, 59–61
Pentecostal denominations, 12
perspicuity of Scripture, 42–43, 48n93
Peter, 36n24, 59, 74, 86, 95, 115–17
Philip, 64, 65
Philippi church, 102
plural-eldership. *See* multiple-elder congregationalism
Plymouth Brethren, 24, 118n47
pneumatology, 44
pneumatophoria, 24
poimainein, 72, 73, 74
poimanate, 74
poimanō, 72
poimēn, 25–26, 71–72, 73–74. *See also* pastor
poimena, 74
Potter, John A., 12n27, 15, 15n37, 15n39, 16
Powers, Beaumont Ward, 76, 103, 126
presbuterion, 18
presbuteroi, 70–71, 119
presbuteros
  antecedent of, 71
  elder as synonymous with, 74
  episcopal polity's separation from *episkopos*, 82
  interchangeability with *episkopos* and *poimēn*, 25–26, 73–74
  occurrences in New Testament, 18, 70–71
  occurrences in Septuagint and papyri, 70
  rendered "old man," 96
  use of term in Greek and Egyptian documents, 119
  See also elders
presbyter
  elder as synonymous with, 74–75
  role in episcopal model, 12–13, 16–17
  See also elders
presbyterian model of polity
  church discipline, 22–23
  governmental connectionalism, 19–21, 85
  hierarchical governing bodies, 17–18, 20, 69, 85–86, 126
  lack of biblical support for, 84–86
  ordination in, 19
  origin of the church, 18, 61
  precise model for church polity, 5
  role of deacons, 22
  role of elders, 18–19, 21–22, 84–85
  role of laity, 21
  roots of, 23
  Whitgift-Cartwright-Harrison debate on, 2
Presbyterian-Reformed tradition, 2n5
prescriptive hermeneutics, 53n125
presuppositionless exegesis, 30–32
pre-understanding, 10n18
priest (Jewish), 12n27, 14, 117–18
priesthood of all believers
  abandonment of plural-eldership and, 130–131
  ability to interpret Scripture associated with, 43
  apostolic succession and, 83
  democracy of congregationalism based on, 25
  elder rule practice as violation of, 85

168

Index

support of congregationalism, 26
primary leader, 140
principlizing, 77–78
private sins, 22–23
proistēmi, 85, 114
prophecy, fulfillment in New Testament, 50, 53
prophets
    as foundation of church, 10, 64–70
    recognition and testing of, 64n47
    role in early church, 13n30
    role in episcopal model, 15
Protestant Reformation, 18, 37–38, 51, 75
public sins, 22–23
Puritan Congregationalists, 3n10, 106–7

The Question of Elders (Radmacher), 132–33
Quick, O. C., 16n45

Radmacher, Earl D., 57n11, 58, 60, 73n91, 85, 98, 104, 132–33
Ramm, Bernard L., 49–50, 53, 76
Ratzinger, Cardinal Joseph, 46, 68
reason, Scripture's supremacy over, 33–47
Reformation, 18, 37–38, 51, 75
"Reformation without Tarrying for Any" (Browne), 24n82
Reformers
    view of church hierarchy, 75
    view of Scripture, 37–38, 42–43
    See also Calvin, John; Luther, Martin
regulative principle of worship, 3n10
revelation, 51–54
Reymond, Robert L., 5n18, 5n19, 20n61–62, 21n64, 21n67
Reynolds, J. L., 68, 107n119
role model, 114–15
Roloff, Jürgen, 82
Roman Catholic Scholasticism, 89
Roman Catholicism
    authority of tradition, 35–39
    church hierarchical interpretation of Scripture, 42–43
    Council of Nicaea, 62
    Council of Trent, 38
    ecclesiology of, 46
    episcopal model of polity, 11–12, 54
    First Vatican Ecumenical Council, 38–39
    Latin Vulgate with apocrypha accepted, 38n37
    sacramentarianism of, 54
    Second Vatican Council, 39
    teaching of magisterium, 51
rule of faith, 35n22
ruling elders, 21, 84–85
Russian Baptist churches, 5n18
Ryken, Philip, 69
Ryrie, Charles Caldwell, 51–52, 58–59, 73n91

sacramentarianism, 54
salvation, 16
Sanhedrin, 120–121
Saucy, Robert L., 15n38, 23, 67, 82, 85
Sawyer, M. James, 105
Scandinavian Lutheranism, 13n29
Schaeffer, Francis A., 5n18
Schneiders, Sandra M., 31
Schrage, W., 122n65
Schupp, James, 134
Schweizer, Eduard, 4, 5n18, 63, 64n47, 74n99, 131n105
Schwöbel, Christoph, 39n43
Scripture
    canonization of, 35, 37, 43–45, 62
    coincidence view, 35–36
    divinely instituted authority over church, 43–44
    episcopal polity's reliance on tradition over, 83–84
    hermeneutics principles for interpretation of. *See* hermeneutics
    illumination doctrine, 40–42
    inerrancy and infallibility of, 30
    interpretation by Scripture, 51
    interpretation from original languages, 51
    interpretation preceding application, 10, 76–80
    literal interpretation of, 10, 47–54, 82, 99

Index

Scripture (*continued*)
  perspicuity of, 42–43, 48n93
  progressive revelation of, 51–54
  relationship to faith, 40
  sufficiency of, 3–4, 5–6, 7–8
  supplementary view, 36
  supremacy over tradition and church, 33–47, 88–90, 98–99
  translation into vernacular, 42n61, 43
  See also New Testament; Old Testament
Scripture references
  Genesis 17:10, 52
  Genesis 43:19, 113n14
  Genesis 44:1, 113n14
  Genesis 44:4, 113n14
  Exodus 18, 27, 54
  Exodus 20:8, 52
  Leviticus 4–5, 61
  Leviticus 16, 61
  Numbers 4:16, 71
  Numbers 11:16–17, 21
  Numbers 27:17, 74
  Numbers 31:14, 71
  Deuteronomy 25:4, 117–18
  Judges 9:28, 71
  1 Samuel 8:4, 120
  1 Kings 16:9, 113n14
  1 Kings 18:3, 113n14
  1 Chronicles 29:6, 113n14
  2 Chronicles 34:12, 71
  2 Chronicles 34:17, 71
  Esther 1:8, 113n14
  Job 20:29, 71
  Psalms 19:7–8, 41n50
  Psalms 22, 50
  Psalms 43:3–4, 41n50
  Psalms 78:38, 61
  Isaiah 7:14, 50
  Isaiah 36:3, 113n14
  Isaiah 53:1–12, 50
  Micah 5:2, 50
  Matthew 4:4, 112
  Matthew 10:1–4, 62
  Matthew 10:5–7, 52
  Matthew 13:52, 21
  Matthew 15:1–9, 118
  Matthew 15:2, 120
  Matthew 16, 62
  Matthew 16:18, 57
  Matthew 16:21, 18n52
  Matthew 18:15–17, 22, 120
  Matthew 18:15–20, 25
  Matthew 18:17, 28, 57, 108, 113n12
  Matthew 18:19, 17
  Matthew 20:8, 113n14
  Matthew 21:23, 18n52
  Matthew 23:34, 21
  Matthew 26:3, 18n52
  Matthew 26:47, 18n52
  Matthew 26:57, 18n52
  Matthew 27:1, 18n52
  Matthew 27:3, 18n52
  Matthew 27:12, 18n52
  Matthew 27:20, 18n52
  Matthew 27:41, 18n52
  Matthew 27:51, 130
  Matthew 28:18–20, 52
  Mark 1:14–15, 61
  Mark 2:1–12, 61
  Mark 3:14, 63, 83
  Mark 7:5, 120
  Mark 8:29–30, 60
  Mark 9:9, 60
  Mark 10:42–44, 98
  Mark 16:16, 16
  Luke, 58
  Luke 4:20, 122n65
  Luke 6:13, 62, 63
  Luke 8:3, 61, 113n14
  Luke 9:3, 52
  Luke 12:44, 113n14
  Luke 15:25, 18n52
  Luke 16:1–8, 113n14
  Luke 22:36, 52
  Luke 22:66, 18, 120
  Luke 24:27, 9
  Luke 24:29, 59
  John 1:17, 52
  John 1:42, 9
  John 3:5, 16
  John 6:63, 41
  John 7:39, 60
  John 8:9, 18n52
  John 10:2, 72
  John 10:10–13, 20

John 10:11, 72
John 10:11-13, 112
John 10:12, 72
John 10:14, 72
John 10:16, 72
John 13:14, 78
John 13:29, 61
John 14:17, 60
John 15:27, 63
John 16:12-15, 41n50
John 16:24, 52
John 17:3, 41n50
John 17:20-21, 20
John 21:25, 116
John 21:26, 72
Acts, 58
Acts 1, 57, 57n13
Acts 1 and 2, 1-3
Acts 1:5, 59, 60
Acts 1:8, 59
Acts 1:13, 63
Acts 1:15, 116
Acts 1:21-22, 63, 73n91
Acts 1:21-26, 25n89
Acts 1:26, 62
Acts 2, 56, 59, 60, 61
Acts 2:2, 59
Acts 2:17, 96
Acts 2:38, 16, 61
Acts 2:40, 63
Acts 2:41, 57
Acts 2:41-42, 4
Acts 2:42, 4, 41n53, 61, 63
Acts 2:42-47, 92
Acts 2:44-45, 61
Acts 2:46, 4, 26n97
Acts 2:46-47, 61
Acts 2:47, 4
Acts 4:5-8, 120
Acts 4:31, 63
Acts 4:33, 63
Acts 5:12, 63
Acts 5:21, 41n53
Acts 5:25, 41n53
Acts 5:42, 41n53
Acts 6, 64n44, 65, 93, 99, 100
Acts 6:3, 25, 134
Acts 9:26-28, 25n89

Acts 9:27, 62n39
Acts 10, 59
Acts 10:44-46, 59
Acts 11, 65
Acts 11:15, 59, 60
Acts 11:16, 59
Acts 11:22, 92
Acts 11:26, 41n53
Acts 11:27, 67
Acts 11:30, 18n52, 21, 94n64, 99, 101, 108
Acts 12:5, 92-93
Acts 12:12, 26n97
Acts 12:17, 26n97, 116
Acts 13, 85
Acts 13:1, 65, 67
Acts 13:1-3, 19-20
Acts 13:2, 67
Acts 13:2-3, 25
Acts 13:13, 116
Acts 14:4, 73n91
Acts 14:4-14, 62
Acts 14:14, 73n91
Acts 14:23, 13, 18n52, 27n105, 91n50, 94, 101
Acts 15, 20, 25n87, 27, 69, 85, 120, 126
Acts 15:2, 18n52, 94, 94n64, 101
Acts 15:3, 19-20
Acts 15:4, 18n52, 20n62, 94n64, 101, 119
Acts 15:6, 18n52, 94n64, 101
Acts 15:7-11, 116-17
Acts 15:13, 13
Acts 15:13-21, 117
Acts 15:22, 18n52, 25, 101
Acts 15:22-23, 94n64
Acts 15:23, 101
Acts 15:28, 63
Acts 15:32, 65, 67
Acts 15:35, 20
Acts 16:4, 20, 27n105, 91n50, 94n64, 101
Acts 18:11, 41n53
Acts 19:6, 67
Acts 20:7, 52
Acts 20:17, 18n53, 27, 27n105, 73, 83, 91n50, 95, 101, 119

Index

Scripture references (*continued*)
  Acts 20:17–18, 91
  Acts 20:20, 41n53
  Acts 20:28, 18, 18n53, 58, 72, 73, 74, 74n97, 83, 91, 101, 102, 112
  Acts 20:28–31, 111, 138
  Acts 20:29–31, 112
  Acts 20:32, 112
  Acts 21:9, 65
  Acts 21:9, 10, 67
  Acts 21:10–14, 65
  Acts 21:18, 26n97, 27n105, 91n50, 94n64, 102, 117, 119
  Acts 21:28, 41n53
  Acts 22:5, 18
  Acts 22:16, 16
  Acts 26:10–11, 92
  Acts 28:31, 41n53
  Romans 12:6, 67
  Romans 12:7, 41n53
  Romans 12:8, 21, 111, 114n17
  Romans 15:4, 4
  Romans 15:5–6, 20
  Romans 16:3–5, 26n97
  Romans 16:7, 62, 73n91
  Romans 16:10–11, 26n97
  Romans 16:14–15, 26n97
  Romans 16:23, 26n97, 113n14
  1 Corinthians 1:10–13, 20
  1 Corinthians 2:9—3:3, 41n50
  1 Corinthians 2:12–13, 40–41
  1 Corinthians 2:13, 63
  1 Corinthians 3:6, 62n36, 64n45, 68
  1 Corinthians 3:10, 62n36, 63, 68
  1 Corinthians 4:1, 113n14
  1 Corinthians 4:2, 113
  1 Corinthians 4:6, 73n91
  1 Corinthians 4:9, 73n91
  1 Corinthians 5:1–13, 120
  1 Corinthians 5:2, 4, 25
  1 Corinthians 5:4, 108, 113n12
  1 Corinthians 5:4, 5, 25n87, 28
  1 Corinthians 5:13, 22
  1 Corinthians 6:4, 25n87
  1 Corinthians 8, 78
  1 Corinthians 9:1, 63
  1 Corinthians 9:1–2, 62n38
  1 Corinthians 9:3, 118
  1 Corinthians 9:4, 118
  1 Corinthians 9:6, 73n91
  1 Corinthians 9:7, 72
  1 Corinthians 9:8, 118
  1 Corinthians 9:9, 118
  1 Corinthians 9:16, 118
  1 Corinthians 9:17, 113n14
  1 Corinthians 10:12, 64n45
  1 Corinthians 11, 67
  1 Corinthians 11:16, 25n87
  1 Corinthians 12, 66
  1 Corinthians 12:12–13, 20
  1 Corinthians 12:13, 60
  1 Corinthians 12:28, 21
  1 Corinthians 12:28–31, 62n36
  1 Corinthians 14, 67
  1 Corinthians 14:27–35, 65
  1 Corinthians 14:29ff, 64n47
  1 Corinthians 15:1–5, 61
  1 Corinthians 15:8–9, 62n38, 73n91
  1 Corinthians 16:2, 4
  1 Corinthians 16:3, 25n89
  1 Corinthians 16:15, 26n97
  1 Corinthians 16:19, 26n97
  Corinthians 12:28, 41n53
  2 Corinthians, 25
  2 Corinthians 2:5–10, 23
  2 Corinthians 2:5–11, 4
  2 Corinthians 2:6, 25, 28
  2 Corinthians 3:2, 63
  2 Corinthians 3:7–11, 52
  2 Corinthians 4:6, 40
  2 Corinthians 8:19, 25n87
  2 Corinthians 8:22–24, 25n89
  2 Corinthians 10–12, 64n47
  2 Corinthians 12:11–12, 62n38
  2 Corinthians 12:12, 63
  Galatians 1:1, 62n38, 63, 73n91
  Galatians 1:8–9, 86
  Galatians 1:11–12, 62n38
  Galatians 1:11–24, 25
  Galatians 1:15–17, 84
  Galatians 1:19, 27, 94
  Galatians 2:6–9, 73n91
  Galatians 2:8, 62n38, 63
  Galatians 2:9, 27
  Galatians 2:12, 27
  Galatians 3:8, 61

Index

Galatians 3:28, 20
Galatians 4:2, 113n14
Galatians 5:2, 52
Galatians 6:1-2, 120
Galatians 6:6, 118
Ephesians 1:17-18, 41
Ephesians 1:20-23, 58
Ephesians 2:14-16, 20
Ephesians 2:19-20, 15
Ephesians 2:19-22, 13n30, 62n36, 64n45, 68
Ephesians 2:20, 66, 67
Ephesians 3:1-10, 58
Ephesians 3:5, 62n36, 66
Ephesians 3:16-19, 41n50
Ephesians 4, 64n45, 66
Ephesians 4:3-6, 20
Ephesians 4:7-12, 59
Ephesians 4:8-11, 58
Ephesians 4:11, 26, 41n53, 66, 72, 112
Ephesians 4:11-12, 62n36
Ephesians 4:11-13, 131
Ephesians 4:11-16, 111
Philippians 1:1, 18n53, 93, 95, 102, 119
Philippians 1:9, 41n50
Philippians 2:2, 20
Philippians 2:25, 25n89
Colossians 3:10, 41n50
Colossians 3:12-14, 20
Colossians 4:15, 26n97
1 Thessalonians 1:1, 73n91
1 Thessalonians 2:7, 73n91
1 Thessalonians 4:8, 63
1 Thessalonians 5:12, 94, 111, 114, 114n17
1 Thessalonians 5:12-13, 101
1 Thessalonians 5:20, 67
2 Thessalonians 3:6, 28
2 Thessalonians 3:14-15, 28
1 Thessalonians 2:6-7, 62
1 Timothy, 144
1 Timothy 2:7, 62n38
1 Timothy 3, 114n22
1 Timothy 3:1, 102
1 Timothy 3:1-2, 95
1 Timothy 3:1-7, 18n53, 94, 111, 126, 138
1 Timothy 3:2, 85, 102, 112, 122
1 Timothy 3:2-7, 88-89n38
1 Timothy 3:4-5, 114n17
1 Timothy 3:8-10, 99
1 Timothy 3:8-13, 65, 88-89n38
1 Timothy 3:14-15, 100
1 Timothy 3:17, 142
1 Timothy 4:3, 52
1 Timothy 4:14, 18
1 Timothy 5:1, 18n52, 96
1 Timothy 5:9, 4
1 Timothy 5:17, 18n52, 21, 27n105, 85, 91n50, 102, 111, 112, 114n17, 117, 118, 122, 137
1 Timothy 5:17-18, 27n103
1 Timothy 5:19, 18n52
1 Timothy 5:19-20, 102
2 Timothy 1:11, 62n38
2 Timothy 2:15, 41
Titus 1, 114n22, 144
Titus 1:5, 13, 18n52, 27n105, 73, 91n50, 95
Titus 1:5-6, 102
Titus 1:5-7, 94, 126
Titus 1:5-9, 18n53, 111, 138
Titus 1:7, 73-74, 95, 102, 113
Titus 1:9, 112
Titus 3:10, 11, 22
Philemon 2, 26n97
Hebrews 2:4, 63
Hebrews 13:7, 96, 102, 111, 112, 113, 114, 115, 133
Hebrews 13:17, 102, 111, 112, 113-14, 133
Hebrews 13:20, 72
Hebrews 13:24, 96, 113
James 2:1, 92
James 5:14, 18n52, 27n105, 91n50, 94, 95, 101, 112, 119
1 Peter 2:2, 112
1 Peter 2:4-10, 26n92
1 Peter 2:5-9, 131n105
1 Peter 2:25, 72, 74
1 Peter 4:10, 113n14
1 Peter 5:1, 27n105, 91n50, 94, 95
1 Peter 5:1-2, 18n53, 102
1 Peter 5:1-4, 74n97, 111
1 Peter 5:2, 72, 73n91, 112

173

Scripture references (*continued*)
1 Peter 5:3, 114
1 John 2:20, 41n50
1 John 2:27, 41n50, 41n53
1 John 4:7, 41n50
1 John 5:9–12, 63
1 John 5:20, 41
2 John 1, 95–96
2 John 12, 95
3 John 9, 100n89
3 John 10, 95–96, 100n89
Revelation 1:3, 67
Revelation 1:5–6, 26n92, 131n105
Revelation 2:1, 27
Revelation 2–3, 15n39, 96–97
Revelation 2:8, 27
Revelation 2:12, 27
Revelation 2:14–16, 25n89
Revelation 2:18, 27
Revelation 3:1, 27
Revelation 3:7, 27
Revelation 3:14, 27
Revelation 5:9–10, 26n92
Revelation 5:10, 131n105
Revelation 5:14, 102
Revelation 10:11, 67
Revelation 11:16, 102
Revelation 16:6, 67
Revelation 18:20, 67
Revelation 18:24, 67
Revelation 19:4, 102
Revelation 19:10, 67
Revelation 20:6, 26n92
Revelation 20–25, 25n89
Revelation 21:14, 69
Revelation 22:6–10, 67
Revelation 22:18–19, 67
authority over the church, 43–44
Second Vatican Council (1962–1965), 39
Separatist church, 24, 24n82
Septuagint
occurrences of *episkopos*, 71
occurrences of *poimēn*, 71–72
occurrences of *presbuteros* and *presbuteroi*, 70
service, 114

seven angels of seven churches, 15n39, 27, 96–97
Sharpening the Focus of the Church (Getz), 139
Shedd, William G. T., 41
Shepherds of Israel, 72
Silas, 62, 65, 73n91
Simeon, 65
single-elder led congregationalism
  basis in tradition, 98–99
  biblical defense of, 26–27, 91–92
  church discipline in, 97
  condemnation of, 100n89
  dangers of, 130–132
  demands on and power of pastor in, 98
  development of, 89–90
  failure of pastors, 105
  lack of biblical support for, 88–97, 110
  as type of congregationalism, 24
Sipes, L. M., 25n87, 65n49, 99
Southern Baptist Convention, 87
Southern Baptists, 126–27, 132
sovereignty of God, 18
spiritual gifts. *See* gifts
spiritual leaders, 139–41. *See also* apostles; elders; pastor; prophets
Spurgeon, Charles Haddon, 105
staff-led congregationalism, 24n85
Stöckhardt, George, 66n51
Strong, Augustus Hopkins, 125–26
A Study of Christianity as Organized (Kern), 23–24
sufficiency of Scripture, 3–4, 5–6, 7–8
supplementary view, 36
supremacy of Scripture, 10, 33–47, 88–90, 98–99
synagogue officers, 121–22
synodical polity. *See* episcopal model of polity
syntax, 51

teachers, 72n87
teaching, 112
teaching elders, 21, 84–85
Terry, Milton Spencer, 47
Tertullian, 13n30, 36

Index

Theodoret, 66n51
theological paradigm for exegesis, 29–32. *See also* hermeneutics
timē, 117
Timothy
  as apostle, 62, 73n91
  appointment of elders, 13
  authority of, 15, 64
  commission of, 83
  as one elder among many, 95
Titus
  appointment of elders, 13
  authority of, 15, 64
  commission of, 83
  as one elder among many, 95
Toon, Peter, 12, 83
Torrance, Thomas F., 56n3, 63–64
tradition
  coincidence view, 35–36
  defined, 34n17
  development of in fifth century, 36–37
  episcopal polity's reliance on, 83–84
  influence on Biblical interpretation, 30–32
  levels of, 34
  maxim for acceptance of, 36n31
  Scripture's supremacy over, 10, 33–47, 88–90, 98–99
  supplementary view, 36
"Treatise of Church Discipline" (Jones), 107
trustee-led congregationalism, 24, 88–89n38
types, 52

unified team of leaders, 139
universal instruction, 77

Van Engen, J., 35m22, 36n24, 38n37
Vincent of Lérins, Saint, 36
Virkler, Henry A., 77, 78
visible Christian unity, 20, 21n64
Von Schlatter, Adolf, 5n18

Waldron, Samuel E., 4, 106, 107, 123n73, 124
Wallace, Daniel B., 73n91, 96
Waterworth, J., 38n37
Watts, Isaac, 24
Webster, John, 39–40, 43–44, 45
White, James R., 5n21, 27n105, 69, 97–98, 107
Whitgift, Archbishop John, 1–3
Whitgift-Cartwright-Harrison debate, 1–3
Williams, Rowan, 52
Williams, William, 85n17
Word of God. *See* Scripture; Scripture references

Yarnell, Malcolm B., III, 39n43, 91n51, 126–28

Zodhiates, Dr. Spiros, 142
Zuck, Roy B., 8–9, 76

www.ingramcontent.com/pod-product-compliance
Lightning Source LLC
Chambersburg PA
CBHW071450150426
43191CB00008B/1294